EXAM *Revision* NOTES

AS/A-LEVEL

Religious Studies

2nd Edition

Sarah K. Tyler

Philip Allan Updates, an imprint of Hodder Education, part of Hachette Livre UK, Market Place, Deddington, Oxfordshire OX15 0SE

Orders
Bookpoint Ltd, 130 Milton Park, Abingdon, Oxfordshire, OX14 4SB
tel: 01235 827720
fax: 01235 400454
e-mail: uk.orders@bookpoint.co.uk

Lines are open 9.00 a.m.–5.00 p.m., Monday to Saturday, with a 24-hour message answering service. You can also order through the Philip Allan Updates website: www.philipallan.co.uk

© Philip Allan Updates 2008
ISBN 978-0-340-94754-8

2006 002632

First printed 2008
Impression number   5   4   3   2   1
Year   2013   2012   2011   2010   2009   2008

Printed in Spain

Hachette Livre UK's policy is to use papers that are natural, renewable and recyclable products and made from wood grown in sustainable forests. The logging and manufacturing processes are expected to conform to the environmental regulations of the country of origin.

Contents

Chapter 2 Philosophy of religion

Chapter 3   Ethics

Specification summary

Introduction

How to use this book

No matter where you are in your AS or A2 course, the examinations are probably looming large in your consciousness. It is therefore never too early to start the revision process — and hence to the purpose of this book! On the other hand, I have had some years' experience of meeting with students in the Easter holidays before their final examinations and discovering to my horror — and theirs — that they know very little indeed. If you fall into that category, then presumably the fact that you have picked up this book is an indication that you now plan to do something about it.

The reason why some students know far too little prior to their exams is because they don't know *how* to work. There may be a number of reasons for this:

- They haven't learned to translate the information given by their teachers into the kinds of answers that will merit high grades.
- They cannot distinguish between what is vital, interesting or completely irrelevant.
- They don't know why the material they have been given is significant.
- They have little knowledge of the scholarly debates relevant to their subject.
- They expect revision just to happen rather than planning how to go about it.

This book addresses all these issues.

Religious studies is a vast subject — its scope is as wide, if not wider, than almost any other arts discipline. As a result this book can only be selective. At first glance some of the sections here may not seem relevant to your specification, but check the appendix (which starts on page 177) and the introductory material at the beginning of each section. This indicates to which specification areas the material is related. You may find some unexpected bonuses this way — for example, there are inevitable overlaps between the philosophy and ethics chapters, and between Old Testament and New Testament. Use the whole book freely, and don't feel constrained to stay only with the topic headings that are on your specification.

Studying and revising for theology, religious studies and philosophy

All the examination boards publish a statement of the aims of any AS or A2 specification. These indicate what you need to learn to do during your course and in the examinations. The aims can be summarised as follows:

- **You must show that you have undertaken a disciplined study of the areas chosen.** You need to show that you are aware of the connections of parts to the whole. Disciplined study involves learning rigorous and systematic working practices and demonstrating them not only in your homework but also in the examination. The disciplined scholar relates everything to the question, alluding to narrative and text, rather than giving a blow-by-blow account of it in a way which may or may not be ultimately relevant. Finally, disciplined answers must be ordered, structured and must build up an argument to its logical conclusion.

- **You must show that you have developed a critical awareness of scholarship relevant to your chosen areas of study.**

  The contribution of scholars — and not just dead ones — is an increasingly important part of your study in this subject. You are not, however, required to list as many scholars as you can remember in the space of 45 minutes. Some candidates' essays — ironically, usually those of intelligent, hard-working and well-taught candidates — resemble a shopping list of scholars that they have diligently learned. But in just listing names candidates demonstrate no real understanding of the value, or otherwise, of the scholars' contributions. You need to obtain a reasonable balance in your work, and not lose sight of the real issues in a forest of scholars' names. Evaluate their contributions, expose the differences, say why some are more convincing than others — but ensure that they are servants and not masters.

- **You must demonstrate an awareness of the historical, cultural and social background to the period studied.**

  You need to show an understanding of the background to the material you study and write about; otherwise you run the risk of being anachronistic. To dismiss Old Testament ethics as 'old-fashioned' would be to fail to appreciate their original setting, in which they would have been modern, forward-thinking — even radical — and certainly directly relevant to the lives of the people of the time. Similarly, it would be arrogant to assume that twentieth-century thinking owes nothing to the past. Nothing emerges in a vacuum or without owing a great deal to the rich heritage of previous generations of scholarship and debate.

- **You must show an understanding of areas of perennial interest and present-day concern.**

  To appreciate that the past leaves a great legacy to the future is to recognise that there are some issues that simply will not die. They are of enduring concern. Issues concerned with human existence, rites of passage, spiritual and psychological mysteries of life and death, morality and ethics, the nature of God, humanity's relationship with the world and its place in the created order are both perennial and current. There are no 'right' conclusions to reach: you are more likely to be given credit for recognising the impossibility of definitiveness than for attempting to reach a conclusion that borders on dogmatism.

- **You must convey knowledge and understanding through the orderly selection and lucid presentation of data.**

  This tests your literacy skills and demands regular practice. Note that selection is required of you — you are not expected to reproduce everything you have learned in the course of your study — indeed to do so would be a waste of time. Thus you need to discern what is important and what is not. This may mean being reasonably selective in your learning, but you must be sure of what is essential, what is useful, what is marginal and what you can leave out entirely.

- **You must evaluate the religious issues raised.**

  Evaluation involves weighing and balancing, demonstrating critical thinking and identifying strengths and weaknesses in arguments, theories and dilemmas. It demands that you lay aside your preferences for certain viewpoints, for the purposes of academic credibility. Learn to recognise the intellectual and moral weaknesses and strengths of the views you study and to convey them in a mature way.

- **You must demonstrate an understanding of the diversity of personal, social and corporate responses, practices and judgements in religious matters, both at the time of the material studied and in the present day.**

This point demands that you understand **why** people think differently. The principles underlying different opinions may be moral, biblical, social, personal or denominational. It is not enough to say 'Roman Catholics are against abortion', since it does not demonstrate that you are aware of the reasons why some, many or all Roman Catholics hold that view. And remember that you must show an understanding of how diversity of opinion is important in all ages. Don't assume that whereas people may disagree on important matters of ethics or biblical interpretation today, 2,000 years ago everyone was of the same mind.

Examinations and exam technique

There are five stages to pass through in the quest to obtain a good grade at AS/A2, and accompanying skills which you need to utilise in order to pass through these stages successfully. Some of them will seem rather obvious, but it is often the obvious that is overlooked by students as they head for catastrophe.

(1) Lessons

First and foremost, lessons are for the **presentation of information**. It is initially your teacher's responsibility to select the right information for your needs, but you need to take responsibility for the way you receive it. Develop the habit of **asking questions**, however banal they may seem. Questions can be used to **clarify** what you have heard: 'So as I understand it, scholar X is suggesting...?' Questions like this are very helpful for verbalising what your teacher has said, thereby putting the material into your own words — a skill that is essential for the examination itself. And, of course, if you don't understand you must ask a question.

Use your lessons to appreciate the contribution that everyone has to make. In religious studies and philosophy it is virtually impossible to find a class in which everyone will have the same opinions, so there should be real fodder for debate. You can learn to evaluate other views from your own by hearing what your classmates have to say.

(2) Homework tasks

First, homework tasks are an opportunity for you to **clarify your understanding** in writing. Homework provides the opportunity for you to practise **past questions**. There's nothing more alarming than going into an exam, opening the paper and seeing on it questions of a style and format that you've never practised before. Homework tasks should enable you to become familiar with the way the relevant examination board asks questions. Your teacher can then use your homework answers to show how the **mark scheme** will be applied to your examination answers. This will enable you to gain enough insight into the system to work out how it may be applied to something less familiar. Every homework exercise should be used as an opportunity to learn the topic you're writing about, so never just store it in the back of your file and forget about it.

(3) Independent learning and consolidation

A good teacher will be able to provide you with **almost** everything you need to get a high grade in the final examination. But it is the student who has actually completed the set reading, or who has shown some initiative in finding an extra scholar's view, or who has simply had the common sense to go over their lesson notes a third or

fourth time, who will emerge with the higher grade. This is where **evaluation** and **critical awareness** come in. These skills can be taught to some extent, but if your independent learning is nothing more than memorising a list of points you will never really develop them. It is only by exposing yourself to a range of views, and practising the skills of weighing and balancing them, that you can gain the extra marks that will move you into the higher-grade bands.

(4) Revision for the examination

The main advice here is simply **it's never too early and it's never too late**. At whatever point you are in your course you can gain from revision — planned, structured and relevant revision — although obviously it is better done early. Your revision strategies must be based on ways to get all your valuable knowledge and understanding into your long-term memory. Different techniques suit different people, and you should not be discouraged if some methods that work for others don't work for you. You can experiment with a range of strategies: index cards, mind maps, audio tapes, essay plans, timed essays.

(5) The examination

It may seem that once you reach the examination hall it's all over — but even at this final hurdle there are still strategies you can use to make the most of the exam situation. First, make sure you **know what is required** of you. It is not unheard of for candidates to answer too few or too many questions, or to ignore the structure of the questions — for example, blending (a), (b) and (c) rather than keeping them distinct. Some are so unfamiliar with the wording of questions that they miss the direction they are intended to take.

Be sure of your **timing**. You will not be able to make the most of the examination if you're still taking 3 hours to write an essay 2 months before the day of the exam. It is your responsibility to use time properly in the examination, and there is never any real justification for spending extra time on one question to compensate for your third or fourth essay being inadequate. Stamina, timing and concentration are your tools and they need to be practised, consolidated and refined. Never take your mind off the question. The question gives you instructions, and if you disobey them you cannot expect to get credit. For every paragraph spend a few seconds checking that you are doing what you have been asked to do; this is a better use of time than writing out mammoth plans and expecting them to be given credit if you run out of time writing out the proper answer.

In the examination room you must **ignore everyone else**. The only person you should be concerned about is you, so don't be distracted by what everybody else is doing. Similarly, ignore everyone else when you come out of the exam room. Post-mortems of what people wrote or didn't write are utterly time-wasting and potentially damaging. The greatest disaster in one paper can be redeemed in the next, so keep your head clear, your emotions under control, and your work over the last year or two will be rewarded.

A Biblical criticism

The material in this section is relevant to questions on:
- the relationship between the gospels
- biblical criticism specifically
- interpreting parallel passages from the synoptic gospels
- comparing important episodes from the gospels, e.g. the death of Jesus
- the interests, purposes and characteristics of the gospel writers

1 *Source criticism and the synoptic problem*

Of Mark's 661 verses, Matthew uses 606 and Luke 320; thus there is a **relationship of dependence** between the three synoptic gospels. This gives rise to the synoptic problem: how can the three synoptic gospels be so similar and yet so different?

Are the similarities because:
- the gospels were written under the inspiration of the Holy Spirit?
- they are an accurate historical record of what Jesus did and said?
- they shared a common oral tradition?

These points cannot entirely explain the relationship, which is clearly **literary**, and the most likely relationship is one between the synoptic gospels themselves. The major suggestions have been:
- **Augustine:** Matthew wrote first, followed by Mark using Matthew and then Luke using Mark (Matthean priority).
- **Griesbach and Farmer:** Matthew wrote first, followed by Luke and then Mark, who used both gospels (Matthean priority).
- **Streeter:** Mark wrote first; Matthew and Luke used both Mark and another common source, **Q** (Markan priority).

Markan priority overtook Matthean priority only in the nineteenth century, since when it has been largely agreed that:

> *Mark's gospel was not the Cinderella among the gospels, as it had been in the early church, but the first gospel to have been written and therefore the gospel with the highest claims to be accepted as a reliable historical source.*
>
> **Graham Stanton, *The Gospels and Jesus*, OUP, 1989, p. 35**

1.1 Reasons for Markan priority

- Mark is the shortest gospel, and it is easier to explain Matthew's and Luke's expansion of Mark than Mark's abbreviation of the other gospels. Key episodes and teaching are not included in Mark; it would be hard to explain Mark's decision to omit the Lord's Prayer, for example.

You may be asked how far Matthew or Luke may be thought to be one of the synoptic gospels. You need to consider whether there are similarities in views and presentation, as well as evidence of a literary relationship with the other gospels.

See how establishing which gospel was written first is essential for establishing the literary relationship between the gospels. If we decide that Matthew wrote first, for example, we reach entirely different conclusions about the relationship between the three synoptics.

In many textbooks you will find extensive material dealing with the question of Markan priority. Most of it is far too complicated and easily misunderstood, so keep things simple. With the time that you will have available in the exam these four points will be more than ample.

- Matthew and Luke appear to have eliminated redundant phrases in Mark, e.g. Mark 1:32: 'At evening, when the sun had set'), and to have tidied up Mark's poorer Greek. Long narratives are abbreviated, e.g. the healing of the Gerasene Demoniac.
- They appear to have softened apparently critical observations about Jesus, e.g. his harshness towards his disciples in the boat (Mark 4:38), and the disciples themselves are presented in a more positive light.
- If Mark wrote first, and was the basis on which Luke and Matthew wrote, there seems to be good reason for the gospel having been preserved in the canon. If Mark copied and abbreviated Matthew and/or Luke, then there seems little reason to have preserved this shorter and in some ways less satisfying account.

1.2 Where does Q fit in?

Holtzmann's two-source theory of 1863 stated that Matthew and Luke used Mark as well as another common source — **Q** — to which Mark did not have access. Q comprises about 230 verses including important sayings of Jesus, parables and material about John the Baptist. Note the following:

The same point applies here. For each main aspect of this huge topic you must establish a quick and easy list of no more than four or five points. Any more than that and you will run out of time, and be in danger of confusing the issue.

- Even when Matthew and Luke are not using Mark there is close agreement between them. Such a coincidence is best explained by a literary source.
- Double accounts of the same incident or saying in Matthew and Luke suggest they were working with two sources.
- Q material can be extracted effectively to form a gospel of its own, suggesting a coherent collection of sayings of Jesus.
- Even though Q is a hypothetical document, it serves better to explain non-Markan agreement than suggesting that Luke used Matthew.

1.3 But what about the differences?

A two-source hypothesis does not adequately explain the differences between Luke and Matthew, however. It is in material found only in one gospel that the particular interests of the evangelists can be traced. **B. H. Streeter's four-document hypothesis** thus incorporated two further sources — **M** and **L**.

1.3a M

About 282 verses of Matthew are unique to him, including his account of the birth narrative, the guard at the tomb, Judas's suicide and Pilate's wife's dream.

> *To source critics, the kind of Christian Community which produced M seemed to be a Jewish-Christian community which felt obliged to keep both the Law and the scribal traditions.*
>
> **F. W. Burnett, in *Dictionary of Jesus and the Gospels*, IVP, 1992, p. 511**

The nature of M is polemical (critical) of a lax interpretation by some factions within the early church of Jesus's relationship to the Law, and is thus thought not to be as reliable as the other synoptic sources. Jesus is presented as the

ultimate interpreter of the Law and as the founder of an eschatological community under the authority of his Father.

1.3b L

L material comprises from a third to a half of Luke's gospel. Indeed, the **proto-Luke theory** argues that Luke may have written a first draft of his gospel before he had access to Mark, the Q and L traditions effectively forming the basis of Luke's gospel. L material includes 14 parables unique to Luke, additions to the passion narrative, and characters including Mary and Martha, and Zacchaeus.

Finally… all three gospels exist independently as well as being interdependent. Any source-critical study must not overlook the fact that each gospel can be read and understood without reference to the others, and using literary critical methods to examine them individually may well do them greater justice than comparing them does. These methods include examining plot, structure, character and the reader's own response to the material in much the same way as a critic might study a modern novel.

> For more about these forms of criticism, look at M. A. Powell, *What is Narrative Criticism?*, SPCK, 1993.

2 | *Form criticism*

Form criticism developed in the early twentieth century as scholars sought to establish the earliest traditions behind the gospels. The main scholars associated with form criticism are **H. Gunkel** and **J. Wellhausen** (Old Testament); and **K. Schmidt**, **M. Debelius** and **R. Bultmann** (New Testament).

2.1 Principles of form criticism

> This is quite a complex form of biblical criticism and you are less likely to be asked to deal with it in detail, so all that is provided here is a broad outline of its main aspects. An understanding of its contribution is important, however.

- The teachings of Jesus and the gospel material about him circulated orally in individual units for some time before being committed to writing.
- Gospel material had many parallels in other traditions of the time.
- The final written form of the gospels was an unreliable account of the life and teaching of Jesus which had been adapted to meet the needs of the early church communities in their *Sitz im Leben*. The gospel writers had little biographical interest in Jesus.
- It was necessary to remove the layers of elaboration and development that had infiltrated the original units of material in any attempt to establish a reliable text.

2.2 Units of material (pericopae)

> Examples are important if you are to convey your understanding of these different forms. Make sure that you have two or three for each.

Form critics identified six broad categories of forms:

(i) **Legends or myths:** considered the most unreliable gospel material, these deal with the divinity of Jesus and his relationship with God, e.g. birth narratives and resurrection stories.

(ii) **Parables:** allegorical or metaphorical narratives that offer teaching on the nature of God or the coming of the kingdom.

(iii) **Miracles:** these can be further divided, e.g. healings, exorcisms, nature miracles.

(iv) **Pronouncement stories:** narratives ending with a climactic teaching point offered by Jesus, e.g. 'The Son of Man is Lord of the Sabbath'.

(v) **Speeches:** sayings of Jesus unified into a continuous whole, e.g. the Sermon on the Mount (Matthew 5–7).

(vi) **Individual sayings:** prophetic or eschatological sayings, church rules, sayings about Jesus's person and purpose.

2.3 The value of form criticism

A discussion of the value of form criticism — or of anything — should include strengths and weaknesses.

- Form criticism identifies the role the gospel material had in the life of the early church rather than being an accurate reflection of the life and teaching of Jesus. As the early church confronted new needs and circumstances, material could be adapted to suit those needs. For example, Matthew 18:15–22 concerns church discipline and is anachronistic on the lips of Jesus. This does not mean that the forms were entirely lacking in historical reliability, however.
- The importance of the oral period was recognised as bridging the gap between the life of Jesus and the emergence of the written gospels — which was the primary interest of the source critics.
- Identifying the separate forms that comprise the gospels permits an appreciation of how each distinct pericope can be interpreted and how the evangelists chose to group the forms. The gospels are not seen as one continuous narrative from which its individual parts cannot be distinguished.
- 'There is no need to insist that the early church was not interested in setting out the "past" life of the life of Jesus … the gospels are concerned with the story of Jesus and also with his significance for his later followers' (Graham Stanton, *The Gospels and Jesus*, pp. 23–24).

3 *Redaction criticism*

Every time you consider the particular characteristics and purposes of the gospel you are studying, you are employing the principles of redaction criticism. So even if you don't know it as such, this is a method already familiar to you.

Again, there is much room for complication here, and plenty of highly detailed information about this method in the major textbooks. For your purposes, a summary of the key principles is really most important.

Redaction criticism is based on Markan priority and concerns itself with examining the way in which the evangelists have used their sources. Redaction critics maintained that the evangelists had been creative in their use of tradition, and that the way in which they compiled the gospels reflected important concerns.

3.1 Principles of redaction criticism

As with form criticism, you need examples to back this up. Make sure you know where your special evangelist has made distinctive changes to his sources, even if you can't give examples of the redactional work of the other evangelists.

- The final gospel form is studied — not the separate sources or units of material — to establish the changes made by each evangelist to his source material.
- It is thought that these changes provide a clue to the evangelists' theological interests and create the distinctive flavour of each gospel. The evangelists are revealed to be authors, rather than cut-and-paste artists who had no creative role in manipulating their sources.
- The role of the early church is again considered important, since the *Sitz im Leben* of the evangelist's church is likely to have influenced his interests.

- Arguably, redaction criticism changed the direction of gospel study away from the teaching of Jesus itself to a study of the evangelists' presentation of the teaching of Jesus.

3.2 The origins of redaction criticism

- **William Wrede and the Messianic Secret (1901):** Wrede proposed that Mark had written a messianic secret onto Jesus's lips. When faced with questions of his identity Jesus encouraged silence or avoided an unambiguous acknowledgement of his messiahship. This had not been part of Mark's original source material, but was imposed by the evangelist onto the narratives to explain why Jesus had been recognised by so few during his earthly life.
- **Gunther Bornkamm and the Storm on the Lake (1948):** Bornkamm published a decisive article based on his analysis of Mark 4:35–41 and Matthew 8:23–27. He argued that Matthew's changes to his Markan source had effected a reinterpretation, changing the focus of the story from Jesus's divine control over nature to discipleship.
- **Conzelmann and Luke:** while it had traditionally been thought that Luke was the historian of the evangelists, Conzelmann argued that he was a theologian, with a special interest in salvation history.

3.3 The value of redaction criticism

- Redaction criticism provides the basis for an understanding of each evangelist's theological interests. The changing of a single word can give an entirely different slant to an episode or saying. The inclusion of distinctive material into the evangelist's primary sources gives the gospels their individual character, and these differences enhance the theological value of the gospels.
- The principle, however, relies on the four-source hypothesis, which although influential is still a hypothesis (a theory).
- The method may pay too much attention to the additions and adaptations and not to the whole tradition.
- Some changes that were made may not necessarily have the significance that redaction critics would claim they have. A consistent pattern of changes should be seen to be more significant than many unrelated ones.
- The combined purpose of the gospels is appreciated: to convey the historical message of the life of Jesus and to interpret it for its readers. 'History and theology are valid aspects of Gospel analysis, and we dare not neglect either without destroying the God-ordained purpose of the Gospels' (G. R. Osbourne, in *Dictionary of Jesus and the Gospels*, p. 668).

B Issues of authorship and dating

Questions on authorship and dating will almost always be ones asking specifically about these issues. It is extremely important, however, to be aware that when and by whom a document was written has real implications for its interpretation.

It would not be practical here to provide details of all the various suggestions and counter-suggestions for the dating and authorship of the New Testament books that appear on the AS/A2 specifications. However, what candidates often stumble over is the **significance** of these debates. An essay on authorship and dating can be nothing more than a list of opinions, and in many cases this can still score well. But if asked why it is important to have some idea of the date of a document or its possible author, candidates are often less confident. The following notes focus on these areas. Use them to enable you to evaluate the significance of the different alternatives offered.

1 *Authorship*

The important considerations are outlined below.

1.1 Is it written by an eyewitness?

If so, there may be grounds for arguing that it has greater authenticity than a document written by a second-hand source. The most likely eyewitnesses would, of course, be disciples of Jesus during his earthly ministry, but the evangelists may have had access to the eyewitness accounts of other observers.

These points are linked with biblical criticism. Look at the previous section on this topic for more detail on the way in which the evangelists have used their sources.

We should be careful not to make assumptions about eyewitness testimony, however. The gospel traditions circulated in oral form for some time before being committed to writing, and the traditions the evangelists used may well have been far removed from their original form. It has been suggested that Luke may have had access to eyewitness testimony from Jesus's mother, and that Mark may have been writing effectively at Peter's instruction.

Some passages do suggest eyewitness testimony. Mark 4:38 describes Jesus being asleep in the boat 'on the cushion', and John 18:5 says that 'Judas, who betrayed him, was standing with them'. However, this need not mean that the whole gospel was written by an eyewitness, but rather that the evangelist made use of the eyewitness testimony of others.

1.2 Is it written by an apostle?

This question is relevant primarily to the Fourth Gospel, which appears to make a claim for apostolic authorship at 21:24: 'This is the disciple who is testifying to these things and has written them, and we know his testimony is true.' The

passage alludes to the mysterious figure of the **Beloved Disciple**, traditionally identified as John, the son of Zebedee. Nowhere in the Fourth Gospel is this identification made, however, even implicitly. Scholars have argued that the character fits the figure of John Zebedee almost by default:

- He is associated with Peter.
- He is present at key events in Jesus's life.
- He is anticipated as having a central role in the early church.

However:

- He is never named, nor is James, his brother.
- The Beloved Disciple could be anyone who was close to Jesus and not necessarily even one of the Twelve.

Interestingly, even if the Fourth Gospel is the work of an apostle, it is strikingly different from the synoptic accounts, which raises important questions about historicity and purpose.

This overlaps with considerations about the reliability of the New Testament canon and the criteria established by the early church for the inclusion of a text.

1.3 What internal evidence is there for authorship?

Internal evidence is that which is provided by the text itself, not from other sources. None of the gospels name their author (the names are traditional, not part of the original texts), and so internal evidence has to be gathered piecemeal. Despite its lengthy statement of purpose Luke's gospel does not name its author, but it is clear that it is by the same hand as the book of Acts. The themes established in Luke are developed in Acts, and the style of writing and use of vocabulary is consistent. The famous 'we passages' in Acts, where the narrator switches from third to first person, suggest extracts from a diary, although not necessarily that of the author.

The letters of Paul are attributed to him within the text, and he frequently makes a point of signing off in his own hand (rather than that of an amanuensis). However, this does not guarantee that they are the work of his own hand.

The letters of John are almost certainly not by the apostle John, and may not even be by the writer of the gospel. Rather, the name that is ascribed to a New Testament document is an indication of the authority held by that name rather than a guaranteed claim to authorship. A document attributed to one of the great heroes of the early church would gain far quicker recognition than one attributed to one of their followers.

1.4 What is the value of the external evidence?

External evidence is the information provided by other sources. This is most usually the testimony of the early church fathers writing from the second century onwards. Papias, Irenaeus, Tertullian, Augustine and Clement of Alexandria are among the most well-known early church writers who suggested candidates for authorship of the gospels and Acts. The weight of their testimony is useful,

Become familiar with the names of some of the apocryphal texts that did not finally make it into the canon. Ultimately, those that did — despite their differences — are those that are most consistent with one another and whose authors were felt to be the most reliable.

especially if we believe them to be unbiased in their reasoning. They may, however, simply have been repeating what had already become tradition, or what they had heard from another source.

Fragments of text may be especially valuable for dating the gospels. The earliest fragment of John is dated AD 110–150, which leads to a speculative dating of AD 95–100 (allowing time for circulation).

1.5 Is finding an author that important?

If we know that the gospel of Mark is the work of a disciple of Peter we may feel more confident about the reliability of the text. If we know that Acts was written by a travelling companion of Paul we may feel sure that he has the details of Paul's missionary journeys correct. However, there are always many arguments raised against traditional claims to authorship, so it is worth considering whether it is such an important issue after all.

The gospels do stand alone and are complete narratives in themselves, even if we do not know who was responsible for their final composition. Modern scholarship also tends to postulate community authorship rather than a single individual being responsible for the gospel. The gospels thus reflect the concerns and experiences of a Christian community, not just of an individual.

Dating **2**

The dating of the texts can tell us something about the **circumstances** and **cultural movements** that may have influenced the writers. The fall of Jerusalem in AD 70 is considered an important benchmark for dating the gospels. Were they written before or after? Did Jesus prophesy it accurately or were the evangelists putting their experience of it into his mouth? The Synagogue Benediction of *c.*AD 85–90 is considered valuable for dating the Fourth Gospel. Were Jesus's followers expelled from the synagogue during his lifetime, as the experience of the blind man (9:22) may suggest, or are the authors writing their own experience back into the lifetime of Jesus?

Dating is also relevant for **eliminating possible authors**. If the Fourth Gospel was written after AD 100 then how likely is it to be an apostolic text? If it was written first — as early as AD 50 perhaps — then the author may be an apostle. But then we are left with the question of why his gospel is so different from the synoptics, when we would expect an apostle to be the most reliable source of evidence. Which tradition is the more authentic?

Dating also tells us something about **how theology was developing** in the first century. Debates about matters of belief and practice continued long after Jesus's death, and there appears to be a world of difference between the narrative of Mark's gospel and the apocalypse of Revelation. The birth narratives of Matthew and Luke appear to be dealing with less weighty christological issues than the cosmological prologue of the Fourth Gospel. It may be possible to trace the development of belief through the New Testament documents if we have some idea of their dates.

> Given that all suggestions about authorship and dating are purely speculative, it is valid to put forward an argument that it is not especially useful to place too much significance on them. Other considerations could be seen to be more important and worthwhile: how authors develop themes, how they use their sources, what the *Sitz im Leben* of the document might be and how it has influenced the text.

C Birth and resurrection narratives

The material in this section is relevant to questions on:
- the content of the birth narratives in Matthew and Luke, and the resurrection narratives in all four gospels
- the person of Jesus (christology)
- redaction criticism
- miracles, virgin birth, myth and symbol
- women in the New Testament
- the use of Old Testament in the New Testament

1 Birth narratives

- The texts are Matthew chapters 1 and 2 and Luke chapters 1 and 2.
- There is no parallel in Mark — the gospel begins with the appearance of John the Baptist.
- The Fourth Gospel jettisons a history-like birth narrative in favour of a **cosmological prologue** tracing Jesus's divine origins back to creation (John 1:1–18).

1.1 Matthew's narrative

1.1a Genealogy (Matthew 1:1–17)
- Matthew is the only gospel to begin with Old Testament-style **genealogy**. Matthew traces the descent of Jesus through the line of **David** from the **patriarchs**, establishing his messianic credentials and the fulfilment of God's promise to Abraham in Genesis 12:2–3.
- **Joseph** is a key figure; his obedient responses to dreams and visions are essential for the preservation of the infant Messiah.
- Five women of apparently dubious background are unusually included in the genealogy. Jesus descends not just from the outwardly pure, but from a gentile (Ruth) and a prostitute (Rahab).
- The genealogy identifies three stages in salvation history before the coming of the Messiah: Abraham to David; David to the exile; the exile to Jesus's birth.

1.1b The birth of Jesus (Matthew 1:18–25)
- The story of Jesus is told from Joseph's perspective. (Luke's narrative suggests Mary's view of the events.)
- Matthew establishes Jesus's divine conception as being through the Holy Spirit, which indicates the beginning of a new age in salvation history.
- 'Jesus' means 'Yahweh is salvation' and is a form of the Hebrew name Joshua. Joseph's naming of Jesus marks his **legal** acceptance of him as his son, but he obediently gives him the prophetic name instructed by the angel.
- The use of Isaiah 7:14 is the first of ten **fulfilment clauses** used by Matthew. The Hebrew *almah* may imply, but certainly not specify, a virgin, and Matthew appears to have made use of the **Septuagint** (Greek translation of the Old

Whenever you are asked to write about the birth narratives you should hear warning bells! You must draw out the significance of their symbolism rather than merely narrating.

Note how these comments are not narrative-based, but concerned with the significance and interpretation of the material important to the evangelist.

Testament), where the noun **parthenos** is more ambiguous. '**Emmanuel**' means 'Jesus is God, tabernacled among his people' (see Isaiah 61:1). Matthew 28:20 echoes this thought.

1.1c The magi (Matthew 2:1–12)

- The magi may represent the gentiles who will come to worship Jesus and to whom the gospel will be spread (28:19), while Herod represents the people of Israel who will reject him (27:25).
- The second fulfilment clause at 2:6 cites Micah 5:2 — the Messiah will be born in the city of David.
- The magi's gifts are prophetic: gold = **royalty**; incense = **divinity**; myrrh = **passion**.
- The third fulfilment clause at 2:15 cites Hosea 11:1 — Jesus is to be the new first-born of God, fulfilling the role that was Israel's.
- The fourth fulfilment clause at 2:18 cites Jeremiah 31:15.
- The fifth fulfilment clause at 2:23 relates to no specific Old Testament text. This reflects the freedom with which Matthew has used his narrative to underline the messianic credentials of Jesus.

1.1d Key issues introduced by Matthew

- Jesus is the fulfilment of Old Testament expectation, and his birth reflects Old Testament traditions.
- In his ministry he will face conflict.
- Jesus's birth and infancy mirror that of Moses.
- God takes the initiative in every aspect of Jesus's birth, compelling man to obey.
- Matthew shows that Jesus is the Son of God. This is Matthew's **evaluative view**.

> *What we are told in these opening chapters ... points forward to the denouement of the story. The beginning ... hints at the ideas which will be made plain at the end.*
>
> Morna Hooker, *Beginnings*, SCM, 1997, p. 42

> *Jesus is God's supreme agent in Matthew's story, and the purpose of the genealogy ... is to advance this claim.*
>
> Jack D. Kingsbury, *Matthew as Story*, Fortress Press, 1986, p. 45

A discussion of Luke's narrative is the one most likely to degenerate into a Sunday school-type fable. Use the headings suggested here to keep your discussion academic.

1.2 Luke's narrative

1.2a John the Baptist and Jesus

Luke **parallels** the births of Jesus and John but always makes it clear that Jesus is the greater:

- Both are born miraculously of pious Jews.
- Their births follow the Old Testament pattern of great men of God and are announced by angelic messengers.

- John is the **Prophet** of the Most High, Jesus is the **Son** of the Most High.
- Some tenuous connection is made between Mary and Elizabeth.
- Both grow up as children with great spiritual wisdom.

1.2b Prophecy

- Luke's narrative contains six **prophetic oracles** concerning the future of both children.
- The spirit of prophecy guarantees the coming of the messianic age.
- God's promises to Abraham are fulfilled.
- Values will be reversed and popular expectations challenged.
- Luke introduces the Holy Spirit, who will direct events in the gospel and in Acts.
- Jesus's visit to the temple aged 12 (the only infancy story in the New Testament canon) anticipates the place of the temple in his later ministry and for the gospel as a whole, which begins and ends in the temple.
- Jesus's passion is anticipated by Simeon (2:34). Jesus is set to be rejected.

1.2c 'He has exalted those of low degree'

Luke anticipates Jesus's ministry to 'seek and save the lost' (19:10):

- The parents of John and Jesus are not of high worldly status.
- Women are given a key role.
- Mary's song (1:46–55) praises God for lifting up the oppressed.
- Mary and Joseph are portrayed as staying in humble accommodation.
- Shepherds are the first visitors to Jesus.
- Jesus's parents offer the poor man's offering of two doves or pigeons at the purification.
- Jesus's 'human' upbringing is stressed.

> *For Luke, this ... is not a sentimental tale to delight his readers; it prepares them for what is to come, and for those who know the events yet to be told it is full of premonition.*
>
> **Judith Lieu, *The Gospel of Luke*, Epworth Press, 1997, p. 20**

Remember that like the birth narratives, the resurrection narratives are not designed simply to amaze, but to link with themes that have already been established as important for the gospel.

2 Resurrection narratives

> *The New Testament asserts that something over and above the Good Friday event happened in the experience of the first disciples, something more than them coming to a new assessment of the meaning of the event of Good Friday. Even the most sceptical historian has to postulate an 'x' as M. Debelius called it.... What is the precise content of this 'x'?*
>
> **R. H. Fuller, *The Formation of the Resurrection Narratives*, SPCK, 1972, p. 2**

Birth and resurrection narratives

2.1 Mark's narrative

The challenge of Mark's resurrection narrative is the **ending**. Traditionally it ends at 16:8, but this was unsatisfactory for early scribes and there are two alternative endings: 16:11 and 16:20. The traditional ending is abrupt and ends on a note of fear. However, there are good reasons for believing it to be the original:

- The reader is left to pursue the risen Jesus for themselves.
- We can trust Jesus's words of 14:28 to be true, so we need no further evidence that the women told the disciples what they had seen and that the disciples went to Galilee as instructed.
- It is a simple narrative, containing no appearances of Jesus that may have been added to give credence to the resurrection story.
- The longer endings appear to be modelled on traditions found in Luke and John.

This early **gospel** resurrection account (**NB:** 1 Corinthians 15:3ff. is earlier) contains the central features of the resurrection tradition:

- The women visit the tomb to anoint Jesus's body.
- The stone is rolled away. (In 16:3 they have already wondered who might do this for them.)
- A young man/angel greets them with the news of the resurrection — news that should not surprise them.
- The women and/or disciples are amazed, and a doubt motif is applied.

2.2 Matthew's narrative

Key additions are as follows:

- An apocalyptic earthquake heralds the angel's appearance, described in Old Testament-type language (27:51ff.).
- The guards placed at the tomb in 27:66 witness the events, and are afraid.
- The women are joyful, not afraid.
- They see the risen Christ and worship him.
- The Jewish authorities ironically plan to cover up the events with a lie.
- The 11 disciples meet with Jesus and receive their commissioning as apostles.

Matthew is concerned to link the beginning and the end of the gospel — see the echoes of the birth narrative throughout.

2.3 Luke's narrative

Key additions are as follows:

- The women's story is not believed.
- The meeting between Jesus and two outer circle disciples on the road to Emmaus is used to explain the purpose of Jesus's death and to correct false thinking.
- At Emmaus they share a quasi-eucharistic meal.
- Jesus appears to Peter (omitted in some manuscripts).
- Jesus appears to the eleven and demonstrates the reality of his resurrection.
- The commissioning is accompanied by a promise of the Holy Spirit.
- The disciples witness the ascension (cf. Acts 1:9ff.).

Luke is concerned to show the necessity of Jesus's death and the reality of his continued presence through the Holy Spirit.

2.4 The Fourth Gospel

The Fourth Evangelist appears to have had access to synoptic traditions about the women going to the tomb. He weaves his own material into these accounts.

- Mary Magdalene apparently goes alone, but refers to 'we' in John 20:2.
- Peter and the Beloved Disciple behave characteristically; the Beloved Disciple grasps the significance of the empty tomb while Peter looks on.
- Jesus makes himself known to Mary and gives her the apostolic commission to tell his disciples that he is risen.
- Jesus personally bestows the Holy Spirit on the disciples.
- Thomas is allowed proof of the resurrection, but those who 'believe and have not seen' are given a special blessing.
- The appearance at the Sea of Galilee may be an addition, addressing issues of concern to early church ministry: discipleship; fulfilling the apostolic mission; the pastoral roles of Peter and the Beloved Disciple; the re-calling of Peter after his denial; the death of the Beloved Disciple.

There are some similarities between the Fourth Gospel and Luke: Peter going to the tomb; the Holy Spirit; a eucharistic-type meal; the catch of fish (see Luke 5).

> The Fourth Gospel narratives raise interesting problems of their own; you need to examine chapters 20 and 21 carefully.

D New Testament miracles

The material in this section is relevant to questions on:

- miracles in the gospel tradition
- christology
- signs in the Fourth Gospel
- redaction and source criticism
- links with philosophical considerations about miracles

The place of miracles in the gospel tradition

> In this topic the examiner knows the story and assumes that you know it, but what you must convey is your understanding of the **significance** of the miracles in the gospel tradition.

Between the four gospels, 34 miracles are recorded and a further 15 summaries of Jesus's miraculous works are made. Despite the considerable differences between the presentation of miracles in the Fourth Gospel and the synoptic gospels, miracles are as integral a part of Jesus's ministry in the Johannine record as they are for the synoptists. Other key episodes, such as the transfiguration and the resurrection, involve miraculous activity and supernatural phenomena. From the beginning of Jesus's life his identity is confirmed by the miracles which accompany his ministry.

2 Background to New Testament miracles

The ancient world made little distinction between the works of God and the works of nature, and tales of the miraculous were virtually taken for granted in both the Hellenism and Judaism of Jesus's time. Arguably, miracles may have been attributed to Jesus as a matter of course, with no consideration for historicity. Hellenistic miracle workers were popular, and Jesus fits the first-century picture of a wonder worker, whose popularity was based on charismatic authority. There are important differences between Jesus and popular miracle workers, however:

- Jesus heals and exorcises with a word, often from a distance.
- He attributes his authority to God alone.
- He does not use incantations or spells.
- In many cases he encourages silence after a miracle.

Jesus's miracles are signs of the kingdom. They point beyond themselves. Interestingly, Geza Vermes classified Jesus as a miracle worker in the tradition of the Hasidim — Jewish holy men — although the evangelists clearly present Jesus as more than a peripatetic miracle worker.

3 The purpose of miracles in the gospel tradition

3.1 To demonstrate the divine authority of Jesus

These points should make it clear that miracles are closely connected with christology, i.e. the revelation of Jesus's divine person.

The miracles in the synoptic gospels serve to demonstrate the source of Jesus's divine power and confirm his identity. Mark 1:1–13 makes it clear that Jesus is the Son of God, but the episodes which follow confirm that identity to the reader. The characters in the narrative wonder about it, asking 'Who is this?' But the authority that Jesus demonstrates can only be attributed to God. He displays authority over areas which were traditionally the province of God alone:

- demons (1:25)
- sickness (1:31)
- the forgiveness of sin (2:5)
- nature (4:39)
- death (5:42)

A good exercise is to go through the Old Testament to find examples of how God is depicted as having supreme control over these areas.

In all these areas Jesus shows that he is engaged in a battle with cosmic forces that he is destined to win. The evil spirits recognise Jesus as Son of God, the one who has the power to overthrow the kingdom of Satan, and when he calms the storm Jesus rebukes the sea as if it were an evil spirit. Such authority is bestowed on believers: when the seventy go out on their own mission (Luke 10:1ff.) they too are equipped to cast out demons, and in Mark 16:17 Jesus promises that all who believe will heal the sick.

Throughout the gospels, Jesus is given a variety of titles, some of which are highlighted by his miraculous works:

- **Jesus** — a common first name for a Jewish male.
- **Christ** — from the Greek 'Christos', which means 'anointed one'.

- **Son of Man** — a title that Jesus used to describe himself when talking about his messiahship and death.
- **Son of David** — from the Old Testament notion that the Messiah would be a descendant of King David.
- **Son of God** — highlights Jesus's unique relationship with God.
- **I am** — the name of God, given to Moses in Exodus 3:14. Jesus uses it to highlight his own divinity.
- **The Lamb** — according to the Old Testament, the Jewish people offered animal sacrifices to God to atone for their sins, often lambs. When Jesus was killed on the cross, he became the final and ultimate atonement for sins. His role as the Lamb of God was predicted by the prophet Isaiah, who said that the 'Servant' (possibly meaning the 'Messiah') would be 'led like a lamb to the slaughter' (53:7).
- **Messiah** — the anointed one who would one day come from God and save Israel. The term 'Messiah' (in Hebrew '*Mashiah*' and in Greek '*Christos*') was used to describe anyone entrusted with a divine mission. Many Jews believed the Messiah would destroy the enemies of Israel and set up a Jewish kingdom, ruled by the line of David. Then, on the Last Day, the Messiah would gather up God's people for judgement and life in paradise.

3.2 To show the kingdom of God has arrived

Miracles are signs of kingdom power. In Luke 1:20 & //s, Jesus declares 'If it is by the finger of God that I cast out demons, then the kingdom of God has come to you'. Even though the reality of the kingdom in its fullness lies in the future, through exorcisms Jesus demonstrates that it has become a reality through his authority exercised on earth. The Fourth Gospel includes no exorcisms, possibly because the writer understands Jesus's cosmic battle with Satan as being already won — 'He has no power over me' (John 14:30). No skirmishes with demons are necessary to demonstrate a gradual take-over.

3.3 As arenas for conflict

Conflict has an important narrative purpose, revealing characters' understanding of Jesus as well as the reason for opposition. The Jewish authorities are frequently presented as failing to recognise the true source of Jesus's authority to work miracles, attributing it instead to Satan (Mark 3:22 & //s) and as blasphemy (Mark 2:7 & //s). Sabbath healings become arenas for conflict as the Pharisees set out to test Jesus (Mark 3:2 & //s).

3.4 To fulfil Old Testament promises

Isaiah 35:5 anticipates the messianic ages when the deaf will hear, the lame will leap and the blind will see. The formerly blind man defends Jesus before the Pharisees, claiming 'Never since the world began has it been heard that anyone opened the eyes of the blind' (John 9:32). When John the Baptist sends messengers to Jesus to establish if he is the one for whom he has prepared, Jesus claims that his miraculous works should speak for themselves: 'Go and tell John what you hear and see: the blind receive their

sight, the lame walk, the lepers are cleansed, the deaf hear, and the dead are raised' (Matthew 11:4–5).

3.5 To reveal misunderstanding

Don't be guilty of making the same mistake as the characters in the narrative. Miracles are not simply stories, but tools that the evangelist uses to illustrate important themes and narrative issues.

Even Jesus's disciples are not able to perceive the significance of his miracles. When they get in the boat after the feeding miracles they still worry that they will not have enough bread: '"Do you not remember? When I broke the five loaves for the five thousand, how many baskets full of broken pieces did you collect?" Then he said to them, "Do you still not understand?"' (Mark 8:19–21). There is no guarantee that Jesus's miracles will lead to a proper understanding of his divine person. Others, however, do understand. The centurion (Matthew 8:5ff.) has sufficient faith in Jesus to know that he does not need to visit his house to heal his servant, drawing the response from Jesus 'In no one in Israel have I found such faith'.

- Miracles must be seen in the context of Jesus's death and resurrection. Mark follows the account of the transfiguration with a passion prediction (9:12 ff.) and again after the healing of a boy with an evil spirit (9:30 ff.). The travellers on the road to Emmaus describe Jesus as a 'prophet mighty in deed and word', but it is not until Jesus explains the significance of his death that their eyes are opened to recognise him.
- Miracles have an inextricable link with faith. Those who urged Jesus to perform miracles out of curiosity or as a challenge are not presented as having true faith. For those with faith, however, miracles are sought in a spirit of humility (Mark 5:28; 7:28). Faith may be demonstrated on behalf of the sick (2:3), but fear suggests a lack of faith that grows out of hardheartedness or misunderstanding (4:40).

4 *Johannine signs*

Almost any question on the Fourth Gospel could involve some discussion of signs, so it is in your interest to be able to understand their significance for the whole gospel and not simply as individual units of material.

The Fourth Evangelist adopts the designation '**sign**' rather than 'miracle'. In other words, Jesus's deeds are pointers to and indicators of his divine identity rather than mighty works to wonder at.

'Now Jesus did many other signs in the presence of his disciples which are not written in this book. But these are written so that you may come to believe that Jesus is the Messiah, the Son of God, and that through believing you may have life in his name' (John 20:30–31). This is often thought to be a statement of the Fourth Evangelist's purpose. If so, then signs are at the heart of his theology. They point to the divine nature of Jesus, which is the means of salvation for man.

Only seven signs are selected, presumably from a much wider store of material available to the Fourth Evangelist. Disputed signs are the walking on the water (6:16 ff.), which is followed by no teaching discourse, and the spear thrust (19:34), which may link with Cana and the feeding of the five thousand (see Joseph Grassi, *The Secret Identity of the Beloved Disciple*, Paulist Press, 1992), but in itself has no miraculous content. The miraculous catch of fish forms part of the post-resurrection appearances and may be modelled on Luke 5.

There are no exorcisms. Jesus's victory over Satan is won before the cross, and his authority over the spiritual world is without question.

E Parables and the teaching of Jesus

The material in this section is relevant to questions on:

- individual parables and parable themes
- the kingdom of God
- discipleship
- the nature of God
- the background to Jesus's teaching and early church interpretation of it

1 Jesus the teacher

> This is the province of narrative criticism. The characters in the gospel wonder about the source of Jesus's authority, but the reader has already been told where it comes from.

Jesus is called ***didaskalos*** (teacher) in all four gospels, and the title **rabbi** — the form of address used for most teachers — is applied in all the gospels except Luke. Luke employs the term ***epistates***, possibly to distinguish Jesus from other teachers of lesser authority. Jesus is not referred to as 'teacher' by the early church, thus is it not a confessional title like Son of God. Rather, it describes the form of his earthly ministry, although Jesus himself is more than a teacher. However, Jesus's hearers perceive his teaching to have a greater authority than that of the scribes (Mark 1:22), so christological significance is applied to Jesus's role as a teacher. For the evangelist and the reader, if Jesus has unique authority as a teacher it is because his teaching, like Jesus himself, comes directly from God.

2 Setting

> Reactions to Jesus's teaching are an important part of the plot. After all, if Jesus never said anything it is unlikely that he would have gained such strong opposition.

Jesus's early teaching is in the **synagogue** — firmly within the structure of Judaism. (Note too that Paul went to the synagogue first to teach on his missionary journeys.) In Luke 4:16ff. Jesus adopts the regular practice of reading the daily portion of scripture, before shocking the crowd by applying it to himself. Teaching in the synagogue is associated with miracles (Mark 1:23ff. & //s; Luke 13:10) and is open and public: 'I have spoken openly to the world; I have always taught in synagogues and in the temple, where all the Jews come together' (John 18:20).

3 Types of teaching

3.1 Conflict

Much teaching is associated with conflict, which serves a dramatic and narrative function to move the plot along. Jesus's teaching on the sabbath (Mark 2:23ff. & //s; John 5:17) and on his own person (John 8:49ff.) serves to heighten opposition against him, which climaxes in the arrest and trials. Conflict scenes are often in the context of debates over legal issues, e.g. the

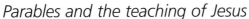

question about divorce (Mark 10:2ff. & //s), and may not originally have been as antagonistic as the evangelists suggest. The later conflicts between the early church and the Jewish authorities may have coloured their interpretation of Jesus's relationship with religious officials. Jesus may have been accepted as a rabbi and been naturally drawn into contemporary areas of debate, interpreted by the early church as tests or tricks.

3.2 Public and private teaching

Jesus speaks to crowds (Matthew 5:1; 15:32) in a teaching ministry often accompanied by miracles: 'Jesus went throughout Galilee teaching in their synagogues…and curing every disease and every sickness' (Matthew 4:23). The **Sermon on the Mount** provides a block of teaching (Matthew 5–7) supposedly to a large crowd. Much of this material is also found in Luke, but here it is scattered throughout Jesus's public ministry. Matthew may have chosen to group a series of teachings together to present Jesus as the archetypal teacher — the new Moses. Key themes in public teaching are the **imminence of the kingdom of God** and the need for **personal repentance** and commitment to its coming. Those ready to make such a commitment are held up as examples (Luke 19:9; Matthew 8:10ff.); those who are not ready risk losing out on the kingdom (Matthew 8:21; Luke 18:18ff. & //s). The inner circle of disciples (usually referred to as the Twelve) receive private teaching on the meaning of parables (Mark 4:10ff.), on their missionary task (Matthew 10; Mark 6:7ff.) and on Jesus's impending passion (Mark 9:9ff.). Their false perceptions of Jesus and his ministry are corrected (Mark 8:33) and they are equipped to be authoritative bearers of teaching (Matthew 28:20).

It is likely that Jesus's inner circle of disciples was bigger than this, but they form a nucleus of followers who receive special teaching appropriate to their close relationship with Jesus and their future role in the early church mission.

3.3 Jewish methods

Jesus's teaching appears to be partly related to typical Jewish methods of teaching. This is characterised in the use of parables, but also in the association of a small group of followers who receive special teaching. Jesus alludes to the Old Testament rather than quoting from it extensively. Issues of interest to scholarly Judaism are raised, e.g. God's continuing creative activity (John 5:17ff.), or the interpretation of the Law (Matthew 5:17ff.). Jesus is presented as fulfilling the Law, not overriding it, despite the tone of some conflict discourses.

The early church was divided over the extent to which it was to be obedient to the Law. Matthew appears to be attacking a lax view that Jesus's teaching had overthrown the Law.

3.4 The use of teaching formulae

As well as parables, Jesus is depicted as using rhetorical devices and repeated aphorisms — 'The Son of Man has come to seek and save the lost' (Luke 19:10); 'Let anyone with ears to hear listen' (Mark 4:9); 'Those who are last will be first, and those who are first will be last' (Luke 13:30). Teaching is prefaced with injunctions: 'Listen', 'I tell you', 'When you', 'Now'. The Fourth Evangelist employs the formula 'Amen, amen', translated variously as 'Truly, truly' or 'Truly I say to you'. Much of Jesus's teaching takes the form of sayings that would have been easily memorised, a basic method in first-century Jewish scholarship. However, it has been suggested that some teachings of Jesus may already have acquired a written form before his death.

See the 'Biblical criticism' section (pp. 10–14) for more discussion of the evangelists' sources and the presentation of their material.

4   *Parables*

Arguably (since there is no scholarly agreement as to what exactly constitutes a parable), Mark's gospel records 6 parables, Matthew's 21 and Luke's 29, of which 9 are from Q, 9 from M and 18 from L. Many of the parables included only in Matthew and Luke reflect the evangelists' particular theological interests.

So central to Jesus's teaching are the parables that Mark 4:34 makes the claim that 'He did not speak to them except in parables, but he explained everything in private to his disciples'. R. Riesner (in *Dictionary of Jesus and the Gospels*, IVP, 1992, p. 809) observes that parables were 'not blurted out *ad hoc*, but show every indication … of being very deliberate and condensed formulations'.

4.1 Characteristics of parables

The word **parabole** is used in a range of ways: it may be a short saying or proverb, a parallel ('With what shall I compare …'), a riddle or paradox, or an allegory. It is most commonly associated with a story form that is used to make an extended metaphor — a fictional scenario is created to illustrate truths of a spiritual nature. They are brief, based on everyday events (typically agricultural settings) but often including a hyperbole (exaggeration), e.g. the servant who owed 10,000 talents (Matthew 18:23ff.). The parables invite hearers to make a judgement about situations described, and often demand a reversal of values. For example, the Samaritan in Luke 10 is the unexpected hero of the story. Most parables invite the listener to change their behaviour or attitude towards others and/or God.

4.2 Themes of parables

The themes of parables are, of course, themes that are prevalent in the gospel tradition as a whole. See the sections 'Salvation, eternal life and the kingdom of God' (pp. 44–48) and 'Discipleship' (pp. 57–60) for more material that is relevant here.

4.2a The nature of the kingdom on earth

The kingdom is compared to a mustard seed, a net, a pearl, treasure, and seed that grows secretly and among weeds. The small beginnings of the kingdom belie the great future that it will have, and its manifestation on earth may appear contradictory — the weeds and the wheat grow up together. It demands a response (the Sower) and is of great value, beyond that of earthly riches (the Pearl and the Treasure).

4.2b The imminence of the kingdom

Parables of the parousia emphasise that the kingdom on earth is to be fulfilled in the future. That fulfilment will be unexpected and no time can be lost in making preparations in the present (e.g. the Wise and Foolish Bridesmaids). Places at the messianic banquet in the kingdom will not necessarily be filled by those who anticipated a place of honour (e.g. the Great Banquet), and how disciples spend the time between conversion and the parousia must be accounted for (e.g. the Talents).

> *Then will the door of the festal hall be closed, and the word will be heard: Too late! (These) closely related parables describe what it means to be too late.*
>
> J. Jeremias, *The Parables of Jesus*, SCM, 1954, p. 171

4.2c The nature of God

The parables are **theocentric** rather than christocentric, i.e. they describe the nature of God rather than that of Jesus. God is shown to be a loving father (e.g. the Lost Son) and a generous employer (e.g. the Workers in the Vineyard), but also as the owner of the vineyard who demands his rightful share in its produce (e.g. the Wicked Tenants). Hearers are warned not to trifle with God, who must call man to account at the end of time, but they are reassured that God's heart is for those who acknowledge their sin (e.g. the Pharisee and the Tax Collector).

4.2d Discipleship

The parables are all aimed at encouraging good discipleship: obedience (e.g. the Two Sons), wisdom (e.g. the Two Builders), compassion (e.g. the Good Samaritan), shrewdness (e.g. the Dishonest Steward) and forgiveness (e.g. the Unforgiving Servant). Luke specially focuses on a correct relationship with wealth (e.g. the Rich Fool, the Rich Man and Lazarus) and on prayer (e.g. the Unjust Judge, the Friend at Midnight).

4.3 The use of parables in the early church

The good biblical scholar will show an awareness of the context of the material: it would be naïve to assume that the gospel text relates the words of Jesus exactly as spoken.

Although the parables include additions by the early church and were clearly adapted to suit its needs, there is evidence that some of their teaching, at least, goes back to Jesus. They reflect the eschatological feeling of his time and the circumstances of everyday life. However, as Graham Stanton observes, 'In the course of their transmission, the parables have undergone more extensive adaptation and reinterpretation than any other part of the traditions about the actions and teaching of Jesus' (*The Gospels and Jesus*, OUP, 1989, p. 205). Many parables have become divorced from their original context and the evangelists have added conclusions or introductions to them. Related parables are grouped together in one gospel, separated in another.

4.4 Guidelines for interpreting parables

- Compare the language, structure and place of the parable with that in other gospels.
- Consider how it fits into the gospel in which it is used.
- Be aware of the cultural background to the parable.
- Consider its application in the following three *Sitz im Leben*: the ministry of Jesus, the evangelist's setting and the early church.
- Consider the context in which it is placed, and its possible original context.
- Consider what place the parable has in the gospel tradition as a whole.

F Special features of the Fourth Gospel

The material in this section is relevant to questions on:
- the Prologue to the Fourth Gospel
- the purpose of the Fourth Gospel

1 The Prologue

> *The Prologue is a popular area, but questions require a detailed knowledge of the text and background as well as the views of scholars. Only attempt such a question if you have an excellent grasp of the material.*

The introduction to the Fourth Gospel is called the Prologue (1:1–18), which provides readers with a concise understanding of the gospel narrative, plot and events.

> *Through him all things were made; without him nothing was made that has been made. In him was life; and the life was the light of men. The light shines in the darkness, but the darkness has not understood it.*
>
> John 1:3–5

> *He came as a witness to testify to the light, so that through him all men might believe.*
>
> John 1:7

1.1 The Word (*Logos*)

> *The term 'Logos' links together concepts from the Old Testament, the Jewish Rabbinic tradition, Hellenistic and Stoic thought and early Christian theology*

In the Prologue, the writer says that Jesus Christ is God himself, who came into the world as a human being. The story of Jesus is the story of the *Logos* or Word. The *Logos* worked alongside God in creation and came into the world as Christ.

There is much religious significance:
- The author brings from Judaism the idea of **God's creative breath (*ruah*)** — his speech, wisdom and purpose from which creation comes.
- The Jews identified the Word of God with the **Torah**; the Word was God's wisdom, embodied in the **Law**, and the Word gave meaning to life.
- The author incorporates the Hellenistic notions of the ideal world and the ideal human.

The Word:
- is a living, distinct being within the Trinity
- is the source of light and life
- was with God 'in the beginning' (v.1)

- is the eternal purpose of God — it is that which gives meaning to life; the author is trying to show to the readers that, in Jesus, the whole purpose of God and creation has meaning

> *The preface to the Fourth Gospel, with its movement from the Word to the Son of God, is both an introduction and a conclusion to the whole work. The relation between creation and salvation, prophets and apostles, history and that beyond history, time and eternity, law and grace, death and life, faith and unbelief — these are the themes of the Fourth Gospel.*
>
> E. Hoskyns and F. Davey, *The Fourth Gospel*, Faber, 1947, p. 43

1.2 Themes of the Prologue

Scholars have differing views concerning the Prologue:
- **J. A. T. Robinson** claims that it is a later addition to the gospel and was put in to bring things to a conclusion.
- **C. F. Burney** says it is an Aramaic hymn.
- **Graham Stanton** suggests it is the **'lens'** through which to view the rest of the gospel.
- **Morna Hooker** describes it as a **'key'** that unlocks the gospel.

1.3 John the Baptist

- John the Baptist was sent from God to announce the coming of the light into the world.
- He bridges the gap between the Old Testament and the New Testament.
- He shows humanity how to recognise Jesus as the Word.
- He is a witness offering testimony to the light; such a testimony was crucial in establishing truth. John shows that the 'light' of the Scriptures is fulfilled in Christ, the incarnate Word of God.

The testimony of a witness as crucial in establishing the truth of a claim. The Word of God is known through testimony — from God himself, or from his divinely inspired messengers.

1.4 The Word Incarnate

The message of the Prologue is that humanity must recognise Christ as the Word Incarnate. However, this is not easy:
- The people live in darkness and do not recognise him.
- Some did receive him. To these are given the right to become 'children of God' (1:12).
- It is not a physical birth, but a spiritual one, achieved through faith in Jesus Christ.
- God became fully human through the Word.

> *He came into the world, and though the world was made through him, the world did not recognise him. He came to his own, but his own did not receive him.*
>
> **John 1:10–12**

1.5 Law, grace and truth

- Jesus is the incarnate word of God, which has existed from the beginning — this is the notion of pre-existence.
- The word becoming flesh is a gift from God to all who believe.
- Humanity will not be saved by obeying the law, but through the grace and truth of God.
- God has become human so that humanity can truly know him.

To become children is a gift of God. This is to be the difference between the Jews — God's chosen people by birth — and Christians, chosen through God's grace.

2 *Purpose*

The author of the Fourth Gospel states his purpose in 20:31:

> *But these are written that you may believe that Jesus is the Christ, the Son of God, and that by believing you may have life in his name.*

The textual narrative supports this in the following ways.

2.1 'Jesus is the Christ...'

The Gospel highlights the fact that Jesus is the Christ, the Messiah who will bring salvation. This is seen in the following incidents:

- Jesus clears the temple (2:13–17) — a promised Messianic action, reflected in Psalm 69:9: 'Zeal for your house will consume me.'
- The healing at the pool, which took place on the Sabbath (5:1–16).
- The disciples will recognise Jesus as Messiah (1:41, 49).
- Jesus tells the Samaritan woman he is the Messiah (4:25–26).
- There are Messianic overtones when Jesus feeds the people (6:1–15).
- Jesus makes a triumphal entry into Jerusalem riding a donkey, in fulfilment of prophecy (12:12–19).
- The Jewish authorities refuse to accept Jesus as the Messiah (5:18, 7:47, 10:33, 19:7).
- The disciples' acknowledgement of Jesus as Messiah (1:41, 1:49, 6:68–69, 7:41).

2.2 'The Son of God...'

There are several references to Christ as the Son of God:

- John the Baptist testifies that 'I have seen and have borne witness that this is the Son of God' (1:34).
- Jesus refers to his intimate relationship to God.
- Jesus knows the Father's will.
- Jesus and the Father are one (3:35, 5:19–20, 8: 4, 14:10).

This is a popular topic for exam questions, which usually require the candidate to consider not only the author's stated purpose, but also other possible purposes.

The author uses Old Testament prophecies to show how the work of the promised Messiah will be fulfilled in Jesus.

Jesus's claim to be the Son of God led directly to the charge of blasphemy levelled against him by the Jews: 'We have a law, and according to that law he must die, because he claimed to be the Son of God' (19:7).

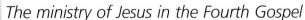

Clement of Alexandria stated: 'Last of all, John, perceiving that the external facts had been made plain in the Gospels, being urged by his friends and inspired by the Spirit, composed a spiritual Gospel.'

B. F. Westcott, comparing the Fourth Gospel with Luke's Gospel, suggested that: 'The real difference is that the earliest Gospel contained the fundamental facts and words which experience afterwards interpreted, while the latest Gospel reveals the facts in the light of their interpretation.'

2.3 '...that by believing you may have life in his name'

Eternal life comes from believing in the teaching of Christ:
- He lays down his life for the sheep (10:11).
- He is 'the Lamb of God, who takes away the sin of the world' (1:29).
- He is lifted up and draws all to him (12:32).
- Those who accept him receive eternal life (3:16).
- He sacrifices himself in order that humanity may have life (12:24, 10:10).

Some scholars believe the author may have other purposes too.

2.4 A spiritual gospel

Some scholars believe the author wrote a spiritual gospel, not to provide an accurate biography of Jesus's life but to express vital truths about Jesus in order to lead his readers into the belief that Jesus was the Son of God. The author does this in the following ways:
- He alters the historical sequence of events in Jesus's life to highlight important theological points. For example, the cleansing of the temple occurs at the start of Jesus's ministry (2:12–25), whereas in the synoptic gospels it occurs near the end.
- He highlights the importance of worship in spirit and truth (4:24)
- He states that Jesus is the place where humanity meets with God (1:51, 2:21).
- He alters the timing of Jesus's death, with events brought forward by 24 hours.
- He states that Jesus's death on the cross is the fulfilment of Scripture.
- He emphasises Jesus's divinity and uses witnesses to support this, for example John the Baptist (1:29) and the Samaritan woman (4:25–26).
- He emphasises the relationship between Jesus and the Father.
- He shows how Jesus is in control of all the events leading up to the Cross.

2.5 Other possible purposes

- To counteract the doctrines of Docetism and Gnosticism.
- To bring the message of Christ to Jews in Gentile nations. (Barrett)
- To convert Jews to Christianity (Robinson).
- To preach salvation to all humanity (Smalley).

G The ministry of Jesus in the Fourth Gospel

The material in this section is relevant to questions on:
- signs
- 'I am' sayings
- women in the Fourth Gospel

In the first part of the Fourth Gospel, the author highlights Jesus's teachings about himself and the nature of salvation. These teachings are sometimes accompanied by signs or 'I am' sayings.

1 The wedding at Cana (2:1–11): the first sign

The story of the wedding at Cana shows how Jesus has come to replace the old Jewish rituals with the new way — with life through him. It contains much symbolism:

- It takes place 'on the third day', with echoes of the resurrection.
- Jesus is invited to the wedding — the Messiah comes to his people.
- The six stone jars contained the water that was needed in the Jewish purification rites.
- Jesus changes the inadequate water into excellent wine and the feast is complete.

The meaning of the first sign is clear: the water of Judaism is inadequate for salvation — the wine/blood of Christ is the path to eternal life.

In the Old Testament, God was depicted as the bridegroom and Israel was the unfaithful bride (Isaiah 54: 5; Hosea 2:19). At this wedding, Jesus is the bridegroom returning to Israel.

2 Cleansing the temple (2:12–25)

The temple market was where faithful Jews could buy animals for sacrifice, in the belief that this could lead to the forgiveness of their sins ('atonement'). Jesus is angry because God's message in the Old Testament was that he did not want animal sacrifices, but worship from the heart (Psalm 51:16). Jesus's message is that salvation will not come through sacrifices but through faith in him.

In the Old Testament, it had been foretold that the Lord would one day come and cleanse his temple (Malachi 3:1; Isaiah 56:7).

3 Jesus and Nicodemus (3:1–21)

The conversation between Jesus and Nicodemus shows the struggle between traditional Judaism and the teaching of Jesus:

- He comes to Jesus at night, symbolising the 'darkness' in which he lives.
- He accepts Jesus as a teacher who has come from God.
- Nicodemus's knowledge of the law and the Scriptures is not enough for salvation.
- Nicodemus can see God's power but he cannot truly experience a personal relationship with God. To do this he must be born again.
- Jesus is saying is that the Jewish rituals will not lead to salvation — rebirth in the spirit is necessary.

Nicodemus represents the best of Judaism. He is a Pharisee and probably a member of the Sanhedrin. He is a Jew who would like to follow Jesus but cannot because he is hampered by his religious situation.

4 Jesus and the Samaritan woman (4:1–45)

In this meeting, Jesus highlights the faith of a Samaritan woman and also reveals his identity to her — something he had not done with his male disciples. He also shows her that the religious traditions of the Samaritans, like those of Judaism, are insufficient for salvation. The main areas of religious significance are the following:

The Samaritans were Jews who had inter-mixed with foreigners. Those who believed themselves to be the true Jews despised them for having abandoned their Jewish faith and traditions.

- The action takes place at Jacob's Well, the place where the patriarch Jacob changed his name to 'Israel'.
- Jesus asks her for a drink. She is surprised, for a Jew would not speak to a Samaritan woman.
- He tells her that he has 'living water' (4:10).
- He tells the woman to call her husband, but she is not married. 'Husband' refers to God.
- The woman called him a 'prophet' (4:19).
- Jesus tells her that he is the Messiah (4:26).
- She acts as a disciple should, going to her people and telling them the 'good news'.
- The townsfolk receive Jesus and accept him.

5. Jesus and the official's son (4:46–54): the second sign

When writing an answer, remember that you do not need to retell the story; it is more important to explain its meaning and significance.

The official is probably a Roman administrator, and he asks Jesus to heal his sick son. Jesus does so with the words: 'You may go. Your son will live' (4:50). The official has such great faith in Jesus that he is able to accept his word without question and goes home to his healed son.

The meaning of the sign is that true belief means obedience and trust in the word and power of Christ.

6. The healing at the pool (5:1–30): the third sign

The crippled man had been there for 38 years, the same length of time that the Israelites had wandered in the desert under Moses (Deuteronomy 2:14).

Jesus meets a crippled man on the Sabbath and asks him if he wants to be healed. He says to the man, 'Arise, take up your bed and walk'. Immediately, the man is made well, and he obeys Jesus's instruction. This causes problems with the Jewish authorities, who say it is against the Law of Moses to work on the Sabbath, and that the man should not be carrying his bed.

Moreover, when the Jewish authorities question Jesus, he tells them of his unique relationship with God and that, as God's Son, he did what God required him to do. He tells them that God will bring judgement and that humanity has been given a chance of eternal life by following him:

> *I tell you the truth, whoever hears my word and believes him who sent me has eternal life and will not be condemned. He has crossed over from death to life.*
>
> **John 5:24**

The later part of Jesus's ministry is characterised by the 'I am' sayings and signs.

The believers shared bread, as the disciples would at the Last Supper. At the end of time, all the faithful would eat with the Messiah according to Revelations 19:17.

7 *The feeding of the five thousand (6:1–15): the fourth sign*

With only five small loaves and two fish, Jesus miraculously feeds a crowd of 5,000 people (6:11). The disciples gather up 12 baskets full of fragments. Sadly, the people do not understand the message of the sign; they think Jesus is a great prophet and want forcibly to crown him as king.

8 *Jesus walks on water (6:16–24)*

Later, the disciples are on a boat in rough weather on the lake and Jesus miraculously walks on the water to them. Jesus is proving to the disciples that he possesses God's authority and power.

In Exodus 3:14, God tells Moses that his name is 'I am': 'God said to Moses, 'I am who I am'.

9 *'I am the Bread of Life' (6:35): the first 'I am' saying*

Jesus proclaims his divinity by describing himself in a series of 'I am' sayings ('*ego eimi*'). Jesus tells the people that:
- under Moses in the desert God gave the people 'bread from heaven' (6:32)
- he is the bread to satisfy their spiritual hunger; this will be understood after his resurrection
- 'whoever eats my flesh and drinks my blood has eternal life and I will raise him up at the last day' (6:54)

Many scholars believe that this incident was not part of the original text of the Fourth Gospel.

10 *The woman caught in adultery (8:1–11)*

The Jews bring before Jesus a woman guilty of fornication before marriage (an offence punishable by death under the Law of Moses — Deuteronomy 22:23). Jesus saves her with the words: 'If any one of you is without sin, let him be the first to throw a stone at her' (8:7). The woman is saved, but Jesus does not excuse her sin. Instead he suggests that the law is not wrong but that it should not be imposed in such a strict and unfeeling way.

The setting for the second 'I am' saying is the last day of the Feast of Tabernacles, and in the evening four golden candlesticks were lit in the temple precincts, symbolising the pillar of flame by which God led the Israelites through the desert (Exodus 13:21).

11 *'I am the Light of the World' (8:12–30): the second 'I am' saying*

This saying has much symbolic significance:
- Humanity lives in darkness and sin.
- Jesus has come with God's light to show humanity the truth.
- Those who follow Jesus will never walk in darkness again.

The Pharisees cannot grasp the spiritual significance. Jesus tells them the light he will bring will show everyone the truth of their situation; being 'Sons of

Abraham' will not be enough. To be freed from the darkness of sin they must believe in him.

12 Healing the blind man (9:1–41): the fifth sign

The blind man probably begged at the gate of the temple. Jesus restores the man's sight by spitting into some clay and anointing the man's eyes with it. Note the following:

- God uses clay in Genesis 2 to create Adam.
- Jesus makes the blind man into a new person.
- The man washes his eyes and receives his sight.
- He has been cleansed in 'living water', and the 'light of the world' has entered into him.
- The Pharisees say that Jesus cannot be from God because this healing happened on the Sabbath.
- The man is thrown out of the synagogue.
- Jesus tells the man who he is.
- The man worships Jesus — he has received both physical 'sight' and spiritual 'sight'.
- Jesus tells the Pharisees they are spiritually blind.

Popular belief at that time held that blindness was a punishment from God because of the sins of the person or his or her parents. Jesus said that this was not true.

To be thrown out of the synagogue meant to be 'excommunicated', and was the most severe of punishments. It meant that no other Jew could associate with him and that God would 'reject' him forever.

13 'I am the Gate for the Sheep' (10:1–10): the third 'I am' saying

In these sayings, Jesus declares that he (and not the chief priests) is the real leader of God's people:

- A shepherd protects the sheep and guards the entrance to the sheepfold.
- Jesus is the real shepherd; the chief priests are false shepherds, who enter by stealth and use threats.
- Jesus is the 'gate' through which the sheep (people) will pass in order to find safety and life.

14 'I am the Good Shepherd' (10:11–42): the fourth 'I am' saying

- A good shepherd sacrifices his own life for his sheep.
- He says ' I lay down my life for the sheep' (10:15).
- Jesus speaks of 'other sheep that are not of this sheep pen' (10:16) in reference to the Gentiles, who will also become part of his flock.
- He says 'I and the Father are one' (10:30).
- The Jews try to stone him but he slips away unharmed.

H Social themes in Luke's gospel

The material in this section is relevant to questions on:
- outcasts and Jesus
- women in the gospels
- the background to the gospels
- parables

In Luke's gospel, Jesus teaches much concerning social issues and, in particular, the treatment of others.

1 *Outcasts*

Within Judaism, certain people were considered to be outcasts or 'sinners', including tax collectors, prostitutes and lepers. Jesus is seen closely associating with such people:
- He calls Levi, a tax collector, to be one of his disciples (5:27).
- He dines with sinners.
- Jesus is the guest of Zacchaeus, a tax collector who receives salvation (19:1–10).
- Jesus teaches of God's concern for outcasts in the parable of the lost son (15:11–32) and the parable of the great banquet (14:15–24).

> *'Why do you eat and drink with tax collectors and sinners?' Jesus answered them, 'It is not the healthy that need a doctor, but the sick. I have not come to call the righteous, but sinners to repentance'.*
>
> **Luke 5:31–32**

2 *Women*

Women had an inferior role in Jewish society. The Law of Moses required them to be obedient and submissive, with their role restricted to raising children and keeping house. However, Jesus emphasised the importance of women and they appear in key roles throughout the gospel. Jesus's relationship with women is characterised in several ways:
- Jesus allows certain women to accompany his group.
- Jesus allows women to listen to his teaching, as a pupil would to a rabbi — a privilege usually given to men.
- Jesus breaks social conventions concerning women. For example, he allows a sinful woman to anoint his feet — an action usually seen as defilement.
- Jesus performs miracles for the benefit of women — the woman with the haemorrhage (8:42), the widow of Nain, Jairus's daughter (8:49) and the crippled woman (13:10).

- Jesus refers to the great faith of women in the parable of the lost coin (15:8) and the parable of the unjust judge (18:1).
- Women are always shown as faithful and obedient.
- It is women who first see the risen Christ.

3 Rich and poor

Luke stresses the importance of Jesus's preaching of the gospel to the poor (4:18) and this is significant:
- Jesus was born into humble circumstances.
- His first visitors were poor shepherds.
- He spoke of the importance of caring for the poor.

'Indeed, it is easier for a camel to go through the eye of a needle than for a rich man to enter the kingdom of God' (18:25).

Jesus warns of the dangers of wealth, because it can keep people from having a proper relationship with God. He does not just mean money, but also power and arrogance. The most important teachings are contained in:
- the parables of the rich fool (12:16), the shrewd manager (16:1) and the rich man and Lazarus (16:19)
- Jesus's conversation with the rich young ruler (18:18–27).
- Jesus's encounter with Zacchaeus, who gives back his property to the poor and receives salvation (19:9)

4 Discipleship

A disciple is a pupil — someone who learns from a teacher. Luke uses the term to mean those who follow Jesus.

The Twelve Disciples named by Luke are Simon (Peter), Andrew, James, John, Philip, Levi, Bartholomew, Thomas, James son of Alphaeus, Simon the Zealot, Judas son of James and Judas Iscariot.

Luke shows the commitment needed to be a disciple:
- repentance
- giving up everything to follow Jesus
- being prepared to accept persecution and death

Luke also emphasises the positive benefits of discipleship, stating that disciples will:
- be helped by the Holy Spirit in times of trouble
- have the authority of Jesus to act in his name
- be filled with joy at their work
- be blessed by God.
- have a unique relationship with God, which will last forever
- achieve great things
- have their prayers answered
- bring in the new age

5 Parables of the lost: Luke 15

Do not just retell the parables. Make sure you can discuss their meaning and significance.

The parables of the lost emphasis Luke's theme of seeking God and finding salvation. They add a fresh dimension; God does not simply wait for people to find him, he actively helps them to do so.

5.1 The parable of the lost sheep

Jesus shows God as a shepherd with 99 safe sheep and one lost sheep. He seeks the lost one and rejoices when he finds it. This highlights the joy of God over the return of one sinner who has repented:

> *There will be more rejoicing in heaven over one sinner who repents than over ninety-nine righteous persons who do not need to repent.*
>
> **Luke 15:7**

5.2 The parable of the lost coin

A woman with 10 silver coins misplaces one and sweeps the whole house in her search for it. When she finds it, she rejoices. In a similar way, God will seek out the repentant sinner and then rejoice in finding him or her.

5.3 The parable of the lost son

This parable shows the nature of God's forgiving love and highlights the contrast between the repentant sinner and those who feel they are righteous. The key features are:

- The younger of two brothers asks his father for his share of the estate.
- The father agrees and the son goes off to another country and spends it on riotous living.
- When the money is spent, the son is forced to feed pigs in order to live.
- He decides to return home and ask his father to give him a job as a servant.
- His father overwhelms him with welcome.
- He gives him the finest robe, a ring on his finger and shoes on his feet. He orders a feast of celebration.
- The eldest brother complains to his father that he has worked hard for him, yet never been given a feast.

The parable is symbolic:
- The father represents God.
- The eldest son represents the 'righteous' Jews.
- The youngest son represents repentant sinners.
- God welcomes the sinner back and does not accept the complaint of the Jews who believe they are righteous.

Feeding pigs was a distasteful job for a Jew, since the pig was regarded as an unclean creature (Leviticus 11:7).

The ring given to the son symbolises authority and he has shoes because only slaves went barefoot.

The message to the Jews was that showing love to repentant sinners is not a threat to those who are already within the kingdom of God.

The death of Jesus

The material in this section is relevant to questions on:
- the passion and resurrection narratives
- redaction criticism

- christology
- early church preaching
- use of Old Testament in the gospels
- political background to the New Testament

1 The significance of Jesus's death

> *For we preach Christ crucified, a stumbling block to Jews and folly to Gentiles.*
>
> **1 Corinthians 1:23**

- All four evangelists record Jesus's death and the events leading up to it in considerable detail.
- Jesus's death is at the heart of early church preaching, despite its being a serious challenge to those who receive it.
- It is the longest continuous narrative in the gospels. This has led form critics to suggest that a passion narrative tradition, older than the gospels, lies behind it.
- It is in the passion narrative that all the evangelists use their most distinctive material.
- In all the gospels, Jesus's death is anticipated from early in the narrative:

Mark 3:6: the Jewish officials make plans to destroy him.

Matthew 2:16: Herod's massacre is a forerunner of Jesus's death at the hands of officials.

Luke 2:34: Simeon prophesies that Jesus will be 'spoken against'.

John 1:11: the prologue to the Fourth Gospel observes that 'He came to his own home and his own people received him not'.

Thus, the theme of Jesus's death is **programmatic** to the gospel — it is not just the substance of the final chapters. Everything in Jesus's ministry and in the evangelists' interpretation of it points towards and prepares for his death.

In questions on Jesus's death you need to show your understanding of how the evangelists prepared for the passion narratives, often from the first chapter of the gospel.

2 Passion predictions

In the synoptic gospels, passion predictions are essential to focus the reader's attention on the real meaning of Jesus's ministry.

- They follow events which exalt Jesus's messiahship (i.e. the transfiguration).
- They emphasise the disciples' misunderstanding of his ministry (see Mark 10:35 — James and John ask for positions of honour in the kingdom after a passion prediction).
- They stress the necessity of Jesus's death; it is not an accident of fate: Luke uses the Greek word *dei* ('must') when speaking of Jesus's impending passion.

These are episodes when Jesus or the narrator explain to characters in the narrative, or to the disciples, that Jesus is to die. Watch out for subtleties here — the use of imagery and symbolism is especially important in the Fourth Gospel.

- They are not understood by the disciples. On the road to Emmaus (Luke 24) the disciples' dismay at Jesus's death shows that they have not grasped why he had to die.
- They also anticipate the resurrection and Jesus's promise to meet the disciples in Galilee after he is raised. It is a matter of some surprise, therefore, that the women go to the tomb to anoint the body (Mark 16:7; Luke 24:5).

In the Fourth Gospel Jesus speaks cryptically about 'going away'. His opponents think he is talking of some geographical location, but his disciples also struggle to understand that Jesus must die — 'Lord, we do not know where you are going; how can we know the way?' (John 14:5).

Symbolism is used amply in the Fourth Gospel: Jesus will be the new temple, destroyed and yet raised in three days (2:19); he is like the serpent lifted up in the wilderness (3:14); he is the heavenly redeemer who comes from heaven and returns to it (3:13). As the bread of life, Jesus gives his flesh for the salvation of the world (6:51); Jesus raises Lazarus from the dead, illustrating that through Jesus's own death there is life (11:25–26).

3 *Conflict and Jesus's death*

The evangelists recognise that the theological significance of Jesus's death makes it unavoidable, however it may have been accomplished. Nevertheless, the culpability of the religious and political authorities in the event is made clear. The passion predictions anticipate that Jesus will be 'delivered into the hands of men' (Matthew 17:22), who are to be the vehicles of God's divine plan. Hence, scenes of conflict prepare for the arrest and trials:

- Sabbath controversies lead to plots against Jesus's life. Under Jewish law blasphemy was punishable by death, although it is questionable whether they had that authority under Roman occupation.
- Despite open conflict, Jesus is able to avoid arrest until his 'time has come'. In Luke 4:30 he passes through a crowd intent on pushing him down a hill, and in John 8:59 he hides himself from an angry mob. These episodes suggest divine concealing and protection.
- The crowds drawn by Jesus's teaching are a primary reason for conflict. After the raising of Lazarus the Pharisees worry that 'If we let him go on thus, every one will believe in him, and the Romans will come and destroy our holy place and our nation' (John 11:48). Jesus's death is seen to be a political expedient to avoid such an outcome: 'One man should die for the people, and the whole nation should not perish' (John 11:50).
- John the Baptist's death is seen as a forerunner of Jesus's passion. He too was a charismatic leader who died at the hands of a weak ruler (Mark 6:14ff.).

Note that Jesus did not die because he healed on the sabbath and annoyed the Pharisees. This may have contributed to the final events that culminate on the cross, but it is by no means the primary reason.

> *Even the most non-political of charismatics took his life in his hands when he preached the good news of God's coming kingdom.*
>
> **Ellis Rivkin, *What Crucified Jesus?*, SCM, 1984, p. 19**

Ellis Rivkin argues that it was the force of Roman occupancy alone that provided the historico-political reason for Jesus's death. Conflict between Jesus and the Jewish authorities would not have led to his death had the issue been entirely religious. Rather, it was the pressure felt by the Jewish authorities to quash the revolutionary spirit of some Jews which forced their hand.

> *Had there been no Roman imperial system, Jesus would have faced the buffetings of strong words, the batterings of skilfully aimed proof texts, and the ridicule of both Sadducees and Scribe-Pharisees, but he would have stood no trial, been affixed to no cross.*
>
> **Ellis Rivkin, *What Crucified Jesus?*, SCM, 1984, p. 75**

> Remember that ultimately, for the evangelists, Jesus dies because it is the only way in which man can be reconciled to God. They use the passion narratives to show how the divine person and purpose of Jesus is revealed in the passion events.

> Other episodes in the passion narratives which the evangelists shape distinctively are the Last Supper, the arrest and the trials before the high priest. Check these over.

4 The evangelists' interpretation of the passion story

> *Even if an early short passion narrative does lie behind all four gospels, the evangelists have all developed their own distinctive emphases both by their choice of supplementary traditions and by their reshaping and adaptation of the narratives.*
>
> **Graham Stanton, *The Gospels and Jesus*, OUP, 1989, p. 249**

Mark's gospel provides the structure followed by all the evangelists: Last Supper, arrest, trials (high priest and Pilate), crucifixion, death, burial. To this structure Matthew, Luke and John add their own material and interpretation of Mark's narrative.

4.1 Matthew's major additions

Emphasis on Jesus as the rejected Messiah
- Judas's suicide, including an Old Testament fulfilment citation from Jeremiah 32.
- Pilate's washing of hands and his wife's dream, removing direct blame for Jesus's death from Pilate.
- Apocalyptic phenomena at Jesus's death and resurrection, adding an Old Testament feel.
- The placing of a guard at the tomb, leading to the officials' lie about Jesus's resurrection.

4.2 Luke's major additions

Emphasis on Jesus as the innocent martyr
- Extended Last Supper and brief farewell discourse.
- Healing of the high priest's slave's ear.

- Night-time trial before the high priest.
- Trial before Herod.
- Weeping women on the way to the cross.
- Jesus's conversation with the criminals.
- Jesus forgives his executioners.
- Crowd repent their complicity.

4.3 The Johannine narrative

Emphasis on Jesus as the Son of God fulfilling his divine commission
- Jesus offers himself up for arrest; he remains in control.
- Not clear if Jesus is tried before one or two 'high priests'.
- Extended conversation between Pilate and Jesus on kingship and truth.
- Pilate goes to considerable lengths to release Jesus, leading the Jewish officials to commit blasphemy themselves.
- Jesus carries his own cross.
- Conversation at the cross between Jesus, his mother and the Beloved Disciple.
- The spear thrust.
- Joseph and Nicodemus bury Jesus.

J Salvation, eternal life and the kingdom of God

This is a popular topic for almost all specifications. You need to be aware of the different ways in which the evangelists deal with the concept of salvation and eternal life, particularly realised and future eschatology. The different interpretations of the kingdom are also significant here, and you need some scholarly support for the alternative ways of interpreting the nature and timing of the kingdom.

1 Salvation

The Greek verb *sozo* is used by the evangelists to convey a range of meanings: to make safe, to make someone well, to offer divine salvation. Whether the intention is to combine them is not clear, but in some passages Jesus tells a healed person: 'Your faith has saved you/made you well' (Luke 7:50). Spiritual and physical well-being run hand in hand since it would be meaningless for Jesus to offer physical health without spiritual wholeness.

1.1 Why does man need salvation?

1.1a Salvation from sin
Jesus is to 'save his people from their sins' (Matthew 1:23). Sin has separated man from God and reconciliation can only be achieved through the saving

> You need to have quick access here to a couple of miracles that illustrate this point. The healing of the woman with a flow of blood (Mark 5:34) is a good starting-point.

work of Jesus on the cross. John the Baptist and Jesus preach a message of repentance of sin in preparation for the coming kingdom (Matthew 3:6) and at the Last Supper Jesus declares that his blood will be poured out for man for the forgiveness of sins (Matthew 26:28). He claims that his mission is to sinful people: 'For I have come not to call the righteous but sinners' (Matthew 9:13).

1.1b Salvation from the world

For the Fourth Evangelist especially, the world represents those who have rejected God and in so doing have forfeited salvation (John 1:10–11). Those who accept Jesus are separated from the world and share a new unity with him, the Father, and all believers. The world has the power to corrupt and is under the rulership of Satan (14:30). But Jesus has authority over Satan and his presumptuous rule: 'The ruler of the world is coming. He has no power over me.'

1.1c Salvation from death

Man's spiritual inheritance after the Fall (Genesis 3) is death. The salvation accomplished by Jesus offers man life once more: 'Very truly, whoever keeps my word will never see death' (John 8:51); 'I am the resurrection and the life. Those who believe in me, even though they die, will live, and everyone who lives and believes in me will never die' (John 11:25). To be saved is the opposite of perishing, the only alternative for sinful man: 'For God so loved the world that he gave his only Son, so that everyone who believes in him may not perish but may have eternal life' (John 3:16). Paul writes, 'The wages of sin is death, but the free gift of God is eternal life through Jesus Christ our Lord' (Romans 6:23). Paul argues that the Law was incapable of releasing man from the penalty of death, but 'There is therefore now no condemnation for those who are in Christ Jesus. For the law of the Spirit of life in Christ Jesus has set you free from the law of sin and death' (Romans 8:1–2).

1.2 Jesus's role in salvation

- Luke speaks of Jesus as coming to 'seek and save the lost' (19:10) and sees Jesus as the culmination of God's long history of salvation for his people. However, there is something of a scandal about this long-awaited salvation: it is for all people. Jesus's ministry symbolises the universal salvation that he offers — he shares table fellowship with sinners and outcasts, allows a 'sinful' woman to anoint his feet and accepts the hospitality of a tax collector.
- Jesus calls his disciples to save their lives by losing their lives (Matthew 16:25). Those who try to preserve their physical life and material attachments will ultimately lose them, because death is inevitable and judgement will not be based on the things of the world. Those who are prepared to die for the sake of the gospel will, however, find that they will enjoy blessings in the kingdom of heaven, far beyond earthly attachments: 'Then Peter said … "Look, we have left everything and followed you. What then will we have?" Jesus said to them "Truly, I tell you … everyone who has left houses or brothers or sisters or father or mother or children or field, for my name's sake, will receive a hundredfold, and will inherit eternal life"' (Matthew 19:27–29).

- For the Fourth Evangelist Jesus, the Son of God, is the agent of salvation. Jesus is the Passover lamb who dies to release his people from slavery to sin, and whose legs are now broken on the cross (John 19:36). He is not only saviour of Israel, but the 'Saviour of the world' (4:42). He breaks the grip of Satan, who has the world in his power, and his death is a victory (19:30). Jesus's work is described in terms of the revelation of God's love, which must be discerned and accepted; if people remain in ignorance of Jesus's saving power, then they will die in their sins (8:21).

2 The kingdom of God

2.1 Background

In the Old Testament, God's kingdom is expressed through his actions on behalf of his people; these display his mighty power. When Israel was disobedient and ignored God's word, it faced disaster, but the prophets continued to hope for some future event that would display God's continued power. In Jesus's time, Roman occupation of the land intensified hope for the coming of God's kingdom, which was described in vivid, apocalyptic terms. Hope for the coming kingdom was expressed in the synagogue prayer: 'May he establish his kingdom in your lifetime and in our days and in the lifetime of all the house of Israel, even speedily and at a near time.'

2.2 Jesus's teaching on the kingdom (synoptic teaching)

- **Schweitzer** claimed that Jesus's kingdom teaching was a call to repentance before an imminent end.
- **C. H. Dodd** drew attention to the present rather than the future kingdom of God — a concept known as **realised eschatology**. The substance of the kingdom was already present in the person and ministry of Jesus and could be enjoyed by believers in the here and now.
- **J. Jeremias** coined the expression 'eschatology in the process of realisation' and claimed that the parables of Jesus were intended to challenge his hearers to respond to the imminence of the kingdom. Jeremias maintained that all Jesus's kingdom references were to a time when the historical order would be culminated and the separation between man and God, brought about by the fall, would be breached.
- **Norman Perrin** claimed that Jesus spoke of the kingdom as a present and future final act of God, which would pour out blessings on his people.
- **Conzelmann** maintained that the time of Jesus was one of eager expectation, but not yet the time of the kingdom.
- **Sanders** argued for the centrality of the future kingdom in Jesus's teaching, dividing Jesus's sayings into two main categories: those suggesting that the kingdom is in heaven and will be entered after death, and those suggesting it will come on earth in the future.

2.2a The kingdom in the present
- Jesus's power in healing, raising the dead, controlling nature, and especially in casting out demons, is seen as evidence that the kingdom is present in his ministry.

Don't get bogged down in a lot of background detail, but remember that you may be asked about the cultural influences on New Testament teaching.

Many questions on the kingdom ask you specifically for scholars' views, so make sure that you don't just summarise a few parables in GCSE style.

- 'The kingdom of God is in the midst of you/within you' (Luke 17:20). The presence of God's kingdom is at work within the individual's experience.
- In Mark 2:18ff. the parabolic images of the wine and wineskins and old and new garments suggest that the disciples are living in the kingdom era and must respond to it appropriately.
- Jesus's ministry to outcasts, and the table fellowship, reminiscent of the messianic banquet in the kingdom of heaven, demonstrate the radical values of the kingdom at work in his ministry.

2.2b The kingdom in the future

The Son of Man sayings point to a future culmination when Jesus will return 'seated at the right hand of Power, and coming with the clouds of heaven' (Mark 14:62). Scholars are divided as to the genuineness of these sayings. Perrin claims that they are from the lips of Jesus; others argue that they belong to the early church's interpretation of him and their development of eschatological hope.

2.3 Jesus's teaching on the kingdom (the Fourth Gospel)

> Fourth Gospel teaching on this area is very different, and its eschatological teaching permeates every chapter of the gospel. Make sure you have studied this thoroughly.

- **R. Bultmann** argued that allusions to a future eschatological event in the Fourth Gospel were additions by an ecclesiastical redactor who found difficulties with the realised eschatology of the Fourth Evangelist and its lack of synoptic features.
- **Painter** claims that the glorification of Jesus is the Fourth Evangelist's way of expressing the nature of Jesus's kingship. The phrase 'kingdom of God' occurs only in John 3:3 and 3:5, and the Fourth Evangelist favours the term 'eternal life'. However, Jesus is referred to as 'king' 16 times and in 18:36 speaks of 'my kingdom' three times. Only when his death is imminent does he accept the designation, while making clear that his kingdom is not an earthly one.

The Fourth Evangelist may have preferred the term 'eternal life' because:
- it does not have the nationalistic overtones of 'kingdom'
- he presents Jesus as the giver of life
- it emphasises the present experience of salvation: 'He who hears my word and believes him who sent me, has eternal life; he does not come into judgement, but has passed from death to life' (John 5:24)
- the gospel was written during the time of the early church, which experienced the presence of Jesus through the Holy Spirit. The delay of the parousia had led to eschatological hopes traditionally associated with the return of Jesus being transferred to the Paraclete

Resurrection looks to the fulfilment of the present experience of eternal life in the future. 'Life' and 'eternal life' are used interchangeably so the believer who has life has eternal life. The Father and the Son both have power to give life and eternal life (John 1:4; 5:26; 6:33; 10:28). The life revealed in Jesus is the Light of the World (8:12), and he gives life through the life-giving Spirit (6:68) and through the giving of his flesh in death (6:51).

> The 'I am' sayings and Jesus's discourses with opponents and with disciples are a good source of material on this topic.

The Fourth Evangelist alludes to future eschatological events in 5:28–29: 'The hour is coming when all who are in the tombs will hear his voice and come

forth, those who have done good, to the resurrection of life, and those who have done evil to the resurrection of judgement.' The themes of resurrection and life are linked here, as they are in the raising of Lazarus.

K The Holy Spirit

The material in this section is relevant to questions on:
- the role of the Holy Spirit in the gospels, especially John
- the early church, especially 1 Corinthians and Acts
- some key episodes, e.g. birth and resurrection narratives
- Old Testament background to New Testament thought
- miracles

1 *Background and terminology*

There is an increasing interest in asking you to demonstrate your knowledge of the religious and cultural background to New Testament issues. In most cases this means the Jewish/Old Testament and/or Hellenistic background or influence. Don't get bogged down in this. A short paragraph is usually enough, although sometimes whole questions may be asked on it. To be honest, my advice would be to avoid such a question altogether unless you have spent some very careful preparation time on it with the guidance of your teacher.

Two primary Greek terms are used for the Spirit: ***pneuma*** and **Paraclete**.

Pneuma (used by all the evangelists) is rooted in the Old Testament traditions, based on the Hebrew **ruach**. Both can be used interchangeably for wind, breath and Spirit. *Ruach* conveys a powerful, life-giving breath — not a transitory puff, as suggested by *hebel*. *Ruach* is used 377 times in the Old Testament in a range of contexts, but most importantly in the divine act of creation: 'You send forth your spirit, and they are created' (Psalm 104:30). God's *pneuma* is an expression of his personality, the living presence of God in a situation or individual.

Unique to the Fourth Gospel is Paraclete, from the Greek *paracletos*. There is no one satisfactory English translation of this multifaceted term, hence a range of interpretations is suggested: comforter, counsellor, helper, advocate, healer, intercessor. In 1 John 2:1 the same Greek word is used of Jesus, where it is almost universally translated as advocate. The anglicisation, Paraclete, is adopted to cover all these possibilities. The roles of the Paraclete appear to be those that Jesus carries out during his earthly ministry and is, to paraphrase Raymond Brown, the presence of Jesus when he is absent. *Paracletos* appears to owe more to a Hellenistic background and to the law courts: the Paraclete is a friend in court, a defence counsel who is called alongside to help. It also has a Jewish overtone, however; Mowinckel identified the Hebraic influence of the interceding angel.

In the intertestamental period there seems to be no significant change in the Old Testament concept of the Spirit, which was believed to have been silent from the end of the prophetic age to the coming of the Messiah. The Qumran community thought of the Spirit as a present possession and a future gift, and believed there were two spirits: the spirit of truth and the spirit of falsehood. Only at the end of time would the battle between these two spirits finally be accomplished.

2 The Holy Spirit in the New Testament

John Rea (in *The Holy Spirit in the Bible*, Marshall Pickering, 1990, p. 119) identifies four 'ages' of the Holy Spirit as presented in the New Testament:
(i) the preparation for the age of the Spirit (Jesus's ministry as recorded in the gospels)
(ii) the beginning of the age of the outpoured Spirit (Acts)
(iii) the work of the Holy Spirit explained (the Epistles)
(iv) the consummation of the age of the Spirit (Revelation)

3 The Holy Spirit in the synoptic gospels

You may think that you know very little about the Spirit, but if you have a good bank of knowledge about miracles, birth narratives, baptism and so on you have the basis of an essay on the Spirit.

The Holy Spirit is present from the beginning of Jesus's ministry, setting him aside as the one anointed for God's purposes.
- Matthew and Luke present the Holy Spirit as instrumental in the **birth of Jesus**. Jesus is conceived by the power of the Holy Spirit (Matthew 1:18). He gives Joseph and the magi the inspiration to believe and respond to the angel's commands (Matthew) and fills Zechariah and Mary with the spirit of prophecy as they foresee the future roles of their children (Luke). John the Baptist too will be filled with the Spirit even from within his mother's womb; he is the first prophet of God at the beginning of the messianic age.
- At the **baptism** in all three synoptics the Spirit descends on Jesus, identifying him as God's beloved son and equipping him for his messianic ministry. It marks him out as the one who will later baptise in the Holy Spirit and as such distinguishes him from John the Baptist, who baptises only in water.
- At the beginning of his public ministry Jesus identifies himself with the prophecy of Isaiah 61:1–4: 'The Spirit of the Lord is upon me ...'. Jesus begins his ministry as the one who is commissioned and equipped to proclaim release to the captives (Luke 4:14–21).
- Jesus's ministry of healing and teaching is Spirit-inspired. In the Old Testament God describes himself as 'The Lord, who heals you' (Exodus 15:26). Jesus continues that healing ministry in fulfilment of Isaiah 53:4. Such charismatic healing may be at a distance, or require the believer only to touch Jesus's clothes to be accomplished. He casts out demons by the power of the Holy Spirit, to which they are subject.
- Jesus promises the Holy Spirit to all believers (Mark 16:9–20), but especially to the disciples, who are instructed to 'stay in the city until you are clothed with power from on high' (Luke 24:49). Through the Spirit, Jesus can promise to be with them 'till the close of the age' (Matthew 28:20).

4 ## The Holy Spirit in the Fourth Gospel

This is an important area in the study of the Fourth Gospel, and one which is not difficult to get to grips with. The Abacus Educational Services booklet on the Holy Spirit (1994) is especially good on this area.

- Jesus receives the Holy Spirit at the beginning of his ministry (note there is no baptism), but much of the gospel anticipates its later outpouring. It will not be until Jesus is glorified (has died and is risen again) that the Spirit can be given. 'Now he said this about the Spirit, which believers in him were to receive; for as yet there was no Spirit because Jesus was not yet glorified' (John 7:39).

- John the Baptist witnesses the descent of the Spirit on Jesus, which singles him out as the one who is uniquely able to baptise in the Spirit. It identifies Jesus to John the Baptist as the Son of God.

- **Water** is used as a symbol for the Spirit. Nicodemus must be 'born of water and Spirit' — not two different processes, but one and the same; 'water that is Spirit' is probably a better interpretation. As water refreshes parched land, so the Spirit will revive the soul that is in need of God's touch. At the Feast of Tabernacles the Fourth Evangelist makes the link clear (7:37–39). The image is implicit too in the conversation with the Samaritan woman who is offered living water at Cana, and at the spear thrust when blood and water flow from Jesus's side (his death having released the Spirit as promised).

- The Fourth Evangelist makes much of the wordplay on *pneuma*. The conversation with Nicodemus compares the Spirit with the wind and alludes to Ezekiel 37 — the valley of dry bones which needs to be revived by God's spirit.

- The true Johannine disciple worships in spirit and truth (4:21–24). The empowering of the Holy Spirit is therefore necessary to make worship genuine, and not merely ceremony and ritual.

- Jesus promises the coming of the Paraclete after his death. The Paraclete will fulfil those functions that Jesus has fulfilled during his earthly ministry, and so the disciples need not be alone. He will teach, remind, comfort, guide and minister to them.

- The Paraclete is the spirit of truth, which comes from alongside the Father, sharing the same divine essence and having the same authority as Jesus.

- Only the Fourth Gospel describes the giving of the Spirit. Jesus breathes the Spirit personally on the disciples, continuing the wordplay on *pneuma*. The disciples are given a new life as they receive the divine breath in this Johannine Pentecost. With it comes the authority to forgive sins.

- The Fourth Evangelist's presentation of the Paraclete addresses the problem of the delay of the Parousia:

> *At a critical stage in the development of the Johannine Community it had been troubled by precisely the same problems that troubled other Christians — the delay of the parousia, and the death of the first-generation Christians.... John's church had solved these problems by the doctrine of the Paraclete as the living presence of Jesus in the church.*
>
> **J. & K. Court, *The New Testament World*, Prentice-Hall, 1990, p. 272**

5 ## The Holy Spirit in the early church

The two main areas you may be asked to consider here are the role of the Spirit in Acts and the use of spiritual gifts. A good discussion of spiritual gifts is found in *The Holy Spirit in the Bible* (1994) by John Rea.

- The Pentecost events (Acts 2:1ff.) fulfil Jesus's instruction to the disciples in Luke 24:49 to wait before beginning their public ministry. This is accompanied by the traditional symbols of God's presence: wind and fire.
- The importance of the Spirit in the missionary work of the church is established; the gift of tongues (**glossolalia**) enables the disciples to reach a wide audience of Passover pilgrims.
- Pentecost fulfils the prophecy of Joel 2:28–32 that God would pour out his spirit in the last days. This is Luke's third period in salvation history about to unfold.
- The influence of the Holy Spirit directs the missionary and pastoral activity of the church. The seven deacons are 'full of the Spirit and of wisdom' (Acts 6:3); the apostles display gifts of healing, raising the dead, performing exorcisms and preaching. The missionary journeys of Paul are under the direction of the Spirit, who gives to the apostles boldness in preaching and under persecution.
- 1 Corinthians testifies to the vital role of spiritual gifts in the early church — not only prophecy and tongues, but also administrative and pastoral gifts for the upbuilding of the church. 1 Corinthians 13 makes it clear that all spiritual gifts must be subject to love.
- John Rea (in *The Holy Spirit in the Bible*, 1994, p. 245) speaks of the charismata as the means by which 'people in every generation must be confronted with the reality of the invisible God'.

L # Key issues in the early church

The material in this section is relevant to questions on:
- the ministry and experience of the early church as described in Acts
- the issues of importance to the Paul's churches

Use the notes below as a checklist if you are studying a specification which demands a knowledge of the issues raised in Acts, Romans and 1 Corinthians especially.

1 ## The spread of the gospel

Perhaps the most important issue here is the gentile outreach and the implications that this had for taking Christianity outside the confines of Judaism.

- The gospel was taken first to Jews, in response to Jesus's command in Matthew 10:5 and Luke 24:47. Peter preaches openly in Jerusalem and the community worship at the temple. Paul goes first to synagogues, wherever he is preaching.
- The missionaries face opposition from the Jewish authorities just as Jesus did. Peter, Paul and Silas are all imprisoned and face trials before the authorities and threats on their lives.

- As the church grows, the question of how gentiles fit in becomes an increasingly vital issue. The Council of Jerusalem (Acts 15) is a watershed, allowing gentiles to become Christians without being circumcised. This was crucial if Christianity was not to become a sect within Judaism.
- Persecution encourages the spread of the gospel. The death of Stephen has the effect of sending Christianity beyond Jerusalem, although the apostles remain in the city.
- The Holy Spirit is presented as the power behind the church's witness. It enables the apostles to speak with authority and inspires people to believe. When gentiles are filled with the Spirit it is impossible for them to be refused entry to the church.
- Early preaching always starts with the Old Testament. Peter's first sermon at Pentecost establishes a pattern for preaching, citing Old Testament support for the ministry, death and resurrection of Jesus.
- It was important for the early church to establish and maintain good relationships with the political authorities. Acts presents the Romans as being essentially benevolent, and opposition primarily coming from the Jewish leaders. Paul urges obedience to the law of the land, paying taxes and submitting to the authority of God-given government.

2   *Authority and ministry*

Here your primary concern is likely to be the role of individual leaders, especially Peter and Paul. Be able to compare and contrast their particular functions and activities.

- The apostles in Jerusalem are the 'pillars' of the church (Galatians 2:9). Peter immediately takes the lead at the beginning of Acts. He officiates over the election of Judas' replacement, preaches the first sermon, performs the first miracle, disciplines Ananias and Sapphira, and — despite the significance of Paul's later role in the gentile mission — baptises the first gentile, Cornelius.
- The seven Hellenistic deacons are appointed for pastoral duties, but Stephen and Philip at least establish a wider brief. All the deacons are appointed for their spiritual maturity and wisdom.
- Paul and Barnabas are appointed as apostles to the gentiles. Paul sees himself as equal in authority to the Jerusalem apostles on the basis of his conversion experience, though clearly some tension existed. Paul and Barnabas themselves split up over a dispute about the reliability of John Mark.
- It seems likely that Paul left elders and overseers in his churches after he had planted them, but he writes clarifying issues of doctrine, ethics and church order. He is concerned to ensure that the churches are loyal primarily to the gospel of Christ and not to any human leader.

3   *The sacraments*

You should be able to pick up marks easily for this topic. Be very clear that baptism and eucharist in the early church bear some, but not very much, relation to the sacraments in today's churches. Make sure you are using the evidence of the text, not your personal experience.

- **Eucharist** and **baptism** are established in Acts. Baptism is an initiation rite which is usually performed when the believer responds to the gospel, e.g. the Ethiopian official (Acts 8).
- Baptism in the Holy Spirit is quite distinct from baptism in water, although it may be simultaneous. In Acts 19 Paul meets disciples of John the Baptist who have only been baptised in water but speak in tongues as soon as they are baptised in the Spirit.

- Baptism in the Holy Spirit is necessary to manifest spiritual gifts, such as tongues, prophecy, healing or wisdom.
- Households and individuals were baptised, but there is no indication of infant baptism. Baptism was probably by total immersion.
- Baptism was into Christ, and symbolised a unity with him in death and resurrection. It expressed commitment to Christ but was not in itself the means of salvation.
- The early church shared a common meal — the breaking of bread — initially more of a fellowship meal in Acts, reflective of community life. In 1 Corinthians 11 Paul rebukes the people of the church for their rowdy behaviour at the meal, reminding them that the primary focus of the meal should be a remembrance of Jesus and an anticipation of his parousia.
- For Paul the meal is strongly sacramental, as it is a sharing in the body and blood of Jesus and in his risen life.

4 Christian life

There is so much to say here that you need to pick your areas carefully. Key issues are Paul's discussion of marriage in 1 Corinthians 7 and Ephesians 5, and the use of spiritual gifts — 1 Corinthians 12–14.

- The members of the early church expected the return of Jesus (the parousia) within their own lifetime. Paul writes with this in mind, urging Christians to make no radical changes to their personal circumstances. However, he also has to warn them not to abandon the responsibilities of daily living.
- Gentile churches with no background in ethical monotheism need guidance on moral and pastoral issues: marriage and divorce, sexual relationships, law suits, co-existing with pagans. Distinctive Christian doctrines need explaining clearly and frequently: the resurrection of Jesus and of all believers, the meaning of Jesus's death, freedom from the Law, justification by faith, the relationship of the Old Testament revelation to the gospel.
- Rules for the administration and hierarchy of the household and the church appear to be strongly patriarchal, despite Paul's belief in the equality and freedom of all men in Christ. Christians should set high standards in family and church life, and leaders must be without blemish. Christ is the model for all believers.

For more material on issues of concern to the early church, look at the sections on the Holy Spirit (pp. 48–51), women in the New Testament (pp. 53–57), and New Testament ethics (pp. 64–68).

- Worship must be orderly and respectful of others, including non-believers, who will be put off by disorder. Spiritual gifts must be exercised in the context of ***agape***. All believers have a vital part to play in the mutual upbuilding of the church and its members.

M Women in the New Testament

The material in this section is relevant to questions on:
- the role and presentation of women in the New Testament books
- birth narratives
- resurrection narratives
- discipleship
- cultural background

1 The first-century picture

> *In both pagan and Jewish society women were considered to be less intelligent than men ... in the wider arena of social life, in politics and religious affairs, women had almost no role at all.*
>
> **Peter Vardy and Mary Mills, *The Puzzle of the Gospels*, Fount, 1995, p. 170**

> *The status of women was markedly inferior to that of men throughout the ancient world, including Judaism.*
>
> **Graham Stanton, *The Gospels and Jesus*, OUP, 1989, p. 202**

You must avoid writing 'In Jesus's time women were second-class citizens'. If you want to make this point, attribute it to a scholar (with book title and page number if you can).

J. & K. Court (in *The New Testament World*, Prentice-Hall, 1990) observe that the relative social status of women in the ancient world was actually rather more complicated than this. Status depended on many factors: family background, employment and employer, and religious background all had an influence on the woman's position relative to the man's. While Roman law stated that all women 'because of their weakness of intellect should be under the power of guardians', Proverbs 31:26ff. speaks highly of a woman who 'opens her mouth with wisdom.... She looks well to the ways of her household'. There are also literary examples of women who were held in high regard: Job's three daughters, who speak the language of angels (the Testament of Job) and traditions about Beruriah, a second-century rabbi.

However:
- Josephus claimed that the Law held women to be inferior in all matters, and that they should therefore be submissive.
- Philo referred to women and female traits as examples of weakness, and claimed that women should stay at home.
- Sirach 42:14 wrote: 'Better is the wickedness of a man than a woman who does good; it is woman who brings shame and disgrace.'
- The rabbinic Tosefta (t.Ber 7.18) included a benediction prayed by a Jewish man, giving thanks that he was not made a woman.

I draw attention to this point to show how important it is to *evaluate* any topic you are required to discuss, especially when you are dealing with one that can so easily lead to one-sided, uncritical answers.

2 Jesus and women

Scholars are careful to point out that even though 'The attitude of Jesus to women was striking' (Stanton, p. 202), at the same time the equality between men and women disciples suggested by Jesus's ministry would only be possible 'in so far as such notions of equality are conceivable in the context of Jewish life and faith' (J. & K. Court, p. 35). The Courts suggest that since Jesus was

acting to renew Judaism, he proposed an alternative to the traditional patriarchal structure rather than something totally at odds with it.

However, in the New Testament 29 women are mentioned by name, and the ratio of named women to named men in Romans is 15:18. There are many other more general references which demonstrate that women had positions of leadership and responsibility in the early church.

Jesus's relationship with women is characterised in various ways:

- Jesus was accompanied by a group of women including at least one (Joanna) of relatively high standing, but also those who had been in some ways on the fringes of society. Note, however, that Mary Magdalene is not described as a prostitute, but as a woman from whom Jesus had cast seven demons (Luke 8:1–3). These women provided for Jesus 'out of their resources' as Lydia appears to have provided for Paul (Acts 16).
- Jesus encouraged women to listen to his teaching in the manner of pupil and rabbi. In Luke 10:38–42 Mary is described as sitting at his feet while he taught. She is favourably compared with her sister Martha, who is preoccupied with traditionally female household tasks.
- Jesus welcomed contact with women. He initiates a conversation with the woman at the well (John 4), defying the convention that a Jewish man would have no contact with a Samaritan woman. At the house of Simon the Pharisee (Luke 7), Jesus allows a 'woman in the city who was a sinner' to anoint his feet. A holy man would usually avoid such contact as defiling.
- A significant number of miracles are for the benefit of women: the woman with a haemorrhage, the widow of Nain, Jairus's daughter, the crippled woman in the synagogue, the Canaanite woman's daughter. Women are shown to have persistence and faith, and to be the recipients of Jesus's compassion.

The evangelists and women

Graham Stanton observes that since the early church did not always follow Jesus's example in its treatment of women, the accounts of his positive and compassionate dealings with them in the gospels is likely to be authentic.

Nevertheless, the evangelists may well have been reflecting in some way the practice of their own communities. Raymond Brown says of the Fourth Evangelist's treatment of key episodes involving women:

> *If other Christian communities thought of Peter as the one who made a supreme confession of Jesus as the Son of God and the one to whom the risen Lord first appeared, the Johannine community associated such memories with heroines like Martha and Mary Magdalene.*
>
> **Raymond Brown, *The Community of the Beloved Disciple*,**
> **Chapman, 1979, p. 191**

This is a useful rule of thumb for ascertaining the reliability of the text. If something is potentially embarrassing for the writers and yet they include it, it is not likely that they made it up.

The evangelists present women positively from the beginning of the gospels:

- Luke's gospel includes three women in the birth narratives — Mary, Elizabeth and Anna the prophetess. They are all shown to be obedient, wise and in tune with God's spirit.
- Matthew's genealogy of Jesus includes five women of dubious background but who nevertheless are essential links in the Davidic line, which culminates in the Messiah.
- Women are used as positive examples in Jesus's teaching: the woman who hunted tirelessly for her lost coin (Luke 15:8–10); the persistent widow (Luke 18:1–8); the widow who puts all she has into the temple treasury (Mark 12:41–44 & //s).
- Women are shown to have perceptive insights into Jesus's divine person. The Fourth Evangelist gives the fullest confession of faith to Martha — 'You are the Christ, the Son of God, the one coming into the world' (John 11:27).
- Women witness the resurrection and are the bearers of the resurrection message. Even though Mark omits any account of the fulfilment of their commission to tell the disciples of Jesus's resurrection and Luke reports that they were not believed, there is no question that the evangelists consider them to be reliable witnesses. Interestingly, Paul omits any mention of the women's testimony in his summary of the resurrection tradition in 1 Corinthians 15. Presumably this is because of doubts about the legal admissibility of women's testimony.

4 *The early church and women*

The early church was clearly made up of both men and women who played significant roles in its development. Luke and Paul refer to women by name who are influential in the churches:

- Chloe (1 Corinthians 1:11), who may have led a group of Corinthian Christians
- Phoebe (Romans 16:1–2), a deaconess
- Priscilla, the wife of Aquila, who taught Apollos and supported Paul in his ministry at Corinth (1 Corinthians 16:19; Romans 16:3)
- Lydia, a wealthy businesswoman who provides hospitality for Paul (Acts 16)
- Tabitha, 'full of good works and acts of charity', who is raised back to life by Peter (Acts 9:36–41)

Paul's teaching on women's role in the church and the household has led to some suggestion that he may not have supported the emancipation of Christian women. He teaches that:

- women should remain silent in church and should not teach (1 Corinthians 14:34ff.)
- women should cover their heads (1 Corinthians 11:2ff.)
- wives are to be submitted to the headship of their husbands (Ephesians 5:22ff.)

Paul's teaching on women in the church is hard to accommodate in the twenty-first century, so it is important to show you have understood that it must be interpreted in its cultural setting.

Although Paul's teaching sounds harsh to modern ears, it is likely that he was concerned to avoid any misunderstandings about the practices of the church in a pagan society. Order and dignity were essential for the church's integrity and to distinguish it from pagan religious groups. Just as Paul imposes order on the

use of spiritual gifts in public worship, he encourages a form of order by instructing women to seek clarification about spiritual matters in the privacy of their homes. Women whose heads were uncovered may have been confused with prostitutes, so Paul's instruction to them to keep their hair covered may be a good example of compromising Christian freedom in the interests of the church's reputation.

The husband's headship over his wife mirrors that of Christ over the church, and as such is not dominating or oppressive. Rather, it is primarily concerned with the well-being of the woman, whose husband is instructed to 'love her as Christ loved the church and gave himself up for her'.

N Discipleship

Questions concerning discipleship may be explicit, e.g. 'Discuss the Fourth Gospel's teaching on discipleship', or more implicit, e.g. 'Examine the teaching of Jesus on poverty and wealth'. Discipleship as a topic covers everything that is involved in being a follower of Jesus, so it is potentially an enormous area to cover. You have to decide which areas you are going to focus on for the purposes of the exam. Think of headings to work under: becoming a disciple; the demands of discipleship; the rewards of discipleship.

1 *Becoming a disciple*

1.1 Terminology

The term 'disciple' is used only in the gospels and Acts. In the Fourth Gospel the designation is used 15 times to refer to a particular individual (usually the Beloved Disciple). In Matthew and Mark it is usually used in the plural to refer to a small group, but Luke speaks of a 'great crowd of his disciples' (6:17), which must indicate a group larger than the Twelve. The Twelve are almost certainly an inner circle chosen from the whole company of disciples. At Matthew 28:19 the Twelve (less Judas) are instructed to 'go therefore and make disciples of all nations, baptising them in the name of the Father and of the Son and of the Holy Spirit, teaching them to observe all that I have commanded you', and in Acts, 'disciples' becomes the distinctive term for those who believed in Jesus.

Try to avoid referring to the Twelve Disciples too often, since it is clear that the teaching on discipleship is not intended to be exclusive to them. For the Fourth Evangelist especially, discipleship is a broad category.

1.2 The calling to discipleship

Becoming a disciple involves making a commitment to following Jesus and learning from him. It is therefore not a category restricted to the Twelve named in Matthew 10:2–4 (note that the evangelists' lists of the Twelve vary), but to all those who chose to follow Jesus — although it does not fully acquire this wider sense until Acts.

In the **Fourth Gospel** the first disciples of Jesus had been followers of John the Baptist, transferring their allegiance to Jesus when the Baptist pointed him out to them (John 1:35ff.). Despite this, it is clear that disciples of John the Baptist continued for a long time after his death (Acts 19:1ff.). At the time of Jesus they were distinguished by their practice of fasting (Mark 2:18ff.), which the evangelist suggests places them within the old order rather then the new order of fulfilment brought by Jesus.

In the **synoptic gospels** the calling of the disciples follows in the tradition of the charismatic calling of Elisha by Elijah in 1 Kings 19. Peter and Andrew, and James and John are called from their fishing boats with the invitation to become 'fishers of men' (Mark 1:17). Only Luke 5 (the miraculous catch of fish) provides the disciples with any reason, other than the compelling power of Jesus's charismatic persona, to follow him.

> Note that the Fourth Gospel's account of the calling of the disciples may therefore be more authentic.

Those who ask to become disciples (as students of the Law sought out a rabbi) are set demanding criteria: the rich man who must sell all he has (Mark 10:17ff. & //s); the scribe who must be prepared to have 'nowhere to lay his head' (Matthew 8:20); and the disciple who must put commitment to the kingdom before family duty: '"Lord, let me go first and bury my father." But Jesus said to him, "Follow me, and leave the dead to bury their own dead."' (Matthew 8:21–22). Those who accept the calling to discipleship make a lifelong commitment: 'No one who puts his hand to the plough and looks back is fit for the kingdom of God' (Luke 9:62).

2 *The demands of discipleship*

The conditions of discipleship are harsh. The would-be disciple must be prepared to count the cost of following Jesus:

- The disciple must 'take up his cross'. Discipleship involves burdens and the real possibility of death in the service of the gospel. When James and John ask to sit at Jesus's side in the kingdom of heaven, Jesus asks in turn whether they are 'able to drink the cup that I drink, or to be baptised with the baptism with which I am baptised' (Mark 10:38 & //s). The disciples are depicted as being slow to grasp the reality of Jesus's impending death and, since 'a disciple is not above his master' (Matthew 10:24), the implications that this will have for them.

> You need to have looked carefully at the importance of Jesus's death here. The disciple who cannot accept that Jesus must die to fulfil his messiahship is operating under an illusion.

- The disciple must be prepared to give up 'houses and brothers and sisters and mothers and children and lands' (Mark 10:29 & //s). Commitment to worldly ties will impede effective discipleship, but a willingness to lay these things down, or to give them second place, will free the disciple to pursue the real rewards of discipleship: 'a hundredfold now in this time ... and in the age to come eternal life' (Mark 10:30 & //s). Luke's description of the early church community indicates that 'all who believed were together and had all things in common; and they sold their possessions and goods and distributed them to all as any had need' (Acts 2:44).

> *In the teaching of Jesus the good news of the kingdom of God was for the poor, and there were stern warnings to the rich about the danger of being kept outside the kingdom by their possessions. The corollary of such warnings is the command to use wealth in the right way.*
>
> I. Howard Marshall, *Luke — Historian and Theologian*, Paternoster, 1970, p. 206

Fourth Gospel students have a wealth of wonderful material here: the 'I am' sayings, the conversations with Nicodemus and the Samaritan woman, the farewell discourses, and the post-resurrection appearance are all important sources of information for this topic.

- Persecution is an unavoidable part of being a disciple. The rewards come 'with persecutions' (Mark 10:30), and Jesus warns the disciples that they will be 'dragged before kings and governors for my sake' (Matthew 10:18). In the Fourth Gospel Jesus warns that the world will hate the disciples because 'it has hated me before' (John 15:18). The disciples' separation from the world sets them apart from it, which guarantees the world's hatred (John 15:19). Ironically, those who persecute the disciples will do so believing that they are 'offering service to God' (John 16:2; cf. 9:22). Unity is vital to preserve the cohesion of the disciples in such trying times, and to serve as a witness to the world of the love which the disciple shares with the Father and the Son (John 17:23).
- Love for one another is an emphatic command in the Fourth Gospel (John 13:34). It is fulfilled through faith in Jesus and an awareness of his love for them, which stems from the Father's love for the Son. This is only possible for those who abide in Jesus, so remaining on the vine (John 15) and as part of the flock (John 10) is essential for growth, unity and fruitfulness.

3 The rewards of discipleship

- Those who 'endure to the end will be saved' (Matthew 10:22). The demands of discipleship are not made without a real promise for the future. The disciple who 'loses his life for my sake will find it' (Matthew 10:39) and the one who acknowledges Jesus before men, despite danger, 'will acknowledge before my Father who is in heaven' (Matthew 10:32).

> *There is an immediate hundredfold reward for those who walk out on their commitments and dependants and join Jesus on the road; there will be even greater rewards 'in the age to come', which here has clearly no connection at all with our traditional ideas of heaven. That age to come will be a new age of the terrestrial world.*
>
> David Bruce Taylor, *Mark's Gospel as Literature and Story*, SCM, 1992, p. 248

See the section on the Holy Spirit (pp. 48–51) for more on this area.

- The disciple receives authority from Jesus to act in his name. The 70/72 who are sent out during Jesus's ministry return full of joy that 'even the demons are subject to us in your name' (Luke 10:17). After the resurrection Jesus promises the disciples that all believers will 'cast out demons ... speak in new tongues ... pick up serpents ... lay their hands on the sick and they will recover' (Mark 16:17–18). In the Fourth Gospel he assures them that 'he who believes in me will also do the works that I do; and greater works than these will he do, because I go to my Father' (John 14:12). Jesus's departure is not to be a source of grief to them, because only if he goes will they be able to enjoy the fulfilment of their own ministry.

- The Holy Spirit can also only come if Jesus goes away. In Luke 24:49 the Eleven are instructed to 'stay in the city until you are clothed with power from on high'. In the Fourth Gospel Jesus promises the disciples that he will 'pray the Father, and he will give you another Counsellor, to be with you for ever' (John 14:16). This spirit of truth will guide, teach, remind, inspire and comfort. It is available only to those who have committed themselves in discipleship, and not to the world which has rejected Jesus.

- Despite persecution, disciples can enjoy a quality of peace that is only possible through their faith: 'Let not your hearts be troubled, neither let them be afraid' (John 14:27). After his resurrection Jesus promises the Eleven that 'Lo, I am with you always, to the close of the age' (Matthew 28:20). The disciple's relationship with Jesus transcends time and space, and is guaranteed in all ages. Like the mother who forgets the pain of childbirth after the child enters the world, Jesus promises the disciples that 'you will weep and lament ... but your sorrow will turn to joy' (John 16:20).

- Answered prayer is assured to all those who believe: 'Whatever you ask in my name, I will do it, that the Father may be glorified in the Son' (John 14:13). The disciple's faith will accomplish great things: 'Therefore I tell you, whatever you ask in prayer, believe that you have received it, and it will be yours' (Mark 11:24). Prayer must be in faith and without public show. The disciple shares an intimate relationship with the Father, who knows his needs before he even asks. Prayer should be persistent, humble and private.

Another vital reward of discipleship is eternal life. See the section 'Salvation, eternal life and the kingdom of God' (pp. 44–48) for a discussion of this topic.

- Discipleship in the new age of the kingdom is universal. No one is excluded from discipleship because they are poor, untaught, female or gentile. Zacchaeus the tax collector is a son of Abraham (Luke 19:9); the Syrophoenician woman quite rightly perceives that 'even the dogs under the table eat the children's bread' (Mark 7:28); and the centurion demonstrates to Jesus that 'not even in Israel [has he] found such faith' (Matthew 8:10).

To be a disciple is the ultimate calling, and disciples — of both sexes — are thus valued highly:

> *Discipleship is the primary Christian category for John, and the disciple par excellence is the disciple whom Jesus loved. But John tells us in 11:5: 'Now Jesus loved Martha and her sister (Mary) and Lazarus.'*
>
> **Raymond Brown, *The Community of the Beloved Disciple*,** Chapman, 1979, p. 191

⓿ Political and cultural background

This is a fashionable area of discussion at the moment, with some examination boards expecting you to be able to relate almost any topic to the cultural background of the time. For the Fourth Gospel, for example, you may be asked to comment on the cultural background to the teaching of the gospel on the Holy Spirit or the 'I am' sayings. Other questions might ask you to consider how the teaching of a gospel, or the experiences of the early Christian mission, are influenced by their Hellenistic or Jewish background. You are also expected to be aware of the main groups and parties within Judaism. You may be asked to explain the beliefs of the Pharisees, for example, for 5–7 marks, but it is also useful to be aware of the political background of the time when considering the interplay between the Jews and Pilate at the trial of Jesus.

1 *Political and religious background to Jesus's ministry*

Bear in mind that the New Testament documents were not written in a vacuum but were deeply influenced by their time. The political setting of the gospels and Acts is extremely important when considering their interpretation of the events that faced Jesus and the early church.

These summaries are given only so that you can relate the various groups to the episodes in the text. You should avoid just giving their main characteristics and failing to show how their ideologies had any bearing on their encounters with Jesus.

The Hasmonean dynasty of the Maccabees ruled Judaea from 165 BC, during which time the key religious parties — Sadducees, Pharisees and Essenes — emerged. In 63 BC, however, the Romans marched on Jerusalem, desecrating the temple and establishing themselves in Palestine. An agreement between Rome and the Herod family allowed the Herods some degree of rulership. At the time of Jesus's birth, Herod the Great ruled in Palestine and Augustus Caesar was emperor in Rome. After Herod's death his sons, Archelaus, Philip, Lysanias and Antipas, ruled over four tetrarchies until the unpopularity of Archelaus led to his deposition. He was replaced by a Roman procurator, the position held by Pontius Pilate from AD 26 to 36. Political unrest between the Jews and their occupiers continued, and the ministry of Jesus was not unaffected by it.

Below are some thumbnail sketches of key characters and various Jewish groups in New Testament times.

1.1 Herod the Great

Popular with Rome; not a Jew and showed little interest in Jewish law or customs. He was more interested in promoting **Hellenism** (Greek culture), although he built the new temple in Jerusalem. Thought to be a cruel man, but there is no evidence of an infant massacre as suggested by Matthew.

1.2 Herod Antipas

Ruled over Galilee. Responsible for the death of John the Baptist. Luke's gospel records that Pilate sent Jesus to Antipas since Jesus was a Galilean.

1.3 The Sanhedrin

The highest court of Jewish law, which dealt with religious and political matters. Its president was the high priest, who was a Roman appointee, with responsibility towards Rome. In the Fourth Gospel Caiaphas, the high priest, advocates putting Jesus to death to reassure Rome that the Sanhedrin were dealing effectively with potential rebels. The Sanhedrin consisted of Pharisees and Sadducees and could technically impose a death penalty, but they could not carry it out while under Roman occupation. Hence the need for Pilate's agreement to put Jesus to death.

1.4 The Pharisees

The progressive party within Judaism, concerned with the studying and the keeping of the Mosaic Law. They can be traced back to the exile in 586 BC but they emerged as a distinct group in the second century BC, when they became known as the 'separated ones'. They resisted Greek influences and aimed to keep the traditional Jewish faith alive. They developed an oral law, equally binding as the written law, which added many regulations and explanations. It was later written down in the Mishnah and the Talmud. The oral law served as a 'hedge around the law', ensuring that the written law was not broken. Although Pharisees are accused of legalism, their concern was to keep the Law alive and relevant. The **Scribes** belonged largely to the Pharisaic party. They were the legal authorities on the religious Law, adding interpretations of their own.

1.5 The Sadducees

These claimed direct descent from Zadok, Solomon's high priest. They controlled the temple, its worship, finances and sacrificial system. More conservative than the Pharisees, they were happy to work in cooperation with the Romans. They accepted only the first five books of the Old Testament as the source of religious, moral and social life, and did not teach any doctrine of resurrection. They did not believe in the coming of the Messiah, and were concerned to put down any force which appeared to be a threat to Rome. After the destruction of the temple in AD 70 their influence died out.

1.6 The Essenes

A monastic group which withdrew from mainstream Judaism, possibly to the Dead Sea area around Qumran. They rejected the temple priesthood, sacrifice and the official calendar, adopting baptismal rites of their own. They lived a communal life in expectation of the final eschatological battle between the 'sons of the light' and the 'sons of the dark'. It may be that John the Baptist was an Essene. Most of our information about the Essenes comes from the work of Josephus and from the Dead Sea Scrolls.

1.7 The Zealots

Political activists who owed their influence to the time of the Maccabees. They maintained that it was unlawful to acknowledge the sovereignty of a

gentile ruler and to pay taxes to that regime. They called for freedom from foreign domination, and obedience to the Law was closely tied up with national independence. They looked forward to an eschatological time when God's kingdom would be triumphantly instated, bringing all alien influence to an end.

1.8 Pontius Pilate

The fifth Roman procurator of Judaea, Samaria and Idumea, a politically turbulent area. His power over non-Roman citizens was absolute, and he was concerned to maintain the authority of Rome rather than understand the Jews over which he ruled. His rulership was characterised by uprisings and threats of violence, which eventually led to his recall to Rome in AD 36.

> **New Testament episodes to consider**
>
> The birth narratives, the teaching and death of John the Baptist, Sabbath controversies, the question about taxes, the question about resurrection, the question about divorce, the adulterous woman (Fourth Gospel only), the passion narratives in all the gospels. You also need to be aware of the encounters between the early church and Judaism, the Council of Jerusalem, the use of the Old Testament by all the New Testament writers, and their assumption that their readers were knowledgeable about it.

This is the important part. Your knowledge of the text and of relevant episodes must dominate an essay about political and cultural influences. You will need lots of examples to illustrate the points you make.

2 Hellenism

Hellenism reflects the background of Greek philosophy, culture, education and language which was widespread in the first century AD. Its influence is due to Alexander the Great, the King of Macedonia, who in 333 BC crossed into Asia Minor, conquered Palestine, the port of Tyre, Egypt and as far as India. Wherever he went he founded Greek-speaking cities and laid the foundations of Greek culture. In Palestine a strongly established Hebrew and Jewish culture was confronted by the rapid invasion of Greek ideas. Some resisted it but others accommodated it, and when in 175 BC a Greek school was established, even some of the Sadducees and Pharisees sent their children to it.

Hellenistic philosophies are much harder to grasp than Jewish influences on the New Testament material. You need a simple but clear understanding of what Hellenism is and where you can find examples of it in the gospel.

Philo of Alexandria was particularly influential in the meeting of Greek and Jewish cultures. His thought combined the two philosophies, interpreting the Old Testament in the light of Greek thinking. It is thought that he had a considerable influence on some of the New Testament writers.

Martin Hengel, in *Judaism and Hellenism* (SCM, 1974), argues that Judaism and Hellenism overlapped so significantly by the time of Jesus that it was difficult to distinguish between them. However, although the New Testament writers appear to have made use of Hellenistic and gnostic influences, it is clear that the gospel message was radically different. In Hellenistic thought the incarnation would be inconceivable, since the divine could not become involved with earthly

matters. Augustine claimed that he had learned the substance of the Prologue to the Fourth Gospel (John 1:1–18) from Hellenism, but nothing had prepared him for the claim that 'The Word became flesh' (1:14).

2.1 Features of Hellenistic thought

- **Dualism:** i.e. light/dark; above/below; flesh/spirit.
- **Gnosticism:** gnostics held that man could be enlightened by a divine spark of knowledge brought by a heavenly revealer who could penetrate the barriers that separated man from the spiritual world.
- **Special knowledge** revealed only to the initiated.
- **Supernatural events** impinging on the natural world order.

> **New Testament episodes to consider**
>
> Birth narratives; miracles; resurrection; the teaching of the Fourth Gospel, especially with respect to dualism and the possible influence of gnosticism (Rudolph Bultmann was particularly influential in arguing that the Fourth Gospel was a gnosticised version of the gospel, and Jesus the gnostic heavenly revealer); the church at Corinth — how far did its problems stem from its Hellenistic environment?; the appointment of Hellenistic deacons in the early church; Paul's missionary journeys into gentile territory; the relationship between Greek and Jewish Christians.

P New Testament ethics

The material in this section is relevant to questions on:
- biblical ethics
- practical ethics
- Jesus's teaching
- discipleship

1 Jesus and the Law

> *Do not think that I have come to abolish the law or the prophets, I have come not to abolish but to fulfil. For truly I tell you, until heaven and earth pass away, not one letter, not one stroke of a letter will pass from the law until all is accomplished…. For I tell you, unless your righteousness exceeds that of the scribes and Pharisees, you will never enter the kingdom of heaven.*
>
> **Matthew 5:17–18, 20**

There is considerable misunderstanding about the relationship between Jesus and the Jewish law and its leaders. Be aware that the accounts of Jesus's clashes with the Pharisees about issues such as the sabbath are not isolated stories which perfectly recall the relationship between Jesus and the leaders. Rather, they are influenced by the experience of the early church and its own hostilities with Judaism. Although Jesus clearly did demand a reappraisal of the Law, he did not court conflict or dismiss it entirely.

The ethical teaching of Jesus must be understood against a background of the Jewish law, which predominated Jewish life and thought at the time of Jesus. Much of his teaching is presented in apparent conflict with the Pharisees over matters of the Law, and as a result the Pharisaic attitude to the Law has been seen as obsessive and oppressive. The Law was a joy for the obedient Jew, however, and the Pharisees were concerned that it should remain relevant to contemporary life, especially under foreign occupation.

Jesus's teaching on matters of the Law has been interpreted in the light of conflict — conflict which in many cases may more accurately reflect that between the early church and the Jewish leaders than between Jesus and the Pharisees. Hence it is not accurate to present Jesus as opposed to the ethical demands of the Torah. Matthew 5:17ff. attempts to set the record straight: those early Christian groups that were teaching antinominanism (rejection of the Law) were not accurately reflecting the teaching of Jesus. Jesus's teaching on the sabbath, tithing and divorce attempts to reinterpret the Law in the light of the imminent kingdom, of which the primary concern is humanitarian and loving.

2 The Sermon on the Mount

Matthew 5–7, it could be argued, presents a summary of Jesus's ethical teaching:

- The first of Matthew's five blocks of teaching, the **Beatitudes** (Matthew 5:3–11) may be a form of commandments urging God-centred living and attitudes.
- The **antitheses** (5:21–47) support Jesus's claim (5:17) to have come not to abolish the Law. In them, all swearing, anger, lust, divorce (except for unfaithfulness), retaliation and hatred are forbidden. The implication in all these is that the Pharisees did not actually go far enough in their application of the Law, dealing only with activities and not with intent and motive. Jesus goes beyond Law to ethics proper:

> *Matthew remembered Jesus and his message of the kingdom and called for a surpassing righteousness ... which might not be reduced to 'scribal' righteousness or distorted into 'Christian' lawlessness.*
>
> **David Atkinson and David Field (eds),** *New Dictionary of Christian Ethics and Pastoral Theology*, IVP, 1995, p. 59

This is an important text for New Testament ethics. Some essay titles may ask you about it specifically, so make sure you have access to a range of good commentaries. Remember to interpret, not summarise.

- Chapter 6 places an ethical standard on the religious practices of fasting, prayer and almsgiving, and encourages a God-centredness in the Christian's relationship with their possessions and the world.
- The 'golden rule' of 7:12 is a reworking of the rabbinic summary of the Torah: 'Do not do to others what you do not wish them to do to you.' Matthew makes this a definite rule and emphasises that true ethics is about positive action, not simply about refraining from prohibited actions.

3   *Kingdom ethics*

See the section 'Salvation, eternal life and the kingdom of God' (pp. 44–48) for more detail here.

Jesus's fundamental message that 'the kingdom of God is at hand' (Mark 1:15) underlies the ethical teaching of the gospels. The concept is of the kingdom as a relationship, which has important implications for Christian behaviour and the lives of the believer and their community.

- **Repentance**, a turning away from the old life of sin, is the necessary pre-requisite for kingdom living. It may involve a radical demand, such as the young man who was required to give up all his wealth (Mark 10:17–31 & //s). Abandonment of homes and families, of material ties and earthly connections must be accepted as the norm for kingdom living.
- The **values** of the coming kingdom are quite the reverse of earthly values. In the kingdom the last will be first, the master will be servant, children and women will be at its heart, the rejected will be welcomed, and those who believed their place to be secure will be shut out.
- The kingdom comes with an **eschatological urgency**, which must affect man's ethical choices: the man whose security lies in his overflowing barn and not in God will find that he has placed his faith only in that which perishes (Luke 12:13ff.). Even the traditional obligations to family are nullified in the light of the kingdom.
- In the kingdom, disciples surrender their will to God. It becomes possible for them to be freed from the obligations of sabbath rest, dietary laws and human ambition, which cuts man off from God. They are free to take up their cross, lay down their life and surrender all things for the kingdom. In all this the disciple is called to obedience — not to a set of laws, but to the will of God.

4   *The Fourth Gospel*

The key chapters here are John 13–17, and these should be learned thoroughly.

You need to be well immersed in the gospel to be able to write effectively about its ethical teaching. Since it is implicit rather than explicit, it permeates the gospel as a whole. Remember that the circumstances of writing the gospel affect its ethical teaching. You need to know about the Johannine community and the importance of love to hold a persecuted community together.

- The Fourth Evangelist appears to show little interest in ethical matters. There is no teaching on ethical issues such as divorce, care for the poor or attitudes to wealth. Discipleship revolves around a relationship of dependency upon Jesus and the Father, which enables the disciples to bear fruit and to be a witness to the world outside their community.

- Sabbath controversies are a catalyst for christological debates, not extended teaching on the Law.
- The concept of the kingdom is replaced by that of eternal life, which a believer enters into not through obedience to ethical demands but because they have recognised the divine person of Jesus.
- The key to the relationship between believers and Jesus is love. The Father has sent the Son whom he loves out of love for the world, and the one commandment that Jesus gives to the disciples is to love one another (John 13:34). It is described as a new commandment, not because it was original (it is rooted in the Old Testament also) but because it alone is sufficient. If the disciples' behaviour is modified by love they will be equipped to make the right ethical choices.
- The indwelling of the Holy Spirit will guide, teach and equip the disciples to live in love for one another and in unity with the Father and the Son.

5 | *Pauline ethics*

This is a huge area, worthy of many books. Decide which areas you are going to concentrate on and avoid saying a little about a lot, otherwise you won't be evaluating your material enough.

- Paul's teaching is heavily influenced by his Jewish background as a Pharisee and his knowledge of Greek and Roman cultures. His understanding of the Christian life is dominated by his passionate conviction in the redemption accomplished for man on the cross. Hence he teaches that while prior to the coming of Christ the Law was the rightful means for man's behaviour to be modified, now that Christ has come and salvation has been won on the cross, continued slavishness towards the Law amounts to a denial of the cross's power.
- Freedom from the Law brings new ethical responsibilities, however. Paul teaches that 'All things are lawful for me, but not all things are beneficial' (1 Corinthians 6:12). Concern for the consciences of others, for the health of the whole Christian community and for the spiritual life of the individual must still be a primary consideration.
- Paul deals with specific ethical situations in the light of this: the man who is living with his stepmother must be removed from the community (1 Corinthians 5), and Christians who bring lawsuits against one another must recognise that this undermines the whole community before the non-Christian world.
- The fruits of the Spirit (Galatians 5:22) must be the key to the believer's behaviour. Even more than the gifts of the Spirit they should be sought as the evidence of God's spirit working in a believer's heart. These fruits enable the believer to withstand temptation, self-indulgence and arrogance.
- Concern for the body of Christ should be a primary consideration for the believer. Paul advocates care in the use of spiritual gifts so that the community is built up by these gifts, respect for others at the common meal and concern for the financial well-being of other churches. His encouragement of generosity and confidence in giving echoes the teaching of Malachi 3:10 on the benefits of obediently tithing.
- Paul demonstrates a special concern for household ethics, the relationship between husband and wife, parents and children, and for the status of

marriage. Paul's hierarchical view of the household may seem inappropriate to the twenty-first century, but he models it on the relationship between the believer and Christ, advocating it not as a means for misuse of power but for the fulfilment of man's potential.

- In all his teaching Paul recognises that his word is not necessarily the final say in ethical matters. He writes to communities, telling them they must exercise discernment and aim to be 'full of goodness, complete in knowledge and competent to instruct one another' (Romans 15:14).

A Proof, probability, faith and reason

The material in this section is relevant to questions on:

- arguments for the existence of God
- the nature of proof and probability
- miracles
- science and religion
- atheism
- the problem of evil
- verification and falsification
- religious experience

1 *Key terms*

An understanding of the key terms is necessary if you are to grapple with the philosophical concept of proof. Many questions are explicit in their demand for you to apply these terms. For example:

- What is meant by a priori and a posteriori arguments?
- Examine the concepts of proof and probability with reference to arguments for the existence of God.

Others are implicit:

- In what ways does the Ontological Argument differ from the Cosmological Argument for the existence of God?
- 'Arguments for the existence of God have some strengths but fail to prove the existence of God.' Evaluate this claim with reference to two arguments for the existence of God.

Some key terms are explained below:

- **Proof:** 'An argument which starts from one or more premises, which are propositions taken for granted for the purpose of the argument, and argues to a conclusion' (Richard Swinburne, *The Existence of God*, OUP, 1979, p. 5). In mathematics and logic a statement is proved if it **cannot be false**. For example, 5 + 5 = 10 cannot be false given the rules of mathematics. It is a logically necessary truth. In the real world a statement is proved if it is **beyond reasonable doubt**. Evidence points towards certain conclusions, and on the basis of that evidence we can say that the conclusion is true. It is possible, however, that some other conclusion could be reached on the basis of the same evidence.

- **Probability:** the measurement of the relative frequency or likelihood of the occurrence of an event. A probable conclusion is not the **only** one that could be reached, although it may be the most likely. This demands that a **judgement** be made and a range of evidence be considered. 'A proposition is probable not in isolation, but in relation to other, evidence-stating propositions' (John Hick, *Faith and Knowledge*, Fount, 1978, p. 153).

Don't make the mistake of thinking that all you need to do to answer these questions is summarise the arguments and their main criticisms. You need to be able to deal with the **principles** of proof.

- **A posteriori:** a proof the premises and conclusion of which are dependent on external evidence or experience.
- **A priori:** a proof the premises and conclusion of which are not dependent on external evidence or experience.
- **Deductive proof:** a set of premises which move towards a logically necessary conclusion.
- **Inductive proof:** a set of premises which move towards a conclusion that is not logically necessary, but is only probable.
- **Analytic proof:** the conclusion of the proof is contained within the premises.
- **Synthetic proof:** the conclusion of the proof is not contained within the premises.

Demonstrate that you understand how these principles apply by using non-religious examples as illustrations.

1.1 A priori/deductive

Premise 1	All bachelors are unmarried	*Bachelor is an analytic term*
Premise 2	Peter is a bachelor	*We already know the conclusion*
Conclusion	Peter is unmarried	*Which is thus logically necessary*

We learn nothing more from the conclusion than we already knew from the premises. It would be nonsense to say 'Peter is a married bachelor' because we know that bachelor means unmarried male. As an analytic term it cannot mean anything else, and thus we don't need anything else to prove the case for us.

1.2 A posteriori/inductive

Premise 1	70% of the pupils at Oakwood School are black-haired	*An observation*
Premise 2	Andrew is a pupil at Oakwood School	*A second observation*
Conclusion	Andrew has black hair	*A probable conclusion*

As you can see, there is a difference in this kind of proof: there is a 30% chance that Andrew does not have black hair. The higher the percentage of black-haired pupils, the more likely, or probable, it is that Andrew's hair is black. But even if 99% of the pupils were black-haired it would not be logically necessary that Andrew was among them. Only 100% black-haired pupils would give us grounds to say **conclusively** that Andrew was among them.

Proving God deductively

Premise 1	God is that than which nothing greater can be conceived
Premise 2	That than which nothing greater can be conceived must exist
Conclusion	God must exist

For details of the Ontological Argument and the other classical arguments for the existence of God, see the section, 'Arguments for the existence of God' (pp. 80–89).

You should recognise this as the **Ontological Proof**. The proof demands that if we accept the definition of God as that than which nothing greater can be conceived (TTWNGCBC) then we must accept that, analytically, he possesses existence, since TTWNGCBC must necessarily possess all perfections — and existence, according to the Ontological Proof, is a perfection.

Proving God inductively

Premise 1   All events require a cause

Premise 2   The universe is an event

Conclusion   God is the cause of the universe

Another familiar proof here — the basis of the **Cosmological Argument**. The proof leads only to a probable conclusion because there is no analytic, logically necessary, a priori reason why God should be the cause of the universe and not anything else. Neither are the premises themselves logically necessary — there is no compelling reason to agree conclusively that 'all events require a cause'. It is only on the basis of our regular experience that we assert that all events have a cause. Experience can be:

- deceptive
- limited
- open to many interpretations

These three points are worth emphasising here. Many issues in the philosophy of religion require you to consider the role and the reliability of experience, whether it be of the world, of God, or of phenomena which may or may not be traced back to God. You should consider whether the experience of others as well as ourselves is a firm foundation for any kind of proof, faith claim or valid statements about the universe.

[A posteriori arguments are] arguments in which the premises report what are (in some very general sense) features of human experience — *e.g. evident general truths about the world or features of private human experience.*

Richard Swinburne, *The Existence of God*, p. 9

See the section on miracles (pp. 97–103) for more on the principle of probability in relation to the occurrence of miracles.

Even if we agree that the universe demands a cause, or that it is inexplicable without one, we need overwhelmingly good reasons to say that God is the **only** possible cause. We need other evidence to support our conclusion before we can say that it has been **proved** that God is the cause of the universe, that the universe has a relationship of dependency on the God of classical theism. The conclusion reached is therefore no more than **probable**, and as such it cannot be said that the existence of God has been decisively proved.

1.3 Weaknesses of deductive proof

- Leads to **apparently** logically necessary conclusions
- Depends on whether we accept the premises are analytically true
- Can only say that **if** there is a God we might be able to make certain claims about him

1.4 Weaknesses of inductive proof

- Relies on accepting the nature of the evidence
- Demands overwhelmingly good reasons for accepting that the conclusion is the most likely
- Alternative conclusions may be just as convincing

2 The purpose of proofs

If proofs are fundamentally flawed, what is their purpose?

- **To provide an explanation — even a complete explanation**
  Classical proofs work on the principle that the universe itself and certain phenomena in the universe are not **self-explanatory** and thus demand an explanation **external** to themselves. The Cosmological and Teleological Proofs claim that God is the simplest explanation for the existence of the universe and its characteristics.

- **They appeal to reason and logical argument**
  The Ontological Proof attempts to establish that it is **logically impossible** not to believe in the existence of God. **Anselm** claimed to be working from the principle of **faith seeking understanding**, i.e. that which is initially accepted by faith can be accepted as a logical necessity.

- **They interpret certain evidence in terms of God rather than anything else**
  Proof attempts to give meaning to phenomena which would otherwise be inexplicable or meaningless. They rely on an agreement that the universe needs to be interpreted in terms of God. Even if a theist accepts the technicalities of a scientific explanation in principle, they will still be inclined to a religious interpretation of such phenomena.

3 The problems of proofs

- **They are dependent on limited experience and resources**
  Not only is experience potentially flawed (see above), but the resources of human reasoning may be said to be inadequate. How can we make claims about the infinite, eternal God of classical theism on the basis of limited human reasoning and logic?

- **They are dependent on empirical evidence**
  We can only argue from what we know, or have experienced ourselves, or from the testimonies of others, whose own experience and reasoning will be limited and flawed.

This could introduce another philosophical concept, that of Ockham's Razor — it is contrary to true philosophy to multiply entities without necessity.

See notes on the Cosmological Argument (pp. 85–87) for more on this point.

 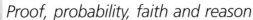

You will doubtless recognise this from another important topic in the philosophy of religion — religious language — and most specifically the 'falsification principle'. Many topics in this area overlap, and you should utilise legitimate connections such as this.

- **Believers do not allow anything to count against proofs**

> *Now it often seems to people who are not religious as if there was no conceivable event or series of events the occurrence of which would be admitted by sophisticated religious people to be a sufficient reason for conceding 'There wasn't a God after all'.*
>
> Anthony Flew, ***Theology and Falsification***, cited in Basil Mitchell (ed.),
> ***The Philosophy of Religion***, OUP, 1971, p. 15

Flew maintains that believers who do not allow — even in principle — anything to count against the existence of God (e.g. the problem of evil) are guilty of making **meaningless** claims about him.

- **The atheist can legitimately reach different conclusions from those of the theist**
  The theist and the atheist are faced with the same data about the universe, but reach differing conclusions about it. There is no reason why atheists should find the conclusions drawn by proofs for God's existence more convincing than the conclusions they have drawn themselves.

- **If the existence of God was self-evident there would be no need for proof**
  The universe and our experience of it is **religiously ambiguous**. Believers choose to interpret it in the light of the existence of God, but this may be on the basis of highly personal experience or conviction, and is therefore not of meaning to others. If God was overwhelmingly evident to man, however, proofs would not be necessary.

This should ring bells for you — the problem of evil addresses this issue. See the section on the problem of evil (pp. 89–97).

4 So who is right?

If, despite proof, believers and non-believers may both claim to adopt a philosophically legitimate stance, can there be any resolution? **John Hick** maintains that the principle of **eschatological verification** may provide a solution. The believer and the non-believer are both travelling the same road. The believer maintains that it leads to the Celestial City, the non-believer maintains that it leads nowhere — the journey is ultimately meaningless. While the evidence they encounter during the journey may be ambiguous, at the end of the road **one of them** will be proved right.

Another important overlap here, of course, this time with life after death. Hick's position is dependent on there being an eschatological future. See the section 'Life after death' (pp. 103–8) for more on this.

> *During the course of the journey ... they entertain different expectations ... about its ultimate destination. And yet when they do turn the last corner, it will be apparent that one of them has been right all the time, and the other wrong ... their opposed interpretations of the road constituted genuinely rival assertions ... whose status has the peculiar characteristic of being guaranteed retrospectively by a future crux.*
>
> John Hick, ***Faith and Knowledge***, pp. 177–78

5 *Faith and reason*

Faith and reason are often thought to be conflicting intellectual approaches. Indeed, faith could be seen to be anti-intellectual, and reason to be the process by which we weigh and balance evidence in an intellectual and academic manner. But faith and reason could also be seen to be complementary:

> *Reason and evidence may legitimately point the direction for faith to go —*
> *and must do so. Indeed, faith must not violate evidence and reason, or it*
> *would be irrational. Faith takes a step beyond reason, but only in the direc-*
> *tion which reason and evidence have pointed.*
>
> **Dave Hunt, *In Defence of the Faith*, Harvest House, 1996, p. 19**
>
> *Where reason is narrow, faith and reason are in opposition; where it is*
> *broad, reason belongs to the total matrix of faith.*
>
> **John Dillenberger, in *A Handbook of Christian Theology*,**
> **Fontana, 1960, p. 132**

It may appear legitimate to reject the application of reason and evidence in theological matters because God is so far beyond human reasoning and comprehension. But believers nevertheless hold certain things about God and the world to be true. This is not because they have taken a blind leap of faith, but because they have weighed the evidence and come to the conclusion that God is the best explanation for the phenomena they experience. This is no more and no less than the process we apply to our understanding of things in the empirical and secular world. It is also the same process that the atheist applies — only in the opposite direction, of course. Both theists and atheists experience the same evidence, only they draw different conclusions. Both have applied **reason** in so doing.

This draws attention to the concept of the religious ambiguity of the universe again. Where there is no overwhelming evidence one way or the other, both the believer and the atheist have to apply reason to come to their own conclusions.

6 *Reasonable faith*

We reach conclusions on the basis of what we consider to be **reasonable**. For example, if we see someone fall from a ten-storey building it is reasonable to believe that they will be killed. However, it may be that they are caught in a fire-fighter's net and are thus safe. Nevertheless, our conclusion was reasonable. We continue to check our beliefs through this application of reason if we are faced with new data which may lead us to modify our beliefs. In many cases there may be no direct link between the individual elements that constitute our belief, but reason still functions to tell us that it is reasonable to associate them.

> *The reasons for our conclusions operate, in a phrase of John Wisdom's, like*
> *the legs of a chair, not the links of a chain. A great mass of facts fit together*
> *in terms of our belief, though no one of them strictly entails it.*
>
> **John Hick, *Faith and Knowledge*, p. 78**

Human reason is fallible because:

- we make mistakes
- it is limited by the information available to us
- it cannot generate the source of religious beliefs, only apprehend their truth and provide intellectual models for what we believe
- humans cannot reason about something that does not exist in the physical world. We can **imagine** that pink elephants exist because 'pink' and 'elephants' do exist. Our imagination is limited by our experience.

Reinhold Niebuhr argued that reason is concerned with pattern and intelligibility but cannot provide a pattern by which to interpret the meaning of life. Revelation is needed to provide an image by which we can make our experience intelligible.

Reason is limited by the laws of **logic**, which serves as a rational check on belief. Logic identifies inconsistencies and contradictory elements which draw attention to problems — such as the problem of evil (see pp. 89–97). Beliefs that violate logic are more likely to be delusion. The classical arguments for the existence of God have served to illustrate that the existence of the deity is capable of being demonstrated logically, but the rebuttal of these arguments has refuted this position. However, **Charles Hartshorne** offered seven possibilities concerning the absoluteness and perfection of God, arguing that one of these alternatives must necessarily be true since the **logical classification** of possibilities cannot be infinite.

Reason makes use of **empirical evidence**. Some religious beliefs have some aspects which are in some sense empirical — the resurrection of Jesus, for example. Even though we cannot provide direct empirical evidence of such an event, it is necessary to believe that such an event did take place in some historical way if the claims of Christianity are to have significance. Some classical arguments for the existence of God are dependent on reasoning drawn from empirical evidence. The **design argument** reasons that the evidence of design in the universe points to the existence of an intelligent designer, namely God.

Reason draws on our experience — not only of the world, but **religious experience** itself. However, religious experiences cannot guarantee the truthfulness of a believer's claims, since truth too is ambiguous and no two experients may reach the same conclusions about their experience. Nevertheless, intense personal experience must be one of the 'legs of the chair' which fit together to form belief and which leads to faith.

7 Defining faith

- **Propositional faith** (*fides*) is the belief that there is a God and that certain propositions (assertions, claims) about him are true.
- **Non-propositional faith** (*fiducia*) is a trust, maintained even in the face of contrary experience or evidence, that God's intentions are loving and beneficial. This religious trust could be compared to trusting a person and must grow out of more than an intellectual acceptance of God's existence, i.e. a personal knowledge of him.

We're back to the question of interpreting the universe again here. If the universe and our experience are self-explanatory there is no need for God, but while they remain ultimately inexplicable an ultimate explanation will be sought.

You can, of course, provide an alternative example here from the religion you are studying or with which you are most familiar.

Basil Mitchell's 'Parable of the Partisan and the Stranger' illustrates this point particularly well. (See the section 'Religious language 1: verification, falsification and language games' on pp. 123–31).

Both types of faith can be thought of as a gift of God (1 Corinthians 12:9), enabling the believer to reach conclusions that they could not deduce by reason alone.

Hick speaks of faith as an 'uncompelled model of experiencing-as' (*Faith and Knowledge*, p. 151). Those who have faith experience the world as a place in which they encounter the transcendent God, leading to propositional faith claims about him and his existence. Faith is a mode by which believers **interpret** their experience, leading to an understanding of the **significance** of that experience.

B The foundations of Judaeo–Christian belief

The foundations of monotheistic religious beliefs lie deep in the pre-Christian philosophical traditions of Plato and Aristotle. Their thinking sheds important light on many key aspects of later theology.

1 Plato

Plato, a follower of Socrates, left Athens after his teacher's execution, not returning until 387 BCE, believing that the only hope for the world would be when 'kings were philosophers or philosophers were kings'.

Plato's works consist of a series of dialogues between Socrates and others, presented in a highly characteristic style known as the 'Socratic Method'. This is a means of discourse that draws out from opponents the error of their reasoning.

The works of Plato are a useful foundation for an understanding of the nature of reality and knowledge, and the distinction between body and soul. Plato uses his famous 'Allegory of the Cave' to draw attention to the difference between the world of appearances and the real world.

Only what is permanent can be the source of true knowledge, not the objects of the physical world, which are always changing. The unchanging realities are those that Plato believed could only be apprehended by the mind, since those we experience through the senses are only imperfect copies. However, the unthinking man simply accepts what he hears and never questions whether it is valuable, good or true, rather than overcoming the difficulties of achieving the goal of perfect reality.

Plato's **theory of the Forms** develops ideas about goodness and reality. The prisoners in the cave would always be condemned to accepting a pale copy of the truth as reality, and so would never be able to apprehend the true, absolute Form of the Good. Aquinas's Fourth Way was clearly influenced

---

You must avoid treating questions on Plato and Aristotle as an opportunity to relate their life stories. Narrative is not important, but it is crucial to show an understanding of their thinking.

In an allegory, the apparent meaning of the characters and events is used to symbolise a deeper moral or spiritual meaning.

H. D. F. Kitto observed that: 'It was Greek philosophy, notably Plato's conception of the absolute, eternal deity, which prepared the world for the reception of a universal religion.'

by Plato, pointing to the need for a highest source of goodness, trust, and nobility, which Aquinas identified as God. These unchanging concepts could never be encountered in the physical world, but Plato believed we have an instinctive, if imperfect, appreciation of them. This, he believed, indicated that man has an immortal, pre-existent soul, which has encountered these forms before becoming imprisoned in the physical body. Upon the death of the physical body, the soul will re-enter the eternal realm from which it came.

2 *Aristotle*

Brian Magee observes that Aristotle was 'working always from inside experience, never trying to impose abstract explanations on it from the outside'.

Aristotle was an empiricist philosopher who was devoted to deepening his understanding of experience. He looked for scientific explanations and asked important questions about the nature of them. Although none of the works he prepared for publication survived, for hundred of years his ideas constituted the largest systematic body of knowledge.

Aristotle rejected Plato's theory of the Forms, believing that reality lay within the empirical world. He sought to answer the question: 'What does it mean for something to exist?' Aristotle identified four causes, which constitute a complete explanation of what causes something to exist:

- The **material cause** of something answers the question 'What does it consist of?'
- The **efficient cause** answers the question 'How did it happen?'
- The **formal cause** answers the question 'What are its characteristics?'
- The **final cause** answers the question 'Why is it here?' or 'What is its purpose?'

Once all four causes have been established, the complete explanation for the existence of an item has been found. The most important of these causes is the final cause, which is **teleological** (that is, concerned with ultimate end or function), since this is what gives an item its ultimate goodness.

Aristotle was also interested in tracing all movements back to a first mover. He concluded that a chain of movers had to begin with an unmoved or prime mover, something which is not itself moved, but which could cause other things to move. He called this prime mover 'God', a final cause in itself, which causes things to be not simply through physical or mechanical momentum but through an act of love. All things are drawn towards God, the necessary being which is eternally good and on whom all other things depend.

Aristotle saw the relationship between soul and body as a psycho-physical unity of the two. The human soul is essentially the body and its organisation, but Aristotle did identify another quality that it possesses — reason, the means by which humans can develop intellectually and morally.

The biblical writers portray God very differently to the ancient Greeks. Although he is a transcendent and sovereign creator, his creation of humanity and the universe is for a purpose and sets the scene for the relationship between God and humanity, which has its culmination in an eschatological future.

3 God as creator

A myth is a symbolic, approximate expression of truth.

The narratives of Genesis 1–2 share remarkable similarities to the creation myths that emerged in the Babylonian traditions, especially the epic *Euma elish*, which recounted the God Marduk's defeat of the sea monster Tiamat and his subsequent creation of heaven and earth. There are also allusions to Baal's defeat of the sea monster Leviathan in the Canaanite texts from Ugarit, which may have influenced the Genesis account.

There are two distinct accounts of creation in Genesis 1 and 2:

Resist the temptation to write out a long account of the creation narratives in Genesis. It will earn you few marks.

- The first account, from the Priestly tradition, is characterised by repeated phrases, and creation takes place over a structured period of 6 days, followed by a day of divine rest. Traditionally, creation is thought to have been *ex nihilo* ('out of nothing').
- The second account is narrative in style, and possibly older. It is linked directly with the events of the fall in Genesis 3 and it begins to address why, if God created a perfect universe (1:31), there are clearly things and situations in the world that we consider to be imperfect.

Look up these verses in Genesis: 1:26; 1:27; 2:7; 2:9; 2:15; 2:19.

There are common features in both accounts:
- The human race is the goal of God's creative work.
- Humans are distinguished from the rest of creation, being in the image of God and given life by the direct and personal action of God's spirit.
- Humans are given authority over the animals and the opportunity to participate in God's creative work.
- Everything necessary for the survival of humans is in the garden in which God places them.

The theme of creation runs throughout the Old Testament, and is expressed vividly in the Psalms and the Wisdom literature. When Job questions God's plans and purposes, God replies rhetorically: 'Where were you when I laid the foundations of the earth?' (Job 38:4). Above all, Isaiah expresses the utter sovereignty of God, who cannot be challenged by man or by the false gods which humanity, in its ignorance, carves and worships.

The Psalmist testifies to God's continued sustaining of the created order:
'Who by thy strength has established the mountains ... who stills the roaring of the seas?' (Psalm 65:6–7).

> *I am the Lord, and there is no other. I form light and create darkness, I make weal and create woe, I am the Lord, who does all these things.*
>
> **Isaiah 45:6–7**

4 God's goodness

The goodness of God is expressed both through the standards he sets for humans and through how he responds to their attempts to live up to those standards. Does God create moral standards that he issues as commands, or does he command that which he already knows as good?

This dilemma is difficult to solve, since religious believers tend to use God's commands as a guide for deciding what is good but are aware that sometimes

this causes problems. The classic example of someone who was called by God to do something that society would condemn as wrong is Abraham's call to sacrifice Isaac. Peter Vardy observes that because Abraham trusted his relationship with God, he was able to hold to two contradictory facts: God's promise to him that he would have many descendents though Isaac *and* that he would sacrifice Isaac, as God had commanded.

For the Israelites, God's goodness was experienced through his covenant relationship with them, first revealed in the giving of the Law, including the Ten Commandments (the Decalogue). Acceptance of these standards of behaviour indicated the willingness of the people of Israel to enter into a covenant relationship with God that separated them from all other nations. It was a free response to a free act of grace by God, but it did bring certain obligations upon the people, who were expected to represent God and his goodness to other nations. It is for this reason that the highest standards of behaviour were expected of the people of Israel.

For the New Testament writers, the ultimate demonstration of God's goodness is, of course, the sending of Jesus whereby God provides the means of redemption.

> *You only have I known of all the families of the earth; therefore I will punish you for all your iniquities.*
>
> **Amos 3:2**

> *I will not execute my fierce wrath against them, I will not return to destroy Ephraim: for I am God and not man; the Holy one in your midst.*
>
> **Hosea 9:11**

> *For God so loved the world that he gave his only Son, so that all who believe in him should not perish but have eternal life.*
>
> **John 3:16**

5 God at work in the world

The biblical writers believed that God is **immanent** and can be known through human experience and the world. This runs counter to the equally important view that God is **transcendent** — that he is beyond the limits of any human experience. The Judaeo–Christian picture is something of a paradox:

> *The God of the Bible stands above the world as its sovereign Lord, its Creator and its Saviour; but he appears in the world to set men tasks to do, speaking to men in demand, in promise, in healing and fulfilment.*
>
> **John A. Hutchinson, *Handbook of Christian Theology*, Fontana, 1960, p.75**

Throughout the Bible, God's action in the world is illustrated by accounts of miraculous events in which he suspends the laws of nature to accomplish his purpose. The biblical writers had no concept of natural law that determined how the universe operates and so when God intervenes in the course of events, it is never portrayed as a violation of natural laws. Whatever the interpretation of biblical events when God intervenes directly, the narratives characteristically attribute all events — both natural and supernatural — to divine providence.

C Arguments for the existence of God

The material in this section is relevant to questions on:
- proof and probability
- faith and reason
- standard issues regarding the arguments
- the problem of evil
- atheism
- religious language

Before pressing ahead with this section you must make sure that you have first read the previous one, on proof and probability. You will not be able to gain all the marks available for a question unless you show a clear understanding of the philosophical principles of proof which are at work in these arguments and in the criticisms levelled against them. Turn back now if you thought that the previous section was not of relevance to you!

This is a vast topic. As you know, there are shelves of fat books on the arguments alone. These revision notes are intended to cover the first principles of the arguments, which will give you enough to answer almost any question you may be asked. But you must combine it with material from the previous section, and bear in mind that there is plenty of scope for going into a lot more detail.

The Ontological Argument

This classic argument is **a priori**, **deductive** and **synthetic**.

1.1 Anselm and the *Proslogion*

In **Anselm**'s (1033–1109) first book, the *Monologion*, he had proposed a chain of arguments which constituted proof for the existence of God. But he wanted to find a single argument which would show, by itself, the irrefutable fact that God must exist. In the *Proslogion* he establishes that: (a) God is **that than which nothing greater can be conceived**; (b) since he is such a being, **his non-existence is inconceivable**.

(a) As 'that than which nothing greater can be conceived', God is the sum of all perfections, and no more perfect being can be described. He is not simply spatially greater, or the most perfect being that exists, but the most perfect **conceivable**. Anselm distinguished between a being existing only in the mind (*in intellectu*) and existing in reality (*in re*). If it exists only in the mind then there may exist a greater being in reality also. Therefore 'that than which nothing greater can be conceived' must exist in reality also if it is **truly** that than which nothing greater can be conceived.

(b) If God is 'that than which nothing greater can be conceived' he must therefore necessarily exist, since by definition it is impossible to conceive of him not existing. At the heart of God's existence is his **aseity** — he is independent of all other beings, not limited by time or space, and so it is impossible to speak of him as having come to exist or ceasing to exist. His non-existence is therefore impossible. Anselm's argument depends on maintaining that it is more perfect to exist necessarily than to exist contingently, and so an unsurpassably perfect being must exist necessarily. Even 'the fool' (the atheist of Psalm 53) who denied the existence of God had comprehended what constituted God's essence, and as such was saying the unsayable when he denied his existence.

> A necessary being cannot not exist
>
> A contingent being comes in and goes out of existence

1.2 Descartes' Triangle

We are paying fleeting visits here to the main players in the argument. Don't spend too long on any one philosopher, as you only have an hour at the most to write your essay in the exam.

Descartes (1591–1650) drew attention to the **analytic** nature of the Ontological Argument. He argued that existence was a quality that belonged analytically to God in the same way that three angles was **analytically predicated** of a triangle. (A predicate is a defining characteristic of a thing or being — something that can be possessed or lacked.) A triangle must possess three angles, otherwise it is not a triangle. Descartes claimed that God possesses existence in the same way — it is part of his nature to exist, and to lack it would be to lack perfection, and hence not to be God. In the twentieth century **Norman Malcolm** added to this by arguing that if God **could** exist then he definitely **must** exist, or he would not be God.

1.3 Plantinga's Possible Worlds

Alvin Plantinga (1932–) suggested that whatever this world is like, God would exist, even if it were considerably different from the world as we know it. Hence God could exist in all possible worlds; there are many possible worlds in which to exist, including our own. Since God could exist in all possible worlds he is, Plantinga maintained, **maximally great**; and if he possess all the attributes of God in all possible worlds he must be **maximally excellent**.

1.4 Gaunilo's Island

Gaunilo, a contemporary of Anselm, claimed that the argument led to absurd conclusions if applied to different examples. He demonstrated a *reductio ad absurdum* (reducing to an absurdity) by suggesting that he could conceive of an island than which no greater could be conceived, and according to Anselm's logic it must exist. **However...** islands are part of the contingent world, and Anselm responded that the proof was only intended to apply to necessary beings.

1.5 Kant rejects the Triangle

Kant (1724–1804) challenged the view that because necessary existence is a characteristic of God then he must exist. All he was prepared to say is that **if** there is an infinitely perfect being then he must exist, just as **if** there is a triangle it must have three angles:

> To posit a triangle and yet to reject its three angles is self-contradictory, but there is no self-contradiction in rejecting the triangle altogether, together with its three angles.

Kant thus rejected the premise that existence is a predicate that can be possessed or lacked. As a defining characteristic it does not add anything to our understanding of a thing: a real £100 is no different in essence from an imaginary £100.

David Hume considered the argument a failure because it made a false assumption about existence — that necessary existence is a coherent concept. He maintained that existence can only ever be contingent (dependent and limited), and that all statements about existence can be denied without contradiction. All things that can be said to exist could also be said not to exist. Hume argued:

> *However much our concept of an object may contain, we must go outside of it to determine whether or not it exists. We cannot define something into existence — even if it has all the perfections we can imagine.*
>
> **Dialogues Concerning Natural Religion**, OUP, 1975, p. 91

Arguments for the existence of God

Russell argued that to say 'Cows are brown' tells us something about cows, but to say 'Cows are brown and exist' adds nothing more to the original definition.

Bertrand Russell (1872–1970) also denied that existence could operate as a predicate, claiming only that it has a propositional function: it asserts that there are beings in the world that answer a particular description, but adds no further information about them. It does not convey their essence or nature.

Norman Malcolm proposed a form of the argument in support of necessary existence, working on the presumption that if God *could* exist, he *does* exist, since he cannot *not* exist. The argument can be framed thus:

1 God is that than which nothing greater can be thought.
2 Necessary existence is a perfection.
3 If God possesses all perfections, he must possess necessary existence.
4 A necessary being cannot *not* exist.
5 If God *could* exist, he would exist necessarily.
6 It is contradictory to say that a necessary being does not exist.
7 God must exist.

Furthermore, Malcolm argues that God's existence is either necessary or impossible, but he cannot possess contingent existence. Hence, God must have necessary existence. Malcolm observes that God is a special case — unlike contingent beings, for whom existence is merely possible. However, as we have already seen, if we adopt Hume's view, necessary existence may be an incoherent concept and so Malcolm's form of the argument will fail. Furthermore, while Malcolm's argument may show that *if* God exists, he exists necessarily, that is not the same as proving that he *does* exist.

Another way of understanding Malcolm's approach is to consider the possible ways of conceiving God's existence:

- God does not exist.
- God exists contingently.
- God exists necessarily.

We are obliged to reject the first claim — by definition, God's non-existence is inconceivable. We must also reject the second claim — if God exists contingently, his existence would be no greater than the existence of any other being. Thus, we have no alternative than to accept that God exists necessarily, since by rejecting the first two claims, we have accepted that he cannot *not* exist.

Alvin Plantinga suggested that since we are able to imagine any number of alternative worlds in which things may be quite different — for example, a world in which Luciano Pavarotti did not choose to become an operatic tenor, but was a house painter instead — there must be any number of possible worlds, including our own. However, if God's existence is necessary, he must exist in them all and have all the characteristics of God in them all. This is because, Plantinga argued, God is both **maximally great** and **maximally excellent**. He proposed that:

A There exists a world in which there is a being of maximal greatness.
B A being of maximal excellence is omnipotent, omniscient and omnibenevolent in all worlds.

Nevertheless, Plantinga's argument only succeeds in showing that God is *possible* in all possible worlds, not that he is *actual* in all possible worlds.

> Obviously, Gasking's *reductio* does not prove the non-existence of God, but in the same way, neither does Anselm's argument prove that he does exist.

1.6 Douglas Gasking: the ontological proof for the non-existence of God

Australian philosopher Douglas Gasking also offered *reductio* to demonstrate the fallacy of the Ontological Proof:

P1	The creation of the world is the most supreme achievement conceivable.
P2	The value of an achievement is measured by its intrinsic quality and the ability of its creator.
P3	The greater the limitation of the creation, the more impressive the achievement.
P4	The greatest limitation of a creator would be non-existence.
P5	Therefore, a world created by a non-existent creator would be greater than one created by an existent creator.
P6	An existing God is therefore not the greatest conceivable being, since an even greater being would be one that did not exist.
Conclusion	God does not exist.

The well-known contemporary atheist, Richard Dawkins, rejects the Ontological Argument, primarily on the grounds that it is 'infantile'. He writes:

> Let me translate this infantile argument into the appropriate language, which is the language of the playground:
>
> 'Bet you I can prove God exists.'
>
> 'Bet you can't.'
>
> 'Right then, imagine the most perfect perfect perfect thing possible.'
>
> 'Okay, now what?'
>
> 'Now, is that perfect perfect perfect thing real? Does it exist?'
>
> 'No, it's only in my mind.'
>
> 'But if it was real it would be even more perfect, because a really really perfect thing would have to be better than a silly old imaginary thing. So I've proved that God exists. Nur nurny nur nur. All atheists are fools.'
>
> *The God Delusion*, **Bantam Press, 2006, p. 120**

Dawkins states that 'the very idea that grand conclusions [that God exists] could follow from such logomachist trickery offends me aesthetically' and supports Bertrand Russell's claim that 'it is easier to feel convinced that the Ontological Argument must be fallacious than it is to find out precisely where the fallacy lies' (cited ibid.). Dawkins argues that the automatic reaction to the argument should be suspicion that that any line of reasoning that lacks a 'single piece of data from the real world' should lead to such a significant conclusion.

Summary

Anselm's argument is not an attempted proof of God's existence, but a revelation of the significance of God to believers as 'that than which nothing greater can be conceived' and who therefore cannot not exist. While this may describe a believer's concept of God, however, it does not prove the actual existence of such a being.

2   *The Cosmological Argument*

This argument is **inductive**, **a posteriori** and **synthetic**. It is based on the claim that everything existing in the universe was caused by something else, and that 'something' was caused by another thing. However, it is necessary for something to have started this chain of causation — an external agent that did not itself need to be caused. The argument is based on three main questions:

● Why is there something rather than nothing?
● Why does the universe possess the form it does, and not some other form?
● How can the series of events that culminated in the universe be explained?

The Cosmological Argument infers the existence of God from the existence of the cosmos. On the principle that nothing causes itself, if the universe exists then it must be caused by something. **Plato** and **Aristotle** had used the argument to postulate a first mover, but the most famous Christian application of the argument is found in the first three of Aquinas's **Five Ways**.

2.1 The First Way — from motion

These three ways are very repetitive. It is not particularly valuable in an exam to go through them in fine detail, so concentrate on evaluating the broader principles of the argument.

● Nothing can move itself, yet things are evidently in motion.
● An infinite chain of movers which has no beginning can have no middle or end.
● Hence there must be a first mover that causes motion in all things — this Aquinas calls God.
● Aquinas described motion as 'the reduction of something from potentiality to actuality'. For example, fire (which is **actually** hot) changes wood (which is **potentially** hot) to a state of being actually hot. Motion, therefore, is a change of state and not just transportation from A to B.

2.2 The Second Way — from cause

● All things are caused, since nothing can be its own cause, otherwise it would be prior to itself — a logical impossibility.
● Thus there must be a first cause (God) on which all other causes depend, and in an infinite chain there can be no first cause.

2.3 The Third Way — from necessity and contingency

● Everything we can point to is dependent upon factors beyond itself and thus is contingent.

Compare the way God's necessary existence is applied here with how it is used in the Ontological Argument. Aquinas is speaking of necessity *de re* (in the nature of things). Anselm speaks of God's necessity being *de dicto* (according to definition).

- Its presence can only be explained by reference to those factors which themselves depend on other factors.
- These factors demand an ultimate explanation in the form of a necessary being — again God — dependent on nothing outside itself.

Summary

The existence of the universe is not explicable without reference to causes and factors outside itself. It cannot be self-causing, since it is contingent. The existence of a first, necessary, cause and mover explains the origin of an otherwise 'brute fact'. The argument assumes that the universe has not always been in existence.

Leibniz argued that even if the universe had always been in existence it would still require an explanation, or a **sufficient reason**, for its existence, since we need to establish why there is something rather than nothing.

Mackie's railway carriage analogy further illustrates the argument: in a series of railway trucks the immediate explanation of the movement of a given truck is that it is being pulled by the one in front of it. But even if we multiply the number of trucks to infinity we shall still not have found the ultimate explanation for the movement of any of them. Only if we postuate an engine — which is not just another truck but which has the power to move without requiring something else to act upon it — can we explain the movement of the trucks.

2.4 Criticisms of the Cosmological Argument

David Hume offered classical criticisms in *Dialogues Concerning Natural Religion*:
- The notion of a necessary being is an incoherent one — there is no being the non-existence of which is inconceivable — and even if there were, why should it be God?
- Why should the first mover be the God of classical theism? Aquinas is guilty of an inductive leap of logic in moving from the need for a first mover to identifying it as God. Similarly, the necessary cause of the universe may yet reveal itself.
- The argument begins with a concept familiar to us — the universe — but reaches conclusions about things that are outside our experience — infinity, God, the origin of the universe.
- Why do we need to find a cause for the whole chain if we can explain each item in a chain of causes?
- The universe could be self-causing — we have no reason to say categorically that it is not.

The argument that the universe is nothing more than a 'brute fact' is useful here.

Bertrand Russell argued that we cannot deduce from the individual parts of the universe that the universe as a whole has a cause, in the same way that we cannot say that because every person in the universe has a mother the human race as a whole has a mother. In his debate with **F. C. Copelston**, Russell claimed that some things 'just are' and require no explanation, and the universe was

such a case in point. To this, Copelston famously replied that 'if one refuses to sit down at the chess-board and make a move one cannot be checkmated'. Russell was effectively withdrawing from the debate.

2.5 The value of the Cosmological Argument

The argument still remains attractive because it addresses questions of perennial concern. We are used to questioning things around us and finding explanations for them. The theist is more likely to find that explanation in the deity, even though the universe is religiously ambiguous and we cannot conclusively prove the existence of God from the existence of the universe. Nevertheless, it could be said to be the simplest explanation for why there is something rather than nothing.

> The Parable of the Gardener deals with the fact that the universe is religiously ambiguous. Even if faced with the same evidence — the universe — there is no reason why any two observers should reach the same conclusion about its origins.

The Teleological/Design Argument

This argument is **inductive**, **a posteriori** and **synthetic**. It suggests that like human inventions, features of the universe are so perfectly adapted to fulfil their function that they display evidence of being deliberately designed by an intelligent, personal designer. Since the works of nature are far greater than the works of humanity, an infinitely greater designer, God, is suggested as the most likely explanation. The argument seeks to explain four features of the world: **order**, **benefit**, **purpose** and **suitability for human life**.

An extension of the Cosmological Argument, Aquinas's Fifth Way — from the governance of the world — identifies the need for an intelligent mind behind the universe. The actions of beings which lack reason (e.g. animals, plants) are inexplicable without reference to an intelligent force external to them.

> Again, these arguments are concerned with the need to find explanations for phenomena which are otherwise inexplicable.

3.1 Paley and the watch

The most popular form of the argument is as an analogy:

> Just as the discovery of a watch on a heath could not be satisfactorily explained by saying it had 'always been there', the order evident in the universe demands an explanation. The watch serves as an analogy for the world: it demonstrates purpose, design and ***telos*** (an end or ultimate function). All parts of the watch unite to fulfil that function and this unity cannot be explained by chance. Even if we have never seen a watch before we could still deduce that it had been designed. And even if parts of it appear to malfunction, or if we cannot work out the function that individual parts contribute to the whole, it does not disprove that it has been designed.

3.2 Weaknesses of the analogy

- **Paley** assumed the presence of order in the universe. This needs to be proved first, and unless we can say what an undesigned universe would be like, how can we presume that this universe is the result of design?

- Is the watch analogous to parts of the universe or to the whole universe?
- The analogy itself is unsound, since the watch and the world are too unlike to withstand comparison.
- The principles of analogy demand that the worldmaker and the watchmaker are as similar as possible. Hence God is anthropomorphosised. David Hume argued that this infers a limited deity, whose creation is not necessarily perfect.
- How is the presence of evil explained if the universe is designed by a benevolent deity?
- The presence of order could be explained by chance or by some impersonal force.
- Most products of human design involve more than one craftsman, hence the universe could have been made by a pantheon of gods, not the one God of classical theism.

Most of these criticisms are found in the *Dialogues Concerning Natural Religion*.

3.3 The probability of design

Richard Swinburne supports the Teleological Argument on the grounds that the probability of design is greater than chance. He identifies seven features of the world that demand an explanation:

- its existence
- its order
- consciousness
- the opportunity to do good
- the pattern of history
- miracles
- religious experience

> *God being omnipotent is able to produce a world orderly in these respects. And he has a good reason to choose to do so: a world containing human persons is a good thing… God being perfectly good, is generous. He wants to share.*
>
> **Richard Swinburne, *Is There a God?*, OUP, 1996, p.54**

3.4 Other forms of the argument

- The **argument from providence** — the universe contains everything needed for human survival and benefit.
- The **aesthetic argument** — the world is beautiful.
- The **anthropic principle** — the purpose of the universe appears to be to support human life.

3.5 Other criticisms

- The features of the universe could be the result of one huge **coincidence** — a cosmic happening producing a result that merely *appears* to be designed. Richard Dawkins suggests that although the universe may be difficult to explain as the result of *one* chance, it could easily be the result of many smaller chances.

- The premises of the argument are flawed: not everyone perceives design in the universe. Moreover, why is God the only explanation for design, even if it *is* present?
- **Evolution and natural selection** could provide just as likely an explanation for the character and appearance of the universe as divine design. As species adapt to their environment, they inevitably appear to be designed to suit it, otherwise they would not survive.
- The aesthetic argument is unconvincing since beauty is subjective, and what one person perceives as beautiful, another does not. Further, since we have no other world to compare with, how do we know this world *is* beautiful?

3.6 The value of the argument

Even David Hume acknowledged that 'a purpose, an intention, a design, strikes everywhere the most careless, the most stupid thinker'. Like the Cosmological Argument, it draws on regular experience and appeals to the beauty evident in the universe. This is the **aesthetic** form of the argument, working on the principle that beauty is not necessary for the basic functioning of the universe. As such it suggests a personal, benevolent designer.

Even scientific explanations of the universe can be made compatible with the argument: the big bang, evolution and the findings of modern cosmology can be seen to be the means that the divine designer has used. In the late nineteenth century **Archbishop Temple** claimed: 'The doctrine of evolution leaves the argument for an intelligent Creator and Governor of the earth stronger than it was before.' It should be said, however, that not all Victorian Christians were able to accommodate the findings of modern science in the same way.

The argument could be said to provide the most reasonable explanation for the features of design which appear to be evident in the universe. **F. R. Tenant** claimed: 'The world is compatible with a single throw of the dice, and common sense is not foolish in suspecting the dice to have been loaded.' Even **Stephen Hawking** has proposed: 'All the evidence points to His [God] being an inveterate gambler who throws dice on every possible occasion.' **Richard Swinburne** observes (in *Is There a God?*, OUP, 1996, p. 68): 'The very success of science in showing us how deeply orderly the natural world is, provides strong grounds for believing that there is an even deeper cause of that order.'

D The problem of evil

The material in this section is relevant to questions on:
- the problem of evil
- the existence of God
- miracles
- biblical responses to the problem of suffering, e.g. the book of Job or the Psalms
- moral issues concerned with suffering and religious responses to it

- life after death
- atheism and religious language

1 *The extent of the problem*

The problem of evil is one which the non-believer is entitled to expect the believer to be prepared to address. It presents a serious challenge to theistic belief, and yet believers are frequently accused of not recognising this challenge. Anthony Flew claims that believers would rather **qualify** God's nature — 'God is all loving, **but** we cannot expect to understand his love' — than recognise the 'full force of the conflict' (Basil Mitchell). Believers should at least suggest an **explanation** for why they live in a world which is so often characterised by evil and yet still hold fast to belief in the omnipotent, omniscient God of classical theism.

The problem of evil has many different aspects, some of which are outlined below.

> A good essay on this topic will not launch straight into the theodicies, or even into classifications of the types of evil, without first having considered the philosophical challenges the problem presents.

1.1 A theological problem

The nature of God is brought seriously into question by the evident problem of evil:

> *Christians, and others who believe in a transcendent, personal God, are faced with the problem of evil. The problem is especially poignant for ... theists who believe in a God who is both good and omnipotent. If God is both good and omnipotent, why is there so much evil expressed in the suffering of so many people throughout the world? If God exists, God is either not completely good or not completely powerful?*
>
> **James Sire, *Why Should Anyone Believe Anything At All?*, IVP, 1994, p. 182**

The whole nature of the theist's experience and relationship with God is brought into question if the nature of God is under threat. For Christians, is it possible to believe both that God sent his son as a sacrifice for human sin, and yet that he allows redeemed humanity to live in a world that has the capacity to destroy them? What about judgement? Would a loving God allow any human being to be consigned to hell? The existence of evil implies that God has **chosen** to allow it.

> *In the place of suffering God could have made happiness. Of his will, and without compulsion, he made suffering. What is he then, but an almighty fiend? His good acts cannot excuse his evil acts.... God must be all good, or else not good at all.*
>
> **Samuel P. Putnam, *400 Years of Free Thought*, 1894, pp. 389–90**

1.2 A philosophical problem

The problem draws attention to the **inconsistent triad**:

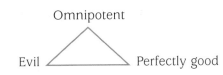

Omnipotent

Evil   Perfectly good

Remove one corner of the triad and the problem goes away, but believers are committed to believing that God is omnipotent and omniscient and to accepting the reality of evil. Yet this is contradictory and inconsistent. Theists are committed to making **conflicting claims**: God is all-powerful and all-loving *and* evil exists. They must therefore have good reasons for maintaining such a contradictory position.

> *There is a problem about why God allows evil, and if the theist does not have (in a cool moment) a satisfactory answer to it, then his belief in God is less than rational and there is no reason why the atheist should share it.*
>
> **Richard Swinburne, *Is There a God?*, OUP, 1996, p. 96**

1.3 A diverse problem

There are many categories and sub-categories of evil, so how can we find a satisfactory definition? You need to consider the following:

- Is evil the opposite of good? Or an absence of good (*privatio boni*)? Or is it parasitic on good?
- Is it sin or the consequence of sin?
- 'The only cause of evil is the falling away from the unchangeable good of a being made good, but changeable, first in the case of an angel, and afterwards in the case of man.' (Augustine)
- How are pain and suffering related to evil? Are they the consequences of it?

> *It is profoundly evil to reject the profoundly good. The consequences are justifiably profound.... The consequences of rejecting the good are the pain and suffering we see so rife around us and in us.*
>
> **James Sire, *Why Should Anyone Believe Anything At All?*, p. 184**

Moral evil has many consequences for individuals, generations and nations:

> *Moral evil I understand as including all evil caused deliberately by humans doing what they ought not to do, or allowed to occur by humans negligently failing to do what they ought to do, and also the evil constituted by such deliberate actions or negligent failure.*
>
> **Richard Swinburne, *Is There a God?*, p. 97**

This is a place where candidates waste a lot of time listing different examples of evil: murder, rape, earthquakes, volcanoes, AIDS, etc. You cannot expect to earn many marks for this, since it does not demonstrate your understanding of the problem.

These simple categories of moral and natural evil are really just the tip of the iceberg. If you are addressing a question on the types of evil or the extent of the problem you should provide more detail.

Natural evil is commonly thought of as that which is beyond man's control — the malfunctioning of the natural order:

> *Natural evil is the evil that originates independently of human actions, in disease, in bacilli, in earthquakes, storms, droughts, tornadoes etc.*
>
> John Hick, *Evil and the God of Love*, Fontana, 1968, p. 18

- What about **animal suffering** or other events which do not directly touch on man as being evil — the extinction of a star or the decay of plants, an earthquake on a uninhabited island? Hick suggests that there is still a 'prima facie challenge to be met'.
- There is a further problem when evils overlap. In the modern world many natural evils are exacerbated by moral evil — war contributes to famine; man's poor stewardship of the natural environment may lead to global warming.
- Consider the contribution of **emotional and psychological pain**. How far may they be considered spiritual in nature?

> *For we are not contending against flesh and blood, but against principalities, against the powers, against the world rulers of this present darkness, against the spiritual hosts of wickedness in the heavenly places.*
>
> Ephesians 6:12

Swinburne's position could be called 'saving theism by adding hypotheses': in order to suggest why God should not be condemned for permitting death he suggests another hypothesis, an afterlife.

- What about **death**? Richard Swinburne maintains that death is not an evil since it is the absolute prerequisite for the benefits that are evident in a world such as the one in which we live. The reality of death gives us responsibility for others and enables us to make a meaningful difference to the world:

> *God does not in general have any obligation to create. That is why death is not itself an evil; death is just the end of a good state, life, (and in any case, one of which God may choose to give us more, by giving us a life after death). Death may be an evil if it comes prematurely or causes great grief to others, but in itself it is not an evil.*
>
> Richard Swinburne, *Is There a God?*, p. 97

1.4 A challenging problem

The problem of evil is a real challenge because it cannot be denied. Among those who have attempted to deny the reality of the problem, the best known are the **Christian Scientists**:

> *Evil has no reality ... it is simply an illusion, and it has no real basis ... when a sufferer is convinced that there is no reality in his belief in pain ... how can he suffer longer?*
>
> **Mary Baker Eddy (Founder of Christian Science), cited in John Hick,**
> ***Evil and the God of Love*, p. 30**

This is not the view presented by the biblical writers:

> *Save me, O God! For the waters have come up to my neck. I sink in deep mire, where there is no foothold; I have come into deep waters, and the flood sweeps over me. I am weary with my crying; my throat is parched. My eyes grow dim with waiting for my God.*
>
> **Psalm 69:1–3**

Is God not able to do anything about the existence of evil? **Process theology** maintains that:

> *Outside of God's nature and existing independently of him, there is material that he did not create, and with which he struggles with only partial success.*
>
> **John Hick, *Evil and the God of Love*, p. 39**

2 Theodicy

A true theodicy must obey three rules:
(i)   It does not deny the existence of evil.
(ii) It does not qualify the nature of God.
(iii) It does not advocate giving up faith when faced with evil and suffering.

Rather, a theodicy demonstrates that God, while being omnipotent, omniscient and perfectly good, has good reasons for occasionally allowing the continued existence of evil and suffering. These good reasons outweigh the existence of suffering and evil. In other words, they provide greater benefits than the benefit of removing evil.

Your learning is not complete until you have done more than just summarise the main points of the two major classical theodicies. As with the problem of evil itself, you need to know the philosophical principles which underlie theodicies.

> *A generous God will seek to give us great responsibility for ourselves, each other, and the world, and thus a share in his own creative activity of determining what sort of world it is to be. And he will seek to make our lives valuable, of great use to ourselves and to each other. The problem is that God cannot give us these goods in full measure without allowing much evil on the way.*
>
> **Richard Swinburne, *Is There a God?*, p. 96**

> It always surprises me when students speak of the free-will defence as something quite independent of these two theodicies; you can only understand how the theodicies work if you accept that they are based on a belief in the true moral autonomy of human beings.

Both the great theodicies of **Augustine** and **Ireneaus** depend on the principle of **free will** — whether it is that God created man in his perfect likeness, from which he fell through the inevitable use of his divinely given free will — or that man's moral development is evolutionary, that is, he has the capacity to grow into the likeness of God through the use of free will.

A world in which humans lacked moral autonomy would be one in which they could be guaranteed always to do good, and one in which it would be meaningless to speak of being able to do others harm. However, the crux of both theodicies is that God did not make that choice, but rather made the better choice of the type of world in which we do live. In such a world:

> *Agents are born and die and during their life give birth, partly through their own choice, to other agents. They can make a difference to the world … agents can make each other happy or unhappy and can increase or decrease each other's **power, freedom and knowledge**. Thereby they can affect the happiness and morality of generations distant in time…. A God has a reason for making such a world.*
>
> **Richard Swinburne, *The Existence of God*, OUP, 1979, p. 195**

This may seem an unreasonably optimistic hope, however, assuming that man will use his free will over many generations to restore the relationship with God and that natural order that has become unbalanced by sin. Perhaps the opposite may be equally likely:

> *We have seen good men made evil wrangling with evil, straight minds grown crooked fighting crooked minds.*
>
> **Edwin Muir, *The Labyrinth*, 1949, cited in John Hick,**
> ***Faith and Knowledge*, Fount, 1978, p. 262**

The balance of good and evil in the world cannot guarantee that good will triumph.

The problem of evil

2.1 The theodicies of Augustine and Ireneaus at a glance

Augustine	Ireneaus
• Soul-deciding	• Soul-making
• Man created in the perfect likeness of God (Genesis 1:27)	• Man created imperfectly with the form but not the content of God
• Man created with true moral autonomy; has freedom to make choices	• Man created with true moral autonomy; has freedom to make choices
• Man's freedom inevitably leads to his fall from grace (relationship with God) and perfection	• Man's freedom gives him the potential to grow into the likeness of God through responsible choices
• The exercise of free will leads to sin and its consequences — evil and suffering	• The exercise of free will enables man to make a difference to his environment
• Man can only be redeemed from the consequences of his sin by Jesus	• Man's positive choices enable him to find redemption through his own actions
• God foresaw man's fall and predestined some for salvation and others for condemnation	• God remains at an epistemic distance so as not to be overwhelmingly obvious to man as he makes free choices
• Sin, evil and suffering are part of the aesthetic pattern of the universe in which man has been placed	• Evil and suffering are necessary for man to grow in power, freedom and knowledge
• Evil is a privation or absence of good	• Evil can lead to good
• The work of Jesus on the cross is essential for man's redemption from sin	• The work of Jesus on the cross does not facilitate man's redemption, but those who do not reach perfection in this life are refined in purgatory
Strengths	**Strengths**
• Biblically based — appeals to conservative beliefs in creation and the Fall	• Evolutionary rather than dependent on a conservative biblical view of humanity
• Values free will as the best choice God could have made for mankind	• Values free will as the means by which man develops morally and spiritually
• God is therefore not responsible for man's evil choices	• God is therefore not responsible for man's evil choices
• Evil is not originally part of God's creative work	• Evil is teleological — its purpose is to facilitate growth
Weaknesses	**Weaknesses**
• May be considered outdated by an evolutionary view of man's development	• Suggests that God's creative work was imperfect
• Begs the question of whether God could have created free beings who always choose what is morally right	• Man's free choices do not always lead to growth in power, freedom and knowledge
• Salvation is reserved for the few who accept Jesus	• Salvation is universal and based on man's own striving
• If God foresaw man's fall then he should have prevented it	• If the completion of man's soul is in purgatory then why face trials in this life?
• Lacks optimism	• Too optimistic

2.2 Process theodicy

Process theodicy stems from the views of A. N. Whitehead and David Griffin. It is a radical theodicy in that it suggests that God is not omnipotent. It maintains that God did not create the universe because the universe is an uncreated process of which God himself is a part.

God is bound by natural laws and therefore suffers when evil occurs. He began the evolutionary process that led to the development of humans, but since he does not have total control, humans are free to ignore him.

God cannot stop evil since he lacks the power to change the natural process, yet he bears some responsibility for it. God's actions are justified on the grounds that the universe has produced sufficient good to outweigh evil.

Process theodicy argues that the reality of God is still developing, and that God is 'bipolar', having one mental pole and one physical pole. The physical pole is the material world itself, which acts almost as God's 'body'. The mental pole is the way in which God apprehends the abstract possibilities of the universe. God is partly distinct from and partly immersed in the world; hence any suffering in creation is also undergone by God. Creation itself is a cooperation between God and all other beings which God cannot force, but can only influence.

2.2a Does God have to be omnipotent?

The claim that God is omnipotent is equivalent to the claim that God possesses the logical limits of power. If this is the case, Whitehead argued that no being could be omnipotent. However, Hartshorne and Griffin argued that while God possesses the *greatest possible power*, that power is not sufficient to bring about a world containing no instances of evil. This is because:

- A being of maximal power has no possible superior and possesses all the power there is to possess.
- In any conceivable world, there must be beings who have power to determine to some degree their own activities and the activity of others (Griffin).
- However, if there were a being that possessed all the power that there is to possess, any other beings would possess no power at all.
- Thus, if some beings can determine their own actions, the notion of a being who possesses all the power is not coherently conceivable.

2.2b Criticisms of process theodicy

Process theodicy denies the monopolistic view of God's omnipotence, which is fundamental to the traditional classical theistic view of God. Is a limited God a being worthy of worship?

Although an omnipotent being *might* prevent all genuine evil in the world, the omnipotent being cannot be the *sufficient cause* of that state of affairs, and hence cannot guarantee it; whether or not it occurs will be partly due to the activities of others. It removes the problem of why God does not put an end to evil and suffering — he simply lacks the power to do so. However, the theodicy may appeal because the fact that God suffers too means that he can identify with the suffering of humanity, and believers are encouraged to fight alongside God against evil.

Process theologians refer to God as 'the fellow sufferer who understands'.

Griffin observed: 'God is responsible for evil in the sense of having urged the creation forward to those states in which discordant feelings could be felt with greater intensity'.

2.3 The free will defence

All the traditional theodicies, as well as process theodicy, depend on the notion that humans have free will. However, the free will defence can run independently of any of specific theodicies.

> 'The less he allows men to bring about large scale horrors, the less freedom and responsibility he gives them' (Richard Swinburne).

If this world forms the logically necessary environment for humans to develop and it does so by providing freedom in the form of real choices, the production of both good and evil is inevitable. Without such choices we would not be free and not be human. God cannot intervene because to do so would compromise human freedom and take away the need for humans to be responsible, and thus they would not be able to develop.

However, as J. L. Mackie observed, God must have been able to make a different world:

> *God was not, then, faced with a choice between making innocent automata and making beings who, in acting freely, would sometimes go wrong: there was open to him the obviously better possibility of making beings who would act freely but always choose right.*
>
> **J. L. Mackie, *Evil and Omnipotence*, Mind, 1955, p. 101**

On the other hand, Richard Swinburne argued:

> *A generous God will seek to give us great responsibility for ourselves, each other, and the world, and thus a share in his own creative activity of determining what sort of world it is to be... The problem is that God cannot give us these goods in full measure without allowing much evil on the way.*
>
> **Richard Swinburne, *The Existence of God*, OUP, 1979, p. 69**

E Miracles

The material in this section is relevant to questions on:
- miracles in the philosophy of religion
- miracles in biblical studies
- science and religion
- the existence of God
- atheism
- the psychology of religion
- the problem of evil
- religious experience

1 Miracles and belief

Do miracles lead people to belief **or** does belief depend on miracles? Do miracles confirm and support belief **or** do they undermine its integrity? How does experience of a miracle affect the existing belief system of the experient? How does the existing belief system of the experient affect their interpretation of the miracle?

Two conflicting views are:

> *Christianity doesn't apologise for miracles or back away ... as though it isn't really important whether miracles happen or not. Christianity requires miracles.*
>
> **Dave Hunt, *In Defence of the Faith*, Harvest House, 1996, p. 81**
>
> *Miracle was once the foundation of all apologetics, then it became an apologetic crutch, and today it is ... a cross for apologetics to bear.*
>
> **Reinhold Seeberg, in Dave Hunt, *In Defence of the Faith*, p. 80**

Hunt's view is that miracles are an essential and fundamental support to Christian belief. Seeberg suggests that miracles were once an important means of defending or justifying the truth of Christian belief (**apologetics**), but have become a stumbling block and an embarrassment to rational belief.

> It is unlikely that you will have heard of either of these scholars; you should not be afraid to cite less familiar scholars in the exam. Your teacher should be able to guide you to some legitimate, but original, contributors in all the areas you will have to study.

2 What did the biblical writers think?

> *Now Jesus did many other **signs** in the presence of his disciples which are not written in this book, but these are written that **you may believe** that Jesus is the Christ, the Son of God and that believing you may have **life in his name**.*
>
> (John 20:30–31)

The writer of the Fourth Gospel suggests four important things about the relationship between miracles and belief:
(i)   Miracles are **signs** — they point to and illuminate something important.
(ii) The writer records them in order that his readers **may believe** — he envisages that miracles can lead to belief or encourage existing belief.
(iii) He gives them a vital role in establishing the divine identity of **Jesus as the Christ, the Son of God**.
(iv) The consequence of this belief is **life in his name** — belief in miracles has led to belief in the divine identity of Jesus, and thus to eternal life. An essential link between miracles and faith has been established.

> Don't be worried about using biblical material in an appropriate way in philosophical questions on miracles. The store of biblical miracles is essential for establishing the relationship between faith and miracles.

The view of the Fourth Evangelist is therefore in agreement with that of Dave Hunt cited at the beginning of this section. But **should** or **could** miracles lead to or confirm faith?

Miracles may confirm or lead to belief because:

- **They are authenticating**
  A miracle may be said to authenticate God's nature as omnipotent and perfectly good. If God is lovingly and passionately committed to man and his relationship with him, then we should expect him to act or intervene in a beneficial way in the lives of his people. Miracles give reason for believers to say 'Yes, that's my God, I know him by his works'.

- **They are encouraging**
  Believers are, or should be, aware that they 'walk through the valley of the shadow of death' and that belief in God does not provide an unassailable guarantee against disaster. However, believers need to be encouraged in their faith. They need sometimes to be able to say 'It's all worthwhile'. Miracles can provide such moments of encouragement.

- **They are expressions of God's love and his response to 'special pleading'**
  Richard Swinburne draws the analogy between God and a loving parent. Natural laws are like rules which parents institute and which children know must be obeyed, or else they face punishment. Loving parents do, however, sometimes break their own rules in response to 'special pleading'. Parents are 'persons in interaction', not just systems of rules. In the same way God will occasionally respond to special pleading — to relieve suffering, to close briefly the epistemic distance, and to show that he cares about all the trials, however trivial or crushing, that man faces. Sometimes this may necessitate a suspension of natural laws, sometimes not.

> *If there is a God, one might well expect him to make his presence known to man, not merely through the over-all pattern of the universe in which he placed them, but by dealing more intimately and personally with them.*
>
> Richard Swinburne, *The Existence of God*, OUP, 1979, p. 225

Just as parents do more than provide a materially secure environment for their children in finding psychologically and emotionally nurturing things for their child to do, so too will God make a difference in the lives of his people **because he loves them**.

Miracles do not confirm or lead to belief because:

- **Faith does not need miracles**
  If man truly believes in God then surely he doesn't need miracles to support that faith. Faith should be self-sufficient, requiring no authentication, encouragement or special intervention. Belief which demands miracles is belief in the miracle, not belief in God. To some extent the biblical writers support

For notes on whether a miracle is by definition a violation of natural laws, see p. 101.

this view. For example, John 6:26: 'Truly, truly, I say to you, you seek me not because you saw signs, but because you ate your fill of the loaves' (i.e. did not understand the real significance of what took place). And yet the Fourth Evangelist also says, in John 2:11: 'This is the first of his signs Jesus did at Cana in Galilee and manifested his glory, and his disciples believed in him' (i.e their existing belief was confirmed, not created, by the sign). In each case the Evangelist has a different quality of belief in mind. Yet critics would be right in saying that belief based on the physical occurrence of a miracle is flawed, because what do you believe when the miracles stop happening?

- **Miracles count against the nature of God**

> *Miracles must by definition be relatively infrequent ... yet even so, it would seem strange that no miraculous intervention prevented Auschwitz or Hiroshima, while the purposes apparently forwarded by some of the miracles acclaimed in traditional Christian faith seem trivial by comparison.*
>
> **Maurice Wiles, *God's Action in the World*, SCM, 1986, p. 66**

We're back to the problem of evil here, for what Wiles is really asking is 'Why does God not intervene to prevent suffering?'

Wiles suggests that miracles contradict classical theistic claims that God is all-loving: if he were, surely he would intervene all the time to relieve suffering, rather than just sometimes. A God who could prevent great tragedy, and yet refrains from doing so, acts arbitrarily and is not worthy of worship.

- **Miracles are open to different interpretations**

  R. F. Holland deals with this in his famous parable of the boy on the railway track. A young child, busily engaged in disentangling his toy car from the railway lines, escapes certain death when a train comes to a halt only inches in front of him. His mother calls it a miracle, even after it is established that the train stopped because at that moment the driver suffered a brain embolism, the medical reason for which could be traced back to hypertension. Holland argues that the most the mother could legitimately claim was **coincidence** and that to impose a religious interpretation on the event goes beyond the evidence. However, although we are not compelled to interpret the event religiously, there is no real reason for the woman **not** to interpret it as an act of God either. It is a question of **interpretation**: the woman presumably felt there were overwhelmingly good reasons to interpret the episode religiously, irrespective of how others may interpret the event.

This is dealt with in more detail on pp. 102–3.

- **We may doubt the reliability of the testimony**

> *'I should not believe such a story were it told me by Cato.'* ... *The incredibility of the fact, it was allowed, might invalidate so great an authority.*
>
> **David Hume, *An Enquiry Concerning Human Understanding*,**
> **Bobbs-Merrill Educational Publishing, 1955, p. 121**

If we have doubts about the reliability of the person testifying to the miracle we are more likely to doubt the occurrence of the miracle. This was Hume's primary concern, along with the issue of probability, and yet we see that the biblical writers were concerned to put this in perspective. If we believe that a person claims to have performed a miracle for their own glory, or for financial gain, we will quite rightly be suspicious. Elijah is depicted as making it clear that the power to raise the widow's son comes not from him but from God: 'O Lord my God, let this child's soul come into him again' (1 Kings 17:21).

3 *What is a miracle?*

It is often argued that a miracle must, by definition, involve a **breach or violation of the natural law**.

David Hume understood miracles (should they occur) to be such breaches, brought about by the 'volition of the deity, or by the interposition of some invisible agent'. To use the term 'miracle' to refer to any other event, even if it has religious significance, would be considered a misapplication — even a trivialisation — of the term. If this is the case, we must accept that the natural laws can be broken and that they exist in the first place. If we maintain, as Hume did, that the laws of nature are inviolate, then we will not accept that such a miracle can take place. On the other hand, if we believe that the laws of nature are nothing more than man's ordering of nature in order to understand or even control it, and that nothing in the universe is fixed, then an event which appears to 'violate' such laws will not be possible, and certainly need not be ascribed to any divine agency.

Aquinas considered three categories of miracle:
(i)   Those that God did which nature could not, e.g. a reversal in the course of the sun
(ii) Those that God did which nature could, but not in the same order, e.g. recovery from paralysis
(iii) Those that God did which nature could, but without the forces of nature, e.g. recovery from a fever

Thus Aquinas allows miracles to include violations of natural law, but the term is not exclusive to it.

Although Hume is not a theist, don't be confused by this. He was concerned with purported reports of miracles, and in order to analyse them he had to establish a working definition.

It is important that you consider a range of definitions of the term 'miracle', not just the traditional association with violations of the natural law.

There are many accounts of modern-day miracles, acts of God, answers to prayer and testimonies to healing available in Christian bookshops — but don't include more than a couple in your essay.

Vardy widens the definition to include **an event with religious significance**. This is a popular definition, although it may be considered to weaken the scope of the term. **Grace Jantzen** gives an example of a woman who has left her bag in a department store and on her return, against all her hopes, finds it where she had left it. She claims that it is a miracle the bag was not stolen. Jantzen maintains that it is a trivialisation of the term to describe the event as miraculous, but if the recipient believes that God was responsible for the bag's safety, then the event has religious significance and can justifiably be called a miracle.

An event with religious significance may, of course, include almost anything that the recipient **believes** to be religiously significant, and some might argue that clearer guidelines are needed. Phenomena such as weeping or drinking statues have been claimed to have such significance, but they may appear to be ultimately valueless. Surely a miracle should make a difference.

There is a close association with religious experience here. See the 'Religious experience' section (pp. 115–19) for notes on this topic.

Vardy also suggests that a **change for the better** in a person might justifiably be called a miracle. This may be the result of a conversion experience, which in itself could be described as miraculous. Believers maintain that the greatest miracle of all is that of salvation, and many conversion accounts include details of dramatically changed lifestyles.

See a full account of Holland's argument on p. 100.

R. F. Holland is critical of those who attempt to designate an event as miraculous when it is no more than a coincidence. This emphasises how open to interpretation miracles are, and even if the recipient maintains that a miracle has occurred, the events can just as easily be interpreted in some equally likely way by others. Thus, definition of miracles and interpretation of them are very closely connected.

4 *The problem of testimony*

> *If the falsehood of his testimony would be more miraculous than the event which he relates, then, and not till then, can he pretend to command my belief or opinion.*
>
> David Hume, *An Enquiry Concerning Human Understanding*, p. 124

Remember that Hume was primarily concerned with testimony and probability. He wasn't setting out to argue that miracles can't happen *per se*, but that philosophically speaking the probability of them is low.

David Hume's critique of miracles is well known for the uncompromising stance he takes. His position is based on his philosophical assessment of the probability of miracles taking place, which he considers to be so low as to be virtually impossible. He argues that 'a wise man proportions his belief to the evidence' (ibid., p. 118), and in order to arrive at the probability of a miracle taking place he should weigh the evidence and 'fix his judgement' on the side which is 'supported by the greater number of experiments' (ibid.) In principle, a person could find more experiments in favour of the miracle than against it, but Hume considers this to be unlikely.

Furthermore, Hume believes that a religious person is:

> *Conscious of a continued miracle in his own person which subverts all the principles of his understanding and gives him a determination to believe what is most contrary to custom and experience.*
>
> **David Hume, *An Enquiry Concerning Human Understanding*, p. 141**

Accounts of miracles strike at a person's deep-seated love for the miraculous which, Hume claims, is only magnified in a religious believer.

Hume controversially claims that accounts of miracles came from 'ignorant and barbarous nations' and from such persons in whom 'the spirit of religion [had joined] … to the love of wonder'. Here, Hume believes, lies 'an end of common sense, and human testimony in these circumstances loses all pretensions to authority' (ibid., p. 125). He argues that since accounts of miracles occur in all religious traditions they cannot all be accurate, and so they effectively cancel one another out.

Neither, he maintains, can there ever be a sufficient number of witnesses whose 'backgrounds, education and reputations' are reliable and authoritative enough for them to have something to lose if their testimonies are discovered to be flawed.

> Consider whether Hume's arguments are really supportable here. How many would he consider to be a reasonable number of reliable witnesses? How would he react if he experienced a miracle himself?

4.1 Responses to Hume

Swinburne maintains that 'we ought to believe things are as they seem unless we have good evidence that we are mistaken' (*Is There a God?*, OUP, 1996, p. 134). He claims that the 'principles of credulity and testimony' should be applied — that is, that we normally believe what people tell us to be the case.

The principle of **Ockham's Razor** is also helpful in responding to Hume. He maintains that the evidence against an occurrence being miraculous will always be too great. The Ockham's principle, however, argues that the simplest explanation for phenomena is usually the most philosophically reliable one. There is no reason why, when all other causes have been considered, the simplest explanation for the unexpected cure of a terminal illness, i.e. God's miraculous activity, might not be true.

F Life after death

The material in this section is relevant to questions on:
- the nature of the afterlife
- the afterlife and verification

- the problem of evil — afterlife as a theodicy
- religious language and the meaningfulness of talk about the afterlife
- the desirability of an afterlife

1 Why is the concept of an afterlife important?

There are interesting questions to consider about why we find the concept of an afterlife a matter of concern. It is relevant to the whole area of religious belief and human nature and interlinks with issues of morality, evil and suffering, and the relationship between God and man.

Mankind is almost universally concerned about the prospect of an afterlife; it is not just a theological issue, since many who would not consider themselves to be believers find the prospect of a *post-mortem* (after-death) existence highly desirable. Why?

- Death has a powerful effect on us; we are saddened, puzzled and angered by it. We have powerful preconceived ideas about life and death and are quick to label death as premature, unjust or cruel. Our feelings for others are often, though not always, expressed in the way we deal with their death.
- Mankind finds it hard to accept that this life is all that there is. We perceive that there must be something beyond this life which gives greater meaning to earthly existence, which to some appears to be empty, trivial and short.
- The alternative — extinction — is inconceivable. As contingent beings there must be a time when we will not be, but we are psychologically unfit to deal with this. The prospect of an afterlife brings comfort to the dying and those who grieve.
- The moral law needs to be balanced, good rewarded and evil punished. Since this is manifestly not done in this life, an afterlife — overseen by a divine moral commander — is necessary in order to do so.
- We want to see the injustices of this life ironed out, suffering compensated and injustice vindicated; we want those whose earthly life is restricted by circumstances to know wholeness and fulfilment. The afterlife is the place where human potential will ultimately be fulfilled.
- 'Following as a corollary from faith in a good and loving God ... that which has been begun by God during man's life on earth, the creation of sons fit for full fellowship with him, will be continued and completed by God, in his own time and in his own ways, beyond the confines of earthly life' (Robert McAfee Brown, in *A Handbook of Christian Theology*, Fontana, 1960, p. 188).
- There is powerful biblical support to convince believers that an afterlife is God's intention for mankind. The resurrection of Jesus is thought of as the first-fruit of the harvest of resurrection for all who believe. It is central to the teaching of Paul, who justifies the whole gospel of Christ and the mission of the early church on the basis of resurrection hope: 'If the dead are not raised at all ... what do I gain, if, humanly speaking, I fought with beasts at Ephesus?' (1 Corinthians 15:29–32). For theistic faiths this afterlife is the gift of God and cannot be earned by human actions.
- Eastern religious traditions claim strong support for the concept of reincarnation — the belief that the soul migrates after death to another body, until it is

Don't just think of life after death in terms of disembodied spirit/resurrected body. Think more laterally as well.

See how these first five points are not directly related to religious beliefs about the afterlife. It is therefore possible to be an atheist and still believe in a post-mortem existence.

On the other hand, many religious believers maintain that the afterlife can be given only by God to those who have made a commitment to him. This can be considered unacceptably exclusivist to non-believers.

finally released from successive incarnations to pass on to a higher form of being. For Buddhists, reincarnation involves the continuous flow of consciousness between successive lives. Actions in the present life can influence whether the next incarnation will be into a higher or lower form of existence.

2 Post-mortem existence and personal identity

In addition to this aspect, the scientific, psychological and philosophical issues arising from the relationship between mind and body may also be on your specification. The booklet *Life After Death* by Jonathan Webber (Abacus, 1996) is particularly good on this aspect.

If life after death is such a desirable prospect, we must want to be sure that it will truly be us, with our personal identity intact, who will enjoy *post-mortem* existence. What would be the good of Paul's sufferings if he were not to be certain of the continuity of personal identity after death? Thus either our personal identity **survives the death process unchanged** or we are given a **new mode of being** by which we can continue to be real and meaningful once we no longer have existence in time and space.

2.1 The disembodied spirit/soul

This has Greek origins, especially with **Socrates**: 'He asks, "How shall he bury me?" And though I have spoken many words in the endeavour to show that when I have drunk the poison I shall leave you and go to the joys of the blessed — these words of mine, with which I was comforting you and myself, have had, as I perceive, no effect upon Crito.' Socrates will no longer need his body in the afterlife, so the means of his burial are inconsequential.

In Hellenistic thought the chief emphasis lay on **dualism** between body and soul. The body is mortal and contingent, the soul is immortal and not subject to decay. Death is therefore a possibility for the mortal body which is discarded, but not for the indestructible soul. **Descartes** conceived of this in his observation 'I think, therefore I am'. Descartes could doubt everything about the physical world, but he could not doubt that he was doubting — a non-physical concept.

2.1a The value of this position
- We are able to enjoy experiences which are separate from the body.
- We can experience feelings and emotions quite different from those which the body is apparently betraying.
- Our bodies change drastically over the years, and yet we know that our personal identity has not changed. Thus it must depend on something non-bodily.
- We find it appealing to be judged not on our external appearance but on our inner selves. It is often thought to be demeaning and trivialising to judge people on their bodily attributes.

However... this view depends on accepting that the essence of personal identity is distinguished from the body. **Aquinas** could not do so: 'Elements that are by nature destined for union naturally desire to be united with each other; for any being seeks what is suited to it by nature. Since, therefore, the natural condition of the soul is to be united to the body ... it has a natural desire for union with the body, hence the will cannot be perfectly at rest until the soul is again joined to a body. When this takes place, man rises from the dead.'

Gilbert Ryle criticised Cartesian dualism for promoting the idea of a '**ghost in the machine**'. He maintained that the concept of a soul distinct from the body was illegitimate because there is no such separate entity to which we should attribute our mental experience — it is an integral part of our existence and should not be separated from the physical.

> *We do not have justification for doing this, indeed the human being is a single entity, one subject of behaviour and experience with a single history. We are not two entities mysteriously laced together. We have made what he [Ryle] calls a **category mistake**.*
>
> **Bryan McGee, *Confessions of a Philosopher*, Phoenix, 1997, p. 77**

> You should be familiar with Ryle's illustration here of the man who, on watching a game of cricket, asks 'But where's the team spirit?', failing to recognise that it was integral to the whole game, not separate from it.

2.2 The resurrected body

Christianity has inherited from Judaism the concept of the resurrection of the body: the body is understood as the total personality which dies and is then raised by the power of God to newness of life with him. Such a view is consistent with the notion that body and soul are not two separate entities: 'Man does not **have** a body, he **is** a body ... he is flesh-animated-by-soul, the whole conceived as a psycho-physical unity' (J.A.T. Robinson, *The Body*, cited in *A Handbook of Christian Theology*, p. 357). Furthermore, the concept of an immortal soul does not do justice to the biblical concern for the ultimate fulfilment of the total life of man, and stresses the worthlessness of the body.

2.2a Personal identity and the resurrected body

> *The principal questions to be asked concern the relationship between the physical world and the criteria of personal identity which are operating when it is alleged that a certain inhabitant of the resurrection world is the same person as an individual who once inhabited this present world.*
>
> **John Hick, *Faith and Knowledge*, Fount, 1978, p. 181**

Hick proposes three scenarios to determine whether the **same person** has survived death. These scenarios are odd but are, Hick maintains, within the bounds of the logically possible.

At a learned gathering in England one of the delegates disappears. At the same moment an exact replica of him — similar in every way — appears at a

This is an odd example, not always easy to learn properly. It is vital, however, and should be reproduced in the most concise form possible.

meeting in Australia. There is everything to suggest that it is the same person except continuity of occupancy of space, and we should have no reasonable alternative but to extend our usage of 'same person' to cover this strange case. In a second scenario the man dies in England, and a replica of him, again identical in every way, appears in Australia. Hick maintains that even now it would still be an extension of 'same person'. In the final scenario Hick supposes that the replica reappears not in Australia but in some different world altogether — one inhabited by resurrected persons. Hick writes:

> *Mr X then dies. A Mr X replica complete with the set of memory traces which Mr X had at the last moment before his death, comes into existence. It is composed of other material than physical matter, and is located in a resurrection world which does not stand in a spatial relationship with the physical world.*
>
> John Hick, *Faith and Knowledge*, pp. 183–84

Hick maintains that it is logically possible to speak of Mr X as having survived the death experience, being replicated by the agency of an omnipotent God, and for that replica to be the same person:

> *The doctrine of the divine creation of bodies — composed of a material other than that of physical matter, but endowed with sufficient correspondence of characteristics with our present bodies and sufficient continuity of memory with our present consciousness for us to speak of the same person being raised up again in a new environment — is not self-contradictory.*
>
> John Hick, *Faith and Knowledge*, p. 185

2.2b The value of this position
- It avoids the complexities of the relationship between the soul and the body.
- It supports biblical teaching.
- It gives the physical body some value.

The point here is that a replica can only ever be a copy, even if it is indistinguishable from the original; the original of anything will always hold more value than the replica.

However... Vardy suggests that Hick does not take seriously the distinction between the same person and a replica; presumably if God can create one replica of Mr X he could create 20 such replicas. Which one would then be the same person? **Bernard Williams** argues that if someone claimed to be Guy Fawkes, having the same memories, 19 others could also claim to be him — and yet they could not logically all be Guy Fawkes:

> We might instead say that one of them was identical to Guy Fawkes and that the others were just like him; but this would be an utterly vacuous manoeuvre, since there would be ex hypothesi *no principle determining which description to apply to which.*
>
> Bernard Williams, *Personal Identity and Individuation*,
> The Proceedings of the Aristotelian Society, Vol. LVII, 1976–77

3 Other issues to resolve

3.1 Is life after death a meaningful concept?

See the section 'Religious language 1: verification, falsification and language games' (pp. 123–31) for a discussion of the logical positivists' criteria of meaningfulness.

Logical positivists would argue that it is not meaningful, since it cannot be verified, and that to speak of life after death is itself a meaningless phrase as it is contradictory. **Flew** claimed that words associated with personal identity — pronouns and proper nouns — must refer to physical beings and not to an immortal or disembodied soul. Furthermore, he suggested that life and death are mutually exclusive categories, and that to speak of 'life after death' was as meaningless as talking about 'dead survivors'. Proponents of language game theory can resolve this by claiming that talk of life after death belongs to the religious language game and has anti-realist (non-literal) meaning only to those who play it.

3.2 Can life after death be verified?

This is an area that you may want to study further. John Hick's classic book *The Philosophy of Religion* (4th edn, Prentice-Hall, 1990) has some very good detail on parapsychology.

Not according to the strong verification principle, of course, but it will be eschatologically verifiable (Hick) and it may be verifiable in principle by other means. Near-death experiences, psychic experiences, occult activity and remembered lives may all point to the possibility of life after death, although most religious traditions discourage attempts to contact the dead or indulge in occult practices.

3.3 Heaven, hell and eternal life

This aspect interconnects with biblical studies, so you can expect to get some useful information from material you have studied for an Old or New Testament option. It also has valuable links with the problem of evil.

For some the concepts of heaven and hell are no more than symbols — pictorial ways of speaking of truths which are beyond human understanding. For others they represent real places which are inhabited in the afterlife. This is a matter of discussion for theology rather than philosophy, but it is important to consider how expectations of an afterlife and the form it may take can be influenced by these beliefs. If life after death is considered a desirable prospect and is anticipated by those who are not religious believers as well as by those who are, then the prospect of hell is a particularly difficult one since it does not suggest a benign existence. Some may argue that a loving God who would allow any of his creatures to suffer in hell is a contradiction. Others maintain that the existence of heaven is essential if there is to be any satisfactory solution to the problem of evil — it would be the ultimate theodicy.

G Atheism

The material in this section is relevant to questions on:
- the nature of atheism
- non-religious interpretations of the world
- critiques of religion
- science and religion debates
- religious language
- the problem of evil

> *The existence of a world without a God seems to me less absurd that the presence of a God, existing in all his perfections, creating an imperfect man in order to make him run the risk of hell.*
>
> **Armand Salacrou, in *The Pan Dictionary of Religious Quotations*, Pan, 1989, p. 41**

1

What is atheism?

If you are asked to define atheism, don't be content just to say 'Atheists don't believe in the existence of God'. Have a handful of these points ready to include, to show that you understand the wider implications of atheism.

An atheist may hold one or more of the following positions:
- The denial that there is such a being to whom the description 'God' can be given.
- The view that what may be interpreted by religious believers as experiences of the divine can be accounted for without reference to God. 'Theist and atheist — the fight between them is as to whether God shall be called God or have some other name' (Samuel Butler).
- The rejection of the supposed nature of the divine being because of apparently contradictory states of affairs in the world, e.g. the problem of evil.
- The opinion that religious believers are deluded in their belief, or have been deluded by religious leaders for unscrupulous purposes.
- A rejection of organised religion, which may lead to a rejection of God.
- The result of personal tragedy which leads to disillusionment in the God of classical theism, and ultimately to his rejection.
- The holding of false beliefs about the nature of God (e.g. that he is powerless, although well intentioned); the denial of expectations propounded in scripture; the rejection of any form of evidence which may point to the existence of God.
- The holding of non-theistic beliefs, e.g. paganism, spiritualism, humanism.
- A hatred of religious beliefs and believers. 'The sort of atheist who does not so much disbelieve in God as personally dislike him' (George Orwell).
- The view that religious beliefs exist only to support those who are emotionally, intellectually or psychologically weak. However, the biblical writers did not really countenance the possibility of atheism or suggest it may have any intellectual or philosophical credibility — it is the fool who says in his heart there is no God (Psalms 10:4; 53:1).

Religious language comes in useful here. Look at the section 'Religious language 2: symbol, myth and analogy' (pp. 131–38) to see how theists are continually grappling with the problem of how to speak meaningfully and informatively about a God who remains outside the realms of regular human experience.

This is an important point to grasp: if you are asked to offer an argument for the non-existence of God and speak only in terms of alternative explanations for **religion**, you are not really addressing the question.

2

What is agnosticism?

Agnosticism holds that it is not possible to know whether God exists, or to know his nature. The term was coined by **Thomas Huxley** in the nineteenth century as the opposite of gnostic, the Greek term used in the early church to describe those who professed to have special revelatory knowledge of the divine. An agnostic, in principle, will keep the door open on belief, but in reality may not be able to say what it would take for them to move from a position of not knowing to knowing. It may be argued, therefore, that agnosticism is merely another form of atheism.

Many theists, however, might argue that even within theistic belief there remains an element of agnosticism, since the transcendent God is ultimately unknowable and cannot be presumed to be known fully.

3

Atheistic arguments

Many atheistic arguments tend to offer critiques of **religion** as well as suggesting that what is attributed to God can be explained in other terms — naturalistic, psychological or scientific, for example.

3.1 Sociological arguments

3.1a Durkheim and religion

Sociologists perceive religion as more than belief in God or the supernatural, but as any system which attempts to provide an ultimate solution to explaining human existence. **Durkheim** (1912) defined religion as 'A unified system of beliefs and practices relative to sacred things ... beliefs and practices which unite into one single moral community called a church, all who adhere to them'. Durkheim's critique assumes a **functionalist** role to religion, maintaining that the primary function of belief in God and to religious systems is to unite and preserve the community.

- Primitive societies were divided into clans, represented by a totem (sacred object) worshipped by the clan. It symbolised God and clan unity, therefore they are one and the same. When the clan member worships God he is worshipping society and the collective force of the clan. God and society are superior to the clan member, who is aware of the restraints imposed upon him by society, but he interprets it as God.
- Religion integrates man into society, unifying him in a shared cultural identity. Shared rituals express shared values and collective identity. It furthers their knowledge of the world, and religion is the first paradigm through which we explain the world. Social stability is promoted and religion acts as a conservative force which discourages social change.
- Religion serves to explain phenomena which make little sense, e.g. death.

Remember that evaluation involves looking at strengths and weaknesses. You do not necessarily have to present them in two separate paragraphs, but can blend them together in a discussion.

3.1b Evaluation

The theory does recognise the important social elements in religion. Religious believers find a special identity in a community of other believers, to whom they owe special loyalty. In times of persecution and struggle that bond strengthens. Religious believers feel accountable to one another and to their leaders. Certain patterns of behaviour are considered acceptable or unacceptable.

However:

- Religious believers distinguish membership of a religious community from belief in God. Their loyalty is ultimately to God, not to the community.
- The theory does not explain how religious believers are prepared to go against, and even reject, society. The Old Testament prophets are a prime example of this, as are Christian reformers who challenged the status quo in their own society.
- Religious beliefs and the nature of God are timeless and unchanging, whereas society is continually mutating.
- Durkheim's theory was modelled on primitive aboriginal societies and therefore cannot be a true reflection of modern expressions of belief in God.

3.1c Marx and religion

For either of these sociological approaches to belief in God you can find a much fuller discussion in a sociology textbook.

> *The first requisite for the happiness of the people is the abolition of religion.*
>
> **Karl Marx**

Marx examined nineteenth-century Christianity. Influenced by **Feuerbach**, he argued that people create God to satisfy emotional needs, and only by loving one another rather than God can man regain his humanity. Marx observed that man creates God, not vice versa, and religion was an alienating force prescribing to God powers that man in fact possessed. Man had therefore lost control of his destiny because of his belief in God.

Religion originated in revolutionary movements, but once detached from its origins, Marx claimed, it was used by ruling classes to dominate and oppress. Inequality was legitimised in the name of religion, discouraging the subject classes from recognising their real situation and seeking to rise above it. Although religion offered a release from distress, it was a false release and thus was 'the opium of the people'. The social conditions which created religion had to be revolutionised and then religion would wither away.

For more detail on liberation theology you need to look at an account of twentieth-century developments in Christian belief and practice.

3.1d Evaluation

- Modern sociologists identify evidence of a greater separation between church and state than Marx assumed.
- **Liberation theology** in countries where there is considerable poverty, such as South America, has blended Marxism and Christianity in an attempt to change the nature of society for the oppressed without rejecting belief in God.
- Religion is a force that is open to interpretation, and so it can be an influence for both change and stagnation. The philosophies of some religions may appear to discourage change, other more radical branches encourage it. The biblical view of God is one who transforms situations and lifts up the oppressed.

- **Weber** (1904) suggested that religion promoted social change and that capitalism had developed in Europe due to the force of the Protestant ethic of hard work and self-denial.

3.2 Psychological arguments

3.2a Freud and religion

Freud argued that religion is a **projective system**, or a product of the human mind. It is a 'universal neurosis' or illusion which, he claimed, we may 'disregard in its relation to reality'. God, therefore, has no reality but is a creation of the human mind.

In *Totem and Taboo*, Freud examined the primitive origins of monotheism, based on the **primal horde**. The tension between the dominant male (father) and the subordinate males (sons) culminates in the overthrow of the father, whom they eat in an act of identification. In their guilt and fear of chaos the sons elevate the father's memory as a totem, which is protected and worshipped. Belief in God thus arises from the **Oedipus Complex**, whereby the sons desire to kill their father and possess their mother. God is the image of the feared father.

The **super-ego**, a form of internalised external authority, takes the place of the father and is derived from socialising influences such as the family, education and the church. It represses antisocial impulses such as killing, and by inducing fear and guilt it is crucial for civilisation. It is this we call the conscience, and God is not only a father substitute but a projection of the super-ego.

Freud claimed that religion was 'born from man's need to make his helplessness tolerable', but man maintains an unhealthy dependency on religious belief which he must overcome if he is to be truly happy.

3.2b Evaluation

- Freud attributed all religious behaviour to the projection of psychosexual drives. He claimed that the individual's relation to God depended on their relationship with their father. However, **Nelson and Jones** (1957) found that the concept of God correlated more highly with a person's relationship with their mother than with their father.
- **Kate Lowenthal** distinguished between **projective** religion, which is immature, and **intrinsic** religion, which is serious and reflective. Freud assumed that all aspects of belief in God were immature, and he neglected the diversity and development of religious beliefs.
- **Arthur Guirdham** argued that Freud overplayed the connection between belief in God and the 'psychopathological' tendencies of much organised religion, and between the feeling of security in the womb (the **oceanic feeling**) and religious belief. He observed that Freud's anti-religious stance may be thought just as neurotic as the religious preoccupations of others.
- Freud's theories of the primal horde have been rejected as mere conjecture.

Similarly, have a look at an AS/A2 psychology textbook in your library for an in-depth discussion of Freudian theories.

See how this is clearly related to belief in God rather than to religion in general.

If you use the problem of evil to answer a question on atheism, you can't then use this material again in a standard 'problem of evil' question on the same examination paper (if you are writing a traditional paper to be marked as a whole).

3.3 Other atheistic arguments

- The **problem of evil** is traditionally thought to make the strongest of all claims for atheism. (See pp. 89–97 for a full discussion of this issue.)
- Many atheists since the enlightenment have rested their position on **rationalism**. If it is possible to explain the phenomena of the natural world without reference to God, then it is philosophically more rational to do so. They take into consideration any of the following:
  - the findings of geology, which in the eighteenth and nineteenth centuries challenged the biblical accounts of creation and the traditional belief that the world had been created only 6,000 years ago
  - Darwin's theories of evolution and natural selection, which challenged the apparent superiority of man in the natural order and suggested that he had developed from more primitive life forms
  - scientific and naturalistic explanations for apparently miraculous phenomena
  - advances in biblical criticism and interpretation, which discouraged a literal interpretation of the text and revealed the biblical writers' use of sources and of influences from their cultural environments
  - modernism, which rejected the literal use of terms such as 'heaven', 'hell' or 'demons' and argued that they merely represented old-fashioned picture language to communicate truths which could not be expressed in any other way. **Rudolph Bultmann** argued that 'It is impossible to use electric light and the wireless, and to avail ourselves of modern medical and surgical discoveries, and at the same time to believe in the New Testament world of demons and spirits'.

A **popularist critique of religion** aims to identify the obvious negative and, in some cases, alarming features of religion, past and present, and to encourage the layman as well as the scholar in the belief that religion is dangerous, outmoded and ridiculous.

A leading figure in promoting this kind of critique is **Richard Dawkins**. A scientist by profession, and the holder of the Charles Simonyi Chair in the Public Understanding of Science at the University of Oxford, Dawkins has become a popular media figure, regularly speaking out on religious issues. His Channel 4 programme *The Root of all Evil?*, was broadcast in January 2006, and his book, *The God Delusion*, reinforced his position as the UK's most vocal atheist.

First, he maintains that the Darwinian worldview makes belief in God unnecessary. He dismisses the idea that there is any ultimate, mystical significance in the world or human beings, arguing instead that the fact that humans exist at all is a remarkable enough coincidence of biology without looking for any greater significance. He furthers this by claiming that religion offers an impoverished worldview:

In 2004, Dawkins topped *Prospect* magazine's poll of the leading intellectuals in the UK, gaining almost twice the votes of his nearest rival.

> *The universe presented by organised religion is a poky little mediaeval universe.*
>
> ***The Third Culture***, ed. John Brockman, Touchstone, 1996

'Growing up in the universe … also means growing out of parochial and supernatural views of the universe … not copping out with superstitious ideas' (Royal Institution Christmas lectures 1991).

While Dawkins claims that the universe we see is one which has 'no purpose, no evil and no other good, nothing but blind, pitiless indifference … DNA neither knows nor cares. And we dance to its music' (*River Out of Eden: A Darwinian View of Life*, Basic Books, 1995), Tinker argues, 'The logical upshot of this is that the Yorkshire Ripper danced to the music of his DNA' (*The Briefing*).

Furthermore, Dawkins holds that religion leads to evil, likening it to a malignant virus that infects human minds. On *The Root of All Evil?*, he dismisses religious faith as 'an indulgence of irrationality that is nourishing extremism, division and terror', and asserts that it is a form of child abuse to refer to the offspring of Christian or Muslim parents as a 'Christian child' or a 'Muslim child'. Dawkins correctly identifies some of the more alarming examples of religious extremism.

Dawkins explains his belief that religion is a virus by reference to 'memes' (Dawkins' own term) — ideas or beliefs that are analogous to genes (the hereditary material that determines our physical characteristics). Memes spread rapidly from one person to another, infecting people's minds. Melvin Tinker suggests that the analogy is false, observing that genes that are biologically transmitted cannot be changed once the process of reproduction is underway, and that while our genetic material cannot be altered, ideas can. History shows that intellectuals can undergo dramatic changes in perspective.

Tinker also criticises Dawkins for reducing everything to scientific terms, a process called **'ontological reductionism'**. Dawkins argues that the sole reason for living is to pass on DNA; Tinker observes that while it is undeniable that biological organisms do pass on their DNA to their offspring, it is by no means their sole purpose.

Tinker addresses Dawkins's accusation that religion is harmful:

> He makes a value judgement that extremism and terror are 'bad' things, but bad for whom? Not for the terrorists who get their way and pass on their genes'
>
> 'Dawkins's Dilemma', 2006, *The Briefing*, Issue 337, October

Finally, Tinker demands that Dawkins be more precise when he talks about religion. Dawkins's sweeping statements suggesting that everything he says about religion applies equally to all religions is considered to be as 'intellectually irresponsible as lumping all animals together and saying that what goes for elephants must go for ants' (*The Briefing*, ibid.).

4 The problem of disproving God

For more on the Parable of the Gardener, see the section 'Religious language 1: verification, falsification and language games' (pp. 123–31).

Ultimately it cannot be any easier to disprove the existence of God than to prove it, as Wisdom's Parable of the Gardener demonstrates.
- Atheistic arguments could be said rather to be agnostic, since they do not offer conclusive proof of the non-existence of God.
- Believers will not allow atheistic arguments to have any real influence, since they will not allow anything to count against their belief.
- Atheistic arguments are just as susceptible to the criticisms of logical positivism, as they deal with non-empirical data, as theistic arguments.
- Atheists are no less likely to offer irrational, biased arguments than are theists.

H Religious experience

The material in this section is relevant to questions on:
- religious experience
- the existence of God
- miracles
- psychology and religion
- the nature of faith

You might typically be asked to look at religious experience from two main perspectives: as an argument for the existence of God, and considering the nature of religious experience itself. The two angles are not entirely divorced from one another, since if an experience is truly religious it would surely in some sense reveal God, and thus prove his existence.

The argument from religious experience is a posteriori. Over the centuries, there have been many thousands of testimonies to religious experience. Such an argument is based on the premise that experience is, in some way, the product of facts about the real world. It could, for example, be set out in premises as follows:

P1	Experience of X indicates the reality of X
P2	Experience of God indicates the reality of God
P3	It is possible to experience God
Conclusion	God exists (i.e. is really present)

1 *Types of religious experience*

1.1 Mysticism

A mystical experience makes the experient overwhelmingly aware of the presence of the ultimately real — becoming one with the divine. In the New Testament church direct experience of the Holy Spirit was common to all, until ascetic specialists seem to have taken over and the expectation of mystical experience was narrowed down to a small élite — although it was still potentially universal. **Ineffability** and a **noetic quality** are associated with mysticism: a state which cannot be communicated or expressed and yet which grants an insight into truths beyond the intellect — a revelation or **apocalupsis** (literally, an unveiling). They can be **numinous** — emphasising separateness from the divine as well as, or instead of, unity. In most cases mysticism requires spiritual discipline and training, leading to a submission of the self to the divine, which enables revelation to take place. Three stages in preparation for a mystical experience may be identified:

(i) **Purgation:** ridding the psyche of those practices which divert its attention from the divine

(ii) **Illumination:** an increasing awareness of the divine in the mind and the emotions

(iii) **Contemplation:** the divine presence penetrates the psyche of the experient

There are a number of technical terms (**emboldened** in the text) associated with mysticism. Learn to use them as simply as possible — you do not need to engage in a complicated analysis of them.

Rudolph Otto defined a mystical experience as 'either a strange fantasy or a glimpse into the eternal relationships of things'.

1.2 Conversion

Paul's conversion from a persecutor of the early church into the leading apostle of the first century was prefaced by a **conversion experience** which took the form of a supernatural encounter with Christ (Acts 9). Other conversion events may be less dramatic and may take place gradually over many years, but can still be described as religious experiences. They lead man into knowledge of God and a changed life as a result of that deepening encounter.

1.3 Charismatic experiences

1 Corinthians 12–14 describes the use of charismatic gifts in the early church. For many Christians these **charismata** are a regular part of their religious experience. Speaking in tongues, gifts of prophecy and knowledge, healing and miraculous transportations are all described in Acts as part of the tools for the early church's ministry. The New Testament stresses that charismatic experiences should be for the benefit of the whole church body, and not employed self-indulgently. Charismatic gifts are received through the baptism in the Holy Spirit, and can be mimicked or used for fraudulent purposes. Thus the test of a genuine charismatic experience, as of all religious experience, will be in its fruits, or results. Both mystical and charismatic experiences may involve visions, or the experient may believe that God has spoken to them.

1.4 Prayer

As a means of communication with the divine, prayer is a form of religious experience. Through prayer a believer will seek to grow in knowledge of the divine, and to enter into a deeper relationship with him. Through answers to prayer that relationship strengthens, as the divine is more fully revealed to the believer. Some forms of prayer, such as meditation, seek only to increase the believer's communion with the divine, not to make petitions. Prayer should be an integral part of worship, in which the believer acknowledges the nature of God in all his aspects and elevates God above the believer's own desires.

1.5 Other types of experience

Religious significance may be found in the beauty of nature; miracles; a retrospective feeling that God has guided a person's life.

2   Interpreting religious experience

2.1 Wittgenstein's interpretation

Ludwig Wittgenstein employed the notion of **seeing-as**. A random series of dots and lines could be perceived as representing a particular form, but each person perceives it differently. 'Experiencing-as' may be mistaken — for example Hare's lunatic don who believes that all his colleagues want to kill him.

Remember that types of religious experience can overlap one another. Any of these types of experience can be mystical.

There is plenty of modern-day information about charismatic experience, including some useful books on the so-called 'Toronto Blessing'. Local Christian groups are useful sources of information here.

This is Hare's notion of 'bliks', of course. See the section 'Religious language 1: verification, falsification and language games' (pp. 123–31) for more on this.

Religious experiences are subject to the same possibly flawed interpretation. What the believer may 'see-as' an experience of God may be seen as something quite different by a non-believer, or even by another believer. No single religious experience can be replicated exactly, unlike a scientific experiment. Personal factors are involved, so interpretations will inevitably vary.

2.2 James's interpretation

William James observed that religious experience draws on the common store of emotions, but is directed at something divine. Happiness, fear and wonder can be directed at both the divine and the non-divine, but in religious experience the emotions are directed at something beyond normal sense experience. The result of such experience will be reverence, a joyful desire to belong to God, a renewed approach to life. Such symptoms will be testimony to the reality of the experience, even if other physiological symptoms are present. James observed that even pathological elements should not detract from its credibility if positive fruits are borne from the experience: 'The results of religious experience are the only reliable basis for judging whether it is a genuine experience of the divine.'

2.3 Other interpretations

Since religious experiences are not subject to objective testing, they can be interpreted variously:

Again, see 'Religious language 1: verification, falsification and language games' (pp. 123–31) for more details on this parable.

Hume's critique of testimonies to miracles argues along these lines.

See the previous section, on atheism, for a discussion of Freud's psychological interpretation of religion.

- If God does not exist, then there can be no experience of him. Hence what appears to be a religious experience must be interpreted in some other way. Certainly religious experience cannot prove the existence of God, since any experience can be interpreted non-religiously as well as religiously. The Parable of the Gardener illustrates how the evidence of a clearing in the jungle can be interpreted as evidence of the existence of a gardener, but this does not prove that the gardener exists.
- Experiences are deceptive. We do not always evaluate everyday experiences correctly. How much more so must this be the case with apparent experiences of the divine.
- The testimony of religious experiences may be regarded as especially unreliable, since religious believers are prone to make claims for the miraculous.
- The sheer variety of religious experiences cancel one another out — they cannot all be veridical.
- Religious experiences are the manifestation of psychological needs and illusions.
- Visual or auditory hallucinations, feelings of separateness from the world, a sense of otherness, can all be explained by biological or neurological factors — e.g. hunger, tiredness, fever.
- If God does exist, he makes himself known in our everyday, universal experience — nature, music, art, poetry, our relationships with others — rather than in experiences which are not made available to all.

Brian Davies argues that we cannot use the fact that not everyone shares a religious experience as grounds to dismiss it. He compares it to a team of explorers discovering an unknown animal in the jungle. A second team goes in search of it, but does not find it. However, this does not prove that the first team did not see it.

Religious experiences may prove the existence of God for those who have good reasons to interpret them as such — this makes them highly subjective. If someone allows nothing to count against his or her claim to have experienced God, he or she could be said to have a **blik**, but this does not make the experience meaningless. However, it is not surprising that religious believers have religious experiences, since they are more likely to know how to identify them.

2.4 Arguments against religious experience as proof for God

- If God does not exist, there can be no experience of him.
- How do we know if we are actually experiencing God?
- There are no tests for verifying that an experience has been of God.
- The testimony of religious believers may be biased.
- Religious experiences may reveal psychological needs.
- If there is a God, why doesn't everyone experience him?

3 *Verifying religious experience*

Richard Swinburne argues: 'How things seem to be is a good guide to how things are. If it seems ... to a subject that X is present, then probably X is present' (*The Existence of God*, OUP, 1979, p. 270). The is the **principle of credulity**.

Swinburne claims further that according to the **principle of testimony**, 'In the absence of special considerations the experiences of others are (probably) as they report them' (ibid., p. 272).

According to these principles we should accept that people normally tell the truth, and that in the absence of clear evidence to the contrary we should believe that what **appears** to be the case **is** the case.

- The principle of **Ockham's Razor** claims that the simplest explanation is the most likely one, thus if an experience appears to be divine and there is no other more obvious explanation, then we should accept that it is an experience of the divine.
- There is a difference between **reports** of religious experience and **having** a religious experience. Ultimately, the truth of a religious experience comes through personal experience rather than the testimony of others.
- Religious experience adds to the **probability** of God's existence rather than proving it. This is the case for all a posteriori arguments for the existence of God. It is always possible to reach an alternative conclusion, so religious experience cannot conclusively prove the existence of God.
- A basic guideline should be that any apparently religious experience should reflect the nature of God as it has been revealed to man through scripture and through the natural world — **and** that the fruits (results) of the experience should similarly reflect the divine nature, leading to a changed lifestyle.

See the section 'Proof, probability, faith and reason' (pp. 69–76) for more on this issue.

In *Is there a God?* (OUP, 1996), Richard Swinburne argued inductively that it is reasonable to believe that God is loving and personal and would seek to reveal himself to humanity as an act of love and to enable people to bring about the good: 'An omnipotent and perfectly good creator will seek to interact with his creatures and, in particular, with human persons capable of knowing him.'

He is suggesting that religious experiences could be felt empirically, through our senses, and interpreted non-empirically, through our 'religious sense'. Thus, if we are told that someone has had a religious experience, we should believe that experience has taken place, even if someone else has had a different experience or no experience at all. Brian Davies in *Philosophy of Religion* (OUP, 2000) writes:

> *We certainly do make mistakes about reality because we fail to interpret our experience correctly; but if we do not work on the assumption that what seems to be so is sometimes so, then it is hard to see how we can establish anything at all...*

Morality and God

The material in this section is relevant to questions on:
- arguments for the existence of God (the moral argument)
- the relationship between religion and morality
- the origins of morality
- issues in practical ethics; reaching moral decisions
- biblical ethics

> *The God of the Old Testament is arguably the most unpleasant character in all fiction: jealous and proud of it; a petty, unjust, unforgiving control-freak; a vindictive, bloodthirsty ethnic cleanser; a misogynistic, homophobic, racist, infanticidal, genocidal, filicidal, pestilential, megalomaniacal, sadomasochistic, capriciously malevolent bully.*
>
> Richard Dawkins, *The God Delusion*, Bantam, 2006, p. 131

1 Morality and religion

It is normally assumed that those who claim to be religious are also making some claim to live a morally good life, based on the teachings of their faith. But is it as simple as that?

- Is it possible to be religious but not moral?
- Or to be moral but not religious?
- What is the relationship between God and goodness?
- Does the existence of a moral law presuppose the existence of a supreme lawgiver?
- If God does not exist, then is everything permissible?

Aquinas and the Fourth Way

The Fourth and Fifth Ways tend to get overlooked, but they are useful since the Fourth Way can also be used when discussing analogy, and the Fifth Way is a form of the Teleological Argument.

Aquinas argued that the gradation to be found in things pointed irrefutably to the existence of God: 'Among beings there are some more and some less good, true, noble and the like. But more and less are predicated of different things according as they resemble in their different ways something which is the maximum ... so that there is something which is truest, something best, something noblest.... Therefore there must also be something which is to all beings the cause of their being, goodness and every other perfection: and this we call God.'

See Plato's myth of the cave for a fuller understanding of this dualistic view of the world — that what we see is only the most superficial perception of reality.

Aquinas's arguments were based on the philosophical principles of **Plato's eternal forms**, or archetypes, which claimed that the contingent realities of which the human mind is aware are merely pale copies of a greater, unseen reality. In this case the goodness found in human beings and in the contingent world is a reflection of the supreme goodness of God, to whom contingent beings owe their lesser goodness. God being perfect in goodness is also perfect in his very being, or existence.

The twentieth-century philosopher **F. C. Copleston**, in discussion with **Bertrand Russell**, claimed: 'I do think that all goodness reflects God in some way and proceeds from Him, so that in a sense the man who loves what is truly good, loves God even if he doesn't advert to God.'

However... Aquinas's Fourth Way does not give a clear indication of how 'good' can be defined. All we know is that God is the supreme source of it and it is in his very essence to be perfectly good.

Kant and the categorical imperative

See the section 'Kantian ethics' (pp. 142–46) for a fuller discussion of Kant's ethical theory.

Kant claimed that only one fact was indisputable, and that was the existence of a moral law which was meaningless unless God existed. His claims amount to what is usually called the **moral argument**, which Kant claimed was based on **practical reason** rather than pure reason. Kant argued that:

- an awareness of the moral law is inherent in all mankind, irrespective of one's background or education
- man has a duty to seek the highest form of good — the ***summum bonum*** (virtue crowned with happiness)
- this duty is the **categorical imperative** which man is obliged, or ought, to pursue
- we should have no other motive for pursuing this end other than the moral rightness of bringing about such a state of affairs
- it is possible to perceive what is good through the use of reason

We know instinctively what we ought to do without reference to the possible consequences. Good is thus **deontological** (good in itself, not because of its outcome); it must be a **free act**, since genuine morality cannot be coerced. The only thing which is truly good is a **good will**; good must be **universalisable** (all people should be able to behave in that way in any given situation).

However... Kant recognised that the fulfilment of these criteria, while they should be man's aim and intention, is not ultimately possible in this life since factors beyond his control prevent him from doing so, and only God can guarantee the realisation of the *summum bonum* in an afterlife. **Thus the existence of God is necessary to satisfy the demands of the moral law.** Kant believed that morality was good in itself and should be pursued irrespective of consequences. However, he held that the existence of God was necessary if the goal of morality were to be realised.

> See how Kant's argument can be used as a proof for the existence of God — the existence of a moral law proves the existence of a moral lawgiver.

3.1 Evaluation

- God is something of an addendum to Kant's theory, existing only to ensure a redress for the disappointments and losses suffered in this life.
- If God guarantees the outcome, what is the point of trying to achieve it in this life?
- Kant assumes that all people are free to discover — by use of reason — what is moral, and that they will come to the same conclusion.
- Kant assumes that man ought to pursue the *summum bonum* — and because he *ought*, he *can*.
- Why can only God ensure the outcome? Why not some being greater than man but lesser than God?
- Why should virtue always be rewarded with happiness? As Kant observes, it is clearly not so rewarded in this life, so why should it be rewarded in the next?
- Kant assumes the existence of an afterlife, which in itself requires proof.

4 *Objective moral laws*

Kant argued that there were clear objective moral laws that were accessible and comprehensible to all and that demanded a moral lawgiver, or commander. **John Henry Newman** claimed too that moral laws have a personal origin in the will of God: 'If, as is the case, we feel responsibility, are ashamed, are frightened, at transgressing the voice of conscience, this implies that there is One to whom we are responsible, before whom we are ashamed, whose claim upon us we fear.' This position depends on certain assumptions:

- Moral laws derive their authority from a divine lawgiver.
- Without such a lawgiver morality would be subjective, relative, emotive or evolutionary.
- When confronted with moral law we are confronted by God himself.
- Human beings must personally respond to God when confronted with his claims.
- **H. P. Owen**: 'It is impossible to think of a command without a commander.... Either we take moral claims to be self-explanatory modes of impersonal existence, or we explain them in terms of a personal God.'

4.1 Non-objective morality

- **Subjective morality** is open to individual interpretation and depends on circumstances.
- **Relative morality** is relative to the culture from which it emerges.
- **Emotivism** argues that something is considered good or bad according to whether we approve of it or not.
- **Evolutionary morality** develops out of a sense of preservation; if we are kind to others we are more likely to survive than if we are confrontational.

5 | *God and morality*

R. B. Braithwaite claims that to be religious and to make religious claims is to be committed to a set of moral values. He uses the instance of religious conversion, which includes a reorientation of the will, to illustrate this position. Religious language is the language of morality and religious believers have committed themselves to particular ways of behaving. This includes refraining from some actions and fulfilling others. However, how do we know what believers are committed to?

Is something good because God commands it? OR

Does he command it because it is good?

The **first** position assumes that a moral action is one that is willed by God; he is the source of morality and man acts morally when he fulfils God's will obediently. The **problems** of this position are:

- Is God's commanding something sufficient grounds to say that it is moral? What if he commanded someone to kill all people with red hair — would that make it morally right to do so? Would man be correctly interpreting what he believed God was commanding?
- How do we deal with situations in which God does not expressly give a command? How do we establish God's will in such situations?
- Many of God's commands are not in themselves moral, e.g. the Book of the Covenant in Exodus 23ff. includes many commands concerning religious ceremonies.
- If something is good because God commands it then what is the nature of God's goodness? Is he good because he obeys his own commands? Surely we should be able to judge God's goodness against some independent standard.
- How can a non-believer act morally, since they are presumably not able to discern God's will? As it is possible for an atheist to be moral, at least in the socially accepted sense, then moral standards cannot wholly derive from God.

The **second** position also assumes that morality and belief in God are interlinked. It suggests, however, that moral values are not established by God's

This is known as the **Euthyphro dilemma.**

This is important for many ethical issues facing the believer in the modern world. There is no objective command laid down in the Bible concerning such matters, so what principles need to be applied to ensure that God's will is to be fulfilled?

will but that God operates according to moral laws already in place in the universe. The **problems** of this position are:

- God is limited by morality, which is above him. He responds to what is good rather than setting moral standards.
- We must wait for God to reveal what is moral by commanding it. He is the channel through which moral values are passed down to man.

So perhaps morality is **opposed** to religion. If belief in God requires man to accept and fulfil his will obediently, then man's freedom is fundamentally violated. If man is not free then he cannot be truly moral, since a genuinely moral action cannot be coerced. Furthermore, a God who demands that man surrender his freedom in this way cannot be worthy of worship. Others may argue that since many atrocities have been carried out in the name of religion, it is not possible to claim that morality either supports or is included in religion.

Kierkegaard argued that we should not confuse ethics or morality with doing the will of God. He used the example of God's command to Abraham to sacrifice Isaac (Genesis 22). Clearly what God commanded was not, according to usual human standards, moral. In this case, however, Abraham was being called to obedience which went beyond such understanding of morality. In such a position, being bound to the moral or ethical would be a hindrance to fulfilling God's will.

J Religious language 1: verification, falsification and language games

The material in this section is relevant to questions on:
- religious language
- the existence of God
- atheism
- the problem of evil
- the nature of God

Religious language has long been something of a Cinderella topic on philosophy of religion papers. Candidates are showing an increasing interest in it — and well they might, since it is a relatively straightforward topic at AS/A2. Even if you have sidelined the issue in the past, it is worth looking at now. The subject overlaps with other, more immediately popular, areas and can give you a new perspective when looking at these more familiar areas.

1 The problem of religious language

This multifaceted problem has many angles:
- How do we use human language about the transcendent, unlimited God?
- If we use other forms of language, how can they be meaningful or comprehensible?
- Should religious language be understandable to those outside the religious community?
- Are those outside the religious community entitled to evaluate religious language critically?
- What use do analogy, symbol, myth, metaphor and other non-cognitive forms of language have?
- Does religious language depend on making factual assertions, or does it serve some other, non-factual, function?

If believers make claims about God, his existence, nature, purposes and relationship with man, then presumably they intend those claims, or assertions, to be meaningful, true and in some way verifiable. For the most part, believers' claims are traditionally **cognitive** — that is, they are intended to be factual assertions about an objective reality, and as such can be proved true or false (verified or falsified): 'God exists'; 'God loves us'; 'God will execute a final judgement'. Such claims are usually made on the understanding that the believer is not uttering 'crypto-commands, expressions of wishes, disguised exclamations, concealed ethics, or anything but assertions' (Anthony Flew, *Theology and Falsification*, cited in Basil Mitchell (ed.), *The Philosophy of Religion*, OUP, 1971, pp. 13–22).

Non-cognitive language is of value for debates about the nature of biblical material, particularly miracles and Old Testament myths such as the creation narratives.

> Non-cognitive language serves some other function — it may be pictorial, or express an emotion or other abstract, subjective feeling: 'God is my rock'; 'Jesus's death washes me clean'; 'The angels will sound the final trumpet'.

2 The verification principle

Although believers may take for granted the factual reliability of their statements, the school of thought known as **logical positivism**, which originated in Vienna' in post-war era, was concerned to find a distinction between sense and non-sense. The issue regarding statements such as 'God exists' was not just a case of person A disagreeing with person B on a matter of objective reality, but rather it became an issue of **meaningfulness**. **Truth** and **meaning** were regarded as distinct concepts by the logical positivists, since it is possible to make a meaningful statement that is not true, for example 'Elephants are red'. This is **meaningful**, since we can test it by sense experience, although it is **false** because elephants are not red.

The logical positivists established three criteria of meaningfulness:
(i) synthetic statements that could be checked by the use of sense experience or empirical testing, e.g. 'The sky is blue'
(ii) mathematics: $2 + 2 = 4$
(iii) tautological or analytic statements, e.g. 'All circles are round'

> This should ring a bell from the Ontological Argument: Anselm's definition of God as 'That than which nothing greater can be conceived' is assumed to be analytically true, and it is only on this basis that the argument succeeds.

The **verification principle** thus demanded that:

> Only assertions that were in principle verifiable by observation or experience could convey factual information. Assertions that there could be no imaginable way of verifying must either be analytic or meaningless.

The members of the Vienna Circle were essentially scientists and mathematicians, and the world view which lay behind the principle was a scientific one.

Analytic statements we know **by definition** to be meaningful, since their meaning is precisely defined. We know that it is meaningless to say 'The man who lives next door to me is a bachelor with a wife and three children' because bachelor means unmarried man. Synthetic statements must be checked, however, by reference to the **evidence** available to us; they are not true in themselves, and therefore, by the logical positivists' definition, not meaningful unless they can be tested. This demands that the evidence is there to be tested. Essentially, the effect of the demand is that either something is scientific or it is capable of becoming a science.

2.1 Implications for religious language

Statements about God cannot be subject to the verification that the logical positivists demanded: his physical, empirical presence cannot be confirmed existentially and — the Ontological Argument aside — 'God exists' is not analytically true. Experience of God may be vividly real to the believer, but that experience is **subjective** — it is not universally shared, not subject to scientific testing, and there are no reliable grounds for establishing a way to verify such claims. Thus all religious language was considered meaningless.

2.2 Weaknesses of logical positivism

- The verification principle renders invalid all statements which express opinions or emotions.
- In its strongest form, historical statements are also invalidated by the principle. The statement 'The Great Fire of London took place in 1666' can only be verified by sense experience, as there is no one alive who could claim to have experienced it.
- Even scientific statements cannot be verified according to the terms of the principle. '**All** water boils at 100°C' cannot technically be verified since we cannot possibly test **all** water.
- Most importantly, the verification principle itself does not fulfil its own criteria.
- Religious statements **could** be verified. **Keith Ward** argued that God can verify his own existence, and **John Hick** observed that religious claims will be verified eschatologically.

So, whereas the principle was initially very popular in philosophical circles, soon 'People began to realise that this glittering new scalpel was, in one operation after another, killing the patient' (Bryan McGee, *Confessions of a Philosopher*,

Hick's principle of eschatological verification is also very useful for other topics: the existence of God and the nature of theological proofs, and life after death.

Phoenix, 1997, p. 55). Furthermore, it was appreciated that there were 'many different and useful ways of talking about the world and our experience of it, each one of which had a *raison d'être* of its own' (ibid., p. 56).

In other words, there are many kinds of meaningful language — not just that which can be verified according to the terms of the verification principle.

3 *The falsification principle*

After the failure of the verification principle, **Anthony Flew** set a new challenge:

> What would have to occur or to have occurred to constitute for you a disproof of the love of, or the existence of, God?

This amounts to the **falsification** debate — what would **count against**, or cause to be falsified, the believer's claims about God?

Flew's thesis is based initially on **John Wisdom**'s 'Parable of the Gardener':

> Two explorers in a jungle come across a clearing which has the appearance of being tended. One believes that a gardener must tend the spot; the other disagrees. After an exhaustive series of tests, the gardener has not been revealed or made himself known. However, the believer continues to maintain that a gardener tends the plot — an invisible, intangible, inaudible gardener. The sceptic is not convinced: how does such a gardener differ from no gardener at all?

The Parable of the Gardener is extremely versatile: it can be used to illustrate the problem of disproving the existence of God in a question about proofs, or about atheism, or about the characteristic nature of faith.

Flew maintains that the believer in God is guilty of the same error — failure to **prove** God's existence does not lead the believer to withdraw their faith claims. Rather, they continue to believe, but in a God who can only be described in terms of negatives, just like the gardener. The believer's definition of God has 'died the death of a thousand qualifications' and amounts to no God at all. Flew challenges the believer to accept that there must be a point when they admit that their claims are open to so great a challenge that they should — hypothetically at least — withdraw them. Only then can their claims be meaningful.

Flew's position is that in order to **assert** something, a proposition must **deny** something. For example:
- If I say 'This table is round' I am also saying 'This table is not square'. In asserting its roundness I am denying its squareness.
- If I say 'God exists' I am denying that 'God does not exist'. In asserting the existence of God I am denying his non-existence.

The first assertions in each case are open to correction and refutation — they are committing to something which may not, in fact, be the case. John Hick describes the position thus:

> *In order to say something which may possibly be true, we must say something which may possibly be false.*
>
> John Hick, *Faith and Knowledge*, Fount, 1978, p. 166

So when the believer says 'God exists' they are making an assertion which they believe to be true, but which — in principle at least — may possibly be false. Flew maintains that this ensures the meaningfulness of their assertions, and that believers should be prepared to admit what would demonstrate for them a denial of their assertion. Perhaps pain and suffering would constitute grounds for such a denial, but religious faith does not put a limit on the amount of suffering which would make belief in God impossible. Believers often face an inordinate amount of suffering and still maintain their faith.

Flew is not satisfied with this. He comments:

> *Now it often seems to people who are not religious as if there was no conceivable event ... the occurrence of which would be admitted by sophisticated religious people to be a sufficient reason for conceding ... 'God does not really love us then'.*
>
> Anthony Flew, *Theology and Falsification*

Flew uses the provocative example of a child dying of a terminal illness:

> *His Heavenly Father reveals no obvious sign of concern. Some qualification is made — 'God's love is not merely human love' ... and we realise that such sufferings are quite compatible with the truth of the assertion that 'God loves us as a father (but of course)'.*
>
> Anthony Flew, *Theology and Falsification*

The believer fails to acknowledge that their assertions about God are threatened by the prevailing circumstances, but in order to go on saying 'God loves us' they **qualify** the nature of his love. What is such love worth? Is it the love of a God worthy of worship? Surely, Flew argues, it is better to recognise the grounds for potential falsification of the believer's claims — that conceivably there are grounds which present a serious challenge to faith.

> Flew's position provides a good reason for the atheist's rejection of belief in God — that the believer's position is logically absurd if they do not allow that anything might constitute a denial of God's existence.

3.1 R. M. Hare and bliks

R. M. Hare responded to Flew's argument by suggesting that religious beliefs are essentially unfalsifiable but that does not make them meaningless, because they are **bliks**. A blik is:

> *A way of regarding the world which is in principle neither verifiable nor falsifiable — but a mode of cognition to which the terms 'veridical' or 'illusory' properly apply.*
>
> John Hick, *Faith and Knowledge*, p. 169

It is a way of regarding the world which makes a significant difference to our lives and affects the way in which we interpret and engage with the universe. If I have a blik that it is fatally dangerous to fly in an aeroplane it will make a difference because I will not take a flight, irrespective of how much proof is offered to me of the safety of air travel. My blik cannot be falsified by reference to any number of safe landings. Hare argues that although religious beliefs by their very nature cannot be verified or falsified, they have a decisive effect on the way in which a person lives their life and so cannot be meaningless.

If I have a blik that God is involved in my life I will interpret the things that happen to me in the light of that blik. It will affect my decision making, my actions, my interaction with others. The fact that others may not share my blik or that they may even attempt to talk me out of it will make no difference — not because I am particularly stubborn, but because it is a blik and bliks cannot be falsified. For the person whose blik is that God exists, and that his existence makes some difference to their life, will live in a way compatible with that blik, irrespective of their critics. It matters to the person, even though they know that it cannot be verified or falsified.

3.2 Basil Mitchell and the 'Partisan and the Stranger'

Basil Mitchell's contribution to the debate also uses a parable — the 'Partisan and the Stranger'. Mitchell disagrees with Flew that believers do not allow anything to count against their assertions. Rather, he maintains that believers are aware of the philosophical problems that are created by the unfalsifiability of their assertions. Mitchell credits believers with recognising the full force of the conflict when faced with evidence which could — or even should — count decisively against the existence of God. He observes that there are three ways in which the believer can react when their assertions are challenged. They can treat them as:

(i) **provisional hypotheses** to be discarded if experience tells against them
(ii) **vacuous formulae** to which experience makes no difference and which make no difference to life
(iii) **significant articles of faith**

If believers are tempted to discard their beliefs when experience is too challenging, the beliefs are clearly of little value. If they treat them as 'vacuous formulae' (e.g. 'God's will is mysterious') when faced with challenges, their faith will not be considered rational or realistic. Thus their claims must be significant articles of faith that are not easily discarded, but which the believer recognises as open to challenge.

Remember Hick's 'Parable of the Celestial City' referred to in the section 'Proof, probability, faith and reason' (pp. 73). This is an example of a blik.

We come to the problem of evil again: if believers are not prepared to recognise the challenge posed by suffering then they cannot expect atheists to be convinced that their faith has anything substantial to offer.

In the Parable of the Partisan and the Stranger, Mitchell suggests the following scenario:

> In times of war a partisan meets a stranger who claims to be the leader of the resistance — to be on the partisan's side. He urges the partisan to have faith in him whatever the circumstances, even if he sees the stranger acting in ways which appear to contradict his claim to be on the partisan's side. The partisan is committed to his belief in the stranger's integrity, even when his friends think him a fool for doing so. When the stranger appears to withhold help, the partisan has the choice to stop believing in him, but he does not do so. Rather, he believes that the stranger must have overwhelmingly good reasons for not helping him when he could have done so.

Note that the partisan **does** recognise the difficulties posed by the stranger's sometimes ambiguous behaviour, and this is where his belief differs from Hare's blik. The man who has a blik does not allow that anything could count against it. The partisan (who is, of course, the believer) recognises the challenge posed.

3.3 The falsification principle in summary

- Flew maintains that a meaningful assertion must be falsifiable, at least in principle.
- Hare claims that because religious beliefs are bliks they are inherently un-falsifiable — but not meaningless, because they have a significant effect on the believer's life.
- Mitchell argues that the believer does recognise the potential falsifiability of their belief, but does not allow circumstances to count decisively against them.

4 Language games

You can be asked to write about more than one topic within religious language in an essay. Common combinations are myth and symbol or analogy and language games, but you should be prepared to combine any two or more.

Language game theory, propounded by **Ludwig Wittgenstein**, turns attention to the **use** of language rather than its meaning. It is an **anti-realist** approach, based on the principle that language as an expression of a form of life does not make statements that are true or false, but rather statements that are correctly or incorrectly used. Wittgenstein maintained that we should not ask for the meaning of language, but rather consider its use. It is also a non-cognitive approach to language, maintaining that the primary purpose of language is not to make factual assertions. Thus each form of life stands alone, with rules that apply only to that game and to no other. One form of life may therefore not be able to understand another, and consequently will not be able to criticise it. Wittgenstein illustrated his theory thus:

> Suppose someone is ill and he says: 'This is a punishment', and I say: 'If I'm ill, I don't think of punishment at all.' If you say: 'Don't you believe the opposite?' — you can call it believing the opposite, but it is entirely different from what we would normally call believing the opposite. I think differently, in a different way. I say different things to myself, I have a different picture. It is this way: if someone says, 'Wittgenstein, you don't take illness as a punishment, so what do you believe?' — I'd say, 'I don't have any thoughts of punishment'.

If a religious believer thinks of illness as a punishment they understand illness in a different way from the person who has 'no thoughts of punishment' in relation to illness. Their understanding of illness is quite different, but to say that one is wrong and the other right would be too simplistic. They both use language in different ways, and the believer who associates illness and punishment is using language in a way appropriate to the language game they are playing. Religious language is therefore a peculiar game of its own.

> Suppose someone were a believer and said: 'I believe in a Last Judgement', and I said, 'Well, I'm not so sure. Possibly', you would say that there was an enormous gulf between us. If he said, 'There is a German aeroplane overhead', and I said, 'Possibly, I'm not so sure', you'd say we were fairly near.

There is a way of responding to religious claims which will indicate whether the hearer is playing the same language game or talking at cross-purposes. If the scientist hears the believer declare 'Here is the blood of Jesus' and grabs the chalice and rushes off to the laboratory to analyse it, they have entirely failed to grasp the context in which religious language is being used. 'For a blunder, that's too big', claims Wittgenstein.

4.1 Strengths of language games

- They recognise the distinctive nature of religious language and distinguish it from other uses of language.
- As a non-cognitive form of language, religious language makes no assertions (factual claims) and therefore cannot be disproved.
- In focusing on use rather than meaning, religious language claims are not assumed to be objectively true.
- Language games unite believers in a common bond.
- They provide boundaries for the correct use of language.
- Believers can be initiated into the rules of language.
- Religious language games provide a defence against criticism from other types of language: religious language does not play by the same rules.

The debate between science and religion is a good example of how language games are used to express different forms of life: if we recognise that they are employing language games and not trying to undermine each other, we will recognise the distinctive contribution each makes.

4.2 Weaknesses of language games

- Language games do not allow for believers' claims to be objectively true.
- In making religious language distinct from all other language it is essentially alienating those outside the game.
- Who makes the rules?
- How can we be sure that the rules are correctly interpreted?
- Can rules be changed? If so, by whom?

K Religious language 2: symbol, myth and analogy

The material in this section is relevant to questions on:
- religious language
- the nature of God
- biblical study of miracles, creation, resurrection, incarnation
- Christian doctrines of incarnation, trinity, creation, christology, atonement

1 *What function does religious language serve?*

If religious language makes claims which can be proved true or false, then it is used to express matters which believers maintain have some objective reality. However, if religious language cannot be confined to these criteria, either in part or in whole, then the verification and falsification principles are invalid.

If religious language claims are in some way non-factual, they will be **non-cognitive** — they serve some other function than that of making factual claims. The language of myth and symbol uses non-cognitive language in such a way. It is complex, bound up with ancient belief systems, literature and history. They are means of expression which go beyond simple assertions about God's love or existence, since myth and symbol are used to express those things which cannot be expressed in anything other than non-literal language, and yet which are nevertheless considered by believers to be true.

Truth has many dimensions in philosophical and theological study. It is possible for believers to claim that something is true not because it is literally or historically the case — that the world was made in 7 days, for example — but that it is religiously true, i.e. it expresses certain things about the nature of God and his actions that cannot be conveyed meaningfully in any other way.

2 *Symbol*

The word 'symbol' originates from the Greek *sumballo* (to throw together) and *sumbolom* (the token or insignia by which someone or something was identified). Symbols could be thought to be interchangeable with words, and words themselves are forms which are arranged and as such are symbols. Hence words could be considered symbolic. **Wallace Stephens** claims that 'we do not live in the world but in a picture of it'. In other words, our entire perception of the world is symbolic.

A symbol could also be described as 'A pattern or object which points to an invisible metaphysical reality and participates in it' (Erika Dinker-von Schubert, in *A Handbook of Christian Theology*, Fontana, 1960, p. 361).

Symbols thus **identify** and **participate**. As identifiers they help man to focus on that which they represent. In religious language, the cross immediately identifies for believers the death of Jesus — it is so well-known a symbol that it is instantly recognisable, even if we do not share the beliefs integral to it. But it does more than identify Jesus's death — it participates in it by bringing to our consciousness what that death signifies:

- salvation from sin — the price paid
- sacrifice and atonement
- victory over death
- the defeat of Satan
- God's love for the world
- Christian hope of eternal life

Paul Tillich used the example of a national flag, which conveys nationalism, patriotism and national identity. It is more than a sign that simply provides information or instructions, such as a traffic light or street sign. Symbols express what the believer feels about what that symbol conveys. Signs are to do with facts; symbols transcend facts. If we try to understand symbol by looking for its literal meaning we will end up like Nicodemus:

> *'Truly I say to you, unless one is born of water and Spirit he cannot enter the Kingdom of God.... The wind blows where it wills and you hear the sound of it, but you do not know whence it comes or whither it goes; so too it is with everyone born of the Spirit.'* Nicodemus said to him, *'How can this be?'* Jesus answered him, *'Are you a teacher of Israel and you do not understand this?'*
>
> **John 3:5–10**

Nicodemus had become so bogged down with trying to work out how it was possible to be born again, what water and spirit meant in this context, and how the wind came to be involved at all, that he missed the rich symbolism of revival, renewal, refreshment and transformation.

It is useful to bear in mind here that symbol is essentially a visual form of language. Remember that language is a means of communication which is not necessarily always verbal.

There are so many religious symbols that you can choose your own, from other religious traditions as well as from Christian literature.

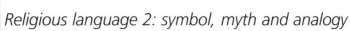

Symbols are enduring because they are born out of revelation. They are flexible in themselves, but the truth they convey is believed to be of eternal value. They are also characteristic of human communication:

> *Symbol expresses what is beyond rational recognition, [it] serves to distinguish the human from the animal world.*
>
> **Erika Dinker-von Schubert, in *A Handbook of Christian Theology*, p. 361**

Symbol is pervasive in human culture, and so we should not be surprised to find it used in religious language:

> *The development of symbolism in religious language is not a process of the encrustation of an original, simple idea, with distracting and extraneous illustration or ornament. Like all other serious human discourse, religious language requires a symbolic foundation.*
>
> **Rowan Williams, in *A Dictionary of Christian Theology*, SCM, 1989, p. 281**

Contemporary religious symbol is still drawn on the ancient symbols used by the biblical writers: God is described as a rock, a shield, shepherd, king, as light. His presence is symbolised by cloud, fire, thunder, rain and a rainbow. The biblical writers made use of symbolism to express or learn truths about the nature of God and his relationship with his people. Hosea married a cultic prostitute in order to experience God's sorrow at Israel's unfaithfulness to him. Jeremiah was sent to the potter's workshop to watch him mould a pot — breaking it down and starting again if necessary — in order to learn how God is the potter and man and his affairs are the clay in the potter's hands.

New Testament symbolism draws on that of the Old, to convey the authors' belief that it has been fulfilled and transcended. An example is the vine, used in John 15 to represent Israel's relationship with God, now expressed in the life and ministry of Jesus. Even animals are used symbolically — lion, eagle, dove and lamb — not to mention the mythical beasts of Daniel and Revelation.

But if religious symbolism draws heavily on everyday experience, can it adequately represent God and participate in his essence?

> *All these images are provided by God in his creative goodness, and to some measure, are true, yet all must be 'denied' in their human sense, so as to lead us back to silence and unknowing.*
>
> **Rowan Williams, in *A Dictionary of Christian Theology*, p. 281**

Note how these symbols are drawn from the natural world or from people's everyday relationships and activities. In this way they facilitate understanding.

In any question about religious language, keep coming back to the original problem which relates to all its forms: how to speak meaningfully of God.

Consider here the importance of symbolic elements such as the Eucharist, and of other central sacraments such as marriage.

See how this highlights the perennial problem of religious language: we are forced to use terms which belong to man, yet we use them to express something of the infinite God. This dilemma frequently leads man 'back to silence' — saying nothing about God at all.

Symbols are not just limited to images, however, but are inherent in actions too: the creed, the *symbolum apostolicum*, originated in the rite of baptism, which is the sacramental core of Christian worship. The sacraments themselves are essentially symbolic, embracing death and resurrection and giving believers a means of participating in the experience of Jesus.

2.1 The weakness of symbol

- Symbols can become the focus of worship in themselves. For example, baptism should not be thought of as the means of salvation, but as a way of demonstrating salvation already accomplished.
- They can be trivialised. The cross, for example, has been appropriated by the secular world in jewellery and art, and the religious significance is lost to many.
- They can appear outdated. Paul Tillich wrote:

> *It is necessary to rediscover the questions to which the Christian symbols are the answers in a way which is understandable to our time.*
>
> Paul Tillich, in **A Handbook of Christian Theology**, p. 363

3 *Myth*

The *Oxford English Dictionary* describes myth as 'purely fictitious narrative'. Such a definition will confuse, rather than illuminate, an understanding of myth in religious language.

In myth, symbols are sustained within a narrative. The vital function of myth is that of a narrative which **embodies and expresses claims that cannot be expressed in any other way**. In this way myth should not be understood as something that is 'not true'.

Rather, myth in religious language is:

> *A symbolic, approximate expression of truth which the human mind cannot perceive sharply and completely, but can only glimpse vaguely, and therefore cannot adequately or accurately express.*
>
> Millar Burrows, **An Outline of Biblical Theology**,
> The Westminster Press, 1946, p. 115

3.1 The origins of myth

This is the province of Old Testament scholarship, and you may find it interesting to follow it up in some of the easily accessible introductions to the Old Testament.

Jewish and Christian myth originate in Greek and oriental antiquity. The great Old Testament myths of creation, the Fall, the flood and the Tower of Babel all present a revised version of Babylonian myth, which **Gunkel** observed had been refashioned according to Israel's faith.

New Testament myth incorporates not only elements of Jewish tradition, but also a Hellenistic worldview of a three-storied universe: heaven, hell and earth. Satan and the demons inhabit Hades, Christ is enthroned with God in heaven, while terrestrial man is poised between divine and demonic forces. **Bultmann and Gunkel** identified the use of Hellenistic saviour or redeemer myths in New Testament literature: Jesus is the heavenly redeemer or saviour who comes down to earth to enlighten man, bridging the gap between these two otherwise incompatible spheres. The Jewish concept of the Son of Man in Daniel 7 combines with the gnostic notion of a heavenly redeemer who descends to earth only to ascend again.

Myth entered **eschatological teaching**, with its special cosmic dimensions, taking its cue from Persian and late Jewish traditions in passages such as 1 Thessalonians 4:16: 'For the Lord himself will descend from heaven with a cry of command, with the archangels' call and with the sound of the trumpet of God … and man, both alive and dead will rise to meet the Lord in the air.'

3.2 A critique of myth

You will find that most discussions of myth revolve around the use of myth in biblical literature. Don't be put off by this. It is the primary source of religious myth and you can't avoid it!

The Enlightenment period brought a new interest in the role of myth. It was suggested that the crude supernatural and miraculous happenings in the biblical narratives owed their form to the fact that the narrators, and those from whom the myths originated, did not understand scientific causality. They described in terms of the supernatural what enlightened humanity would ascribe to natural causes.

- In 1806 **De Wette** proposed that a historical kernel of truth could be recovered from biblical myths, which reflected the concerns of the people in the time when the narratives were being compiled.
- In the mid-nineteenth century **F. Max Miller** suggested that myths were originally poetic descriptions of natural phenomena.
- **D. F. Strauss**'s book *The Life of Jesus Critically Examined* (1835) adopted the term 'myth' to cover all the miraculous elements in the gospels. He shifted his focus from 'the story of a **miraculous occurrence**' to 'the **story** of a miraculous occurrence'. Myth was the expression or embodiment of an idea, not a historical event. Myths were not something positive — a proof of Jesus's messiahship — but something problematic once history was concerned with an observable train of cause and effect and not the intervention of forces outside the historical range of observation.
- **Rudolph Bultmann**, in the 1940s, maintained that: 'It is impossible to use electric light and the wireless, and to avail ourselves of modern medical and

Note these key terms, which should be part of your personal glossary.

surgical discoveries, and at the same time to believe in the New Testament world of demons and spirits.' In the twentieth century the reader had to release the essential message from its mythical framework — a process Bultmann called **demythologisation**. Bultmann's purpose was **apologetic**. He did not intend to destroy the Christian message, but to find the essence of the **kerygma** — the kernel of religious truth that had become overwhelmed by the details of myth. In this way, Bultmann maintained, it would be possible to re-experience and re-express the gospel in a way that twentieth-century minds could grasp.

However... mythological language is so deeply ingrained in religious talk that it may well be indispensable. If religious language is **anti-realist** — expressing subjective, rather than objective, truths — then mythological language need not be a burden to understanding. It is only when we attempt to find a literal understanding to myth that problems can occur. Mythological language is part of the religious language game. What is necessary is to ensure that myths are used effectively and without undue concern for establishing what 'really happened'.

> *Because myths have their birth not in logic, but in intuitions of transcendence, they are of value to traditions that seek to describe the action of the other worldly in the present world. However, the term 'myth' must be a servant and not a master.*
>
> J.W. Rogerson, *A Dictionary of Biblical Interpretation*, SCM, 1990, p. 482

4 *Analogy*

The use of analogy, like all forms of religious language, attempts to solve the problem of how can we talk significantly about God. What is the difficulty in saying:

- God is wise?
- God is our father?
- God is omnipotent?
- God is our rock?

You will notice that these include terms that are symbolic or metaphorical. Thus all the forms of religious language interlink with each other.

David Hume, of course, criticised the Design Argument for depending on analogy and the anthropomorphism inherent in it.

All these descriptions of God draw on things that are part of everyday, human, earthbound existence. Yet they are used to describe characteristics of God, who believers would say is completely different from anything of which we have empirical experience. The danger of using such terms is that we fall into **anthropomorphism** — we bring God down to human level in order to say anything meaningful about him at all. **David Hume** said: 'Wisdom, thought, design, knowledge — these we justly ascribe to him because those words are honourable among men, and we have no other language by which we can express our adoration of him.'

4.1 Does the answer lie in negation?

The principle of **negation** involves speaking of God in terms of what he is not, rather than ascribing to him positive characteristics, e.g. 'God is not evil'.

- **Strength:** negation emphasises the unknowability of God. **Aquinas** observed that an affirmative statement has to have a subject, and God cannot be a subject.
- **Weakness:** it tells us nothing positive about God and so we are no closer to understanding his nature in its fullest essence.

4.2 Or in equivocal and univocal language?

Equivocal language speaks of two things as being entirely different. A common example used is the word 'bat'. It can be used to describe a small, furry flying mammal or an object used in the game of cricket. Although they share the same terminology, we would not be confused as to which was being spoken of as they are being used in entirely different ways. Is this how language is used of God and man? When we say 'John is wise' and 'God is wise', do we mean that their wisdom is as completely different as a cricket bat is from a fruit bat?

- **Strength:** it emphasises the difference between God and man.
- **Weakness:** it only tells us that God is completely different from man, so are we any closer to knowing him?

Univocal language uses the same term to describe two different things to identify their similarities. The word 'coat' may be used to describe a short cotton jacket or a full-length fur coat, and yet we know that it is being used in exactly the same way. Thus if we say 'John is wise' and 'God is wise' univocally, we mean that their wisdom is of the same nature.

- **Strength:** we learn exactly what God's wisdom entails.
- **Weakness:** God's wisdom is reduced to the level of man's wisdom.

Aquinas said: 'To say "God is wise" goes beyond our understanding of the word "wise". God is so distant from his creatures that nothing can be said to be the same of God and creatures.'

4.3 The use of analogy

Analogies are 'proportional similarities which also acknowledge dissimilar features' (D. Burrell, in A *Dictionary of Christian Theology*).

Aquinas observed that we can speak analogically of God because he is the cause of all things. God is good because he is the cause of goodness, which we see imperfectly mirrored in his creation. Goodness, love, wisdom, even being, in creatures, pre-exists in God in a higher way.

Even when using analogy, however, we speak of man before we speak of God; our knowledge is of man before it is of God. Our ideas can reach no further than our experience. This makes God the **secondary analogate**, and yet because

---

Although these types of language are not examples of the use of analogy, they lay the groundwork for analogy, which attempts a compromise between the two.

Even if you don't think you are familiar with analogy you probably are, since the design argument is based on an analogous relationship between the world and the objects of human design.

Turn to the fourth of Aquinas's Five Ways for this principle; he used it as one of his 'proofs' for the existence of God.

God's wisdom is perfect it must come before man's, even though we learn of man's first. Ways around this are as follows:

- **Remotion and excellence:** all creaturely concepts are removed from a word, and we learn by this that God has no defects. Remaining qualities are projected without limit, and we come to the conclusion that God possesses wisdom with no ill-effect to the utmost degree.
- **Models and qualifiers:** we take a human attribute and ascribe it to God, qualifying it to make clear that it is infinitely enhanced when applied to God.
- **Analogy of proportion:** goodness, wisdom, justice and so forth belong proportionately to God, man, angels, dogs, etc. Thus we know that God's wisdom is proportionate to God's nature and must therefore be greater than man's wisdom.
- **Analogy of attribution:** God is the cause of wisdom in man and other beings and thus attributes it to them. It belongs to God first in a greater and higher sense.

A Utilitarianism

The material in this section is relevant to questions on:
- utilitarianism specifically
- ethical theories in general
- solving dilemmas in practical ethics

1 Background

In an essay, cut down on the length of time and space you devote to the history of the various ethical theories. There are few marks available for biographical and historical details. Get quickly on to the evaluation.

- Utilitarianism is a nineteenth-century ethical theory most often attributed to **Jeremy Bentham**, **John Stuart Mill** and **Henry Sidgwick**. They adopted the principle that **right actions are those which produce the greatest total pleasure for everyone affected by their consequences and wrong actions are those which do not produce the greatest total happiness**. The goal of many utilitarians was to address social inequalities in the workplace, education, social opportunities, housing and many other areas. Hence, it is best seen as a political and social tool, rather than a metaphysical way of approaching ethics.
- In the mid-twentieth century, 'ideal utilitarians' such as **G.E. Moore** agreed in principle with the philosophy of the nineteenth-century proponents, but held that some things other than pleasurable experiences were intrinsically good.
- Bentham discovered the phrase 'greatest good of the greatest number' in Joseph Priestley's *Essay on Government*, which led him to propose the principle of utility.
- Bentham was motivated by the desire to establish a universal theory which could be applied to all ethical situations.
- His influence on nineteenth-century society and beyond was considerable: he was involved in parliamentary and penal reform, the development of savings banks and the post office, and the registration of births and deaths.

2 The principle of utility

This is where the examiner is going to want to be sure that you understand the technical terminology and can use it efficiently.

- The principle is **teleological**: it is a means by which the moral value of an action can be judged by reference to the likely consequences. It is thus not concerned with motives or with the intrinsic rightness of an action (as in a deontological theory of ethics). It is a forward-looking **consequentialist theory** which holds that actions are made right or wrong by something after the action in time: the consequences.
- The principle claims that we should choose the action most likely to bring about the greatest happiness of the greatest number. Thus in one set of circumstances action A may be the most appropriate, while under other circumstances action B might bring more happiness to more people. Therefore no action is judged solely on its own merits, but rather in terms of its uscfulncss in any one particular set of circumstances.

Keep case studies to a minimum. In many essays candidates fail to gather marks because they spend far too long detailing possible scenarios and fail to evaluate the theory.

- The theory is thus one of universal ethical hedonism: if an action brings or increases pleasure, then it is right. Bentham proposed the **Hedonic Calculus** to calculate the most pleasurable action. Seven elements are taken into consideration: the intensity, duration, certainty, propinquity (remoteness), fecundity (chance of there being further pleasures), purity (not followed by pain) and extent of the pleasure. It would therefore be theoretically possible to calculate whom it was morally right to rescue first from a fire: a child, a pregnant woman, an old man or a scientist who possessed the formula for the ultimate cure for cancer.

Vardy and Grosch (in *The Puzzle of Ethics*, Fount, 1994, p. 74) cite the case of a young pregnant woman who is planning a skiing trip. If she chooses to abort the pregnancy in order to ski, the pleasure will be minor and temporary; if she chooses to abandon the holiday, the long-lasting and intense pleasure of having the child will outweigh her initial disappointment. However, this example simply highlights the difficulty of using this theory to deal with personal moral dilemmas that do not affect a sufficient number of people to justify its application.

John Stuart Mill developed the principle by referring to **qualitative** rather than quantitative pleasure, recognising some of the problems inherent in Bentham's formulation. He argued that pleasures of the mind should take precedence over physical pleasures and that once basic human requirements for survival were fulfilled, a human being's primary moral concerns should be for the higher-order 'goods'. He claimed: 'It is better to be a human being dissatisfied than a pig satisfied; better to be Socrates dissatisfied than a fool satisfied.' More interestingly, he suggested: 'If Bentham thought at all of any of the deeper feelings of human nature, it was but as idiosyncrasies of taste.'

Instead of a Hedonic Calculus, Mill proposed that general rules should be used as guides in decision making concerning moral actions — rules that promote happiness, such as keeping promises and not stealing. **Rule utilitarianism** suggests that a person should follow established rules and consider the practical consequences of an action before carrying it out.

- **Strong rule utilitarianism** maintains that certain rules have universal value and should always be kept.
- **Weak rule utilitarianism** argues that there will sometimes be circumstances in which it would be better to allow exceptions.
- Mill's approach has also been called **'ideal utilitarianism'**, as it includes ideals (such as compassion or justice) in his understanding of human happiness.
- **Negative utilitarianism** argues that maximising pleasure is not as important as minimising pain; the priority is to reduce suffering in the world.
- **Preference utilitarianism** works on the principle that people are happiest if given the opportunity to exercise their preferences.

Strengths of the theory

The strengths revolve around its consideration of consequences:

- The evaluation of moral choices is influenced only by personal preferences if there is no consideration of consequences.

- Utilitarian theories hold with the general consensus that human well-being is intrinsically good and actions should be judged according to their effect on this well-being.
- Jesus preached an ethic of love, requiring men to work for the well-being of others: 'Do to others as you would have them do to you' (Matthew 7:12).
- Motives may be good or bad, but only consequences have a real effect on human well-being.
- The principle encourages a democratic approach to decision making. The majority's interest is always considered, and a dangerous minority is not allowed to dominate.
- Present circumstances can be judged without reference to precedents. Just because it would be wrong for woman A to have an abortion, it does not necessarily follow that in woman B's completely different circumstances it would be wrong for her.

4 Weaknesses of the theory

The weaknesses also take into consideration the governing principle that the consequences of an action are all that is important:

- The practical application of the theory requires the ability to predict the long-term consequences of an action, and to predict those consequences with unfailing accuracy. Past experience can to some extent guide future experience, but we know that there is no guarantee that circumstances will turn out exactly the same. People may suffer at second or third hand, even if the immediate consequences of an action fulfilled the conditions of the principle.
- The theory gives no credit to motivation. Not every action done out of goodwill is going to result in good consequences, but the attitude with which it is performed should be worthy of some credit.
- The theory cannot be used to determine what is really universally good. Under Bentham's theory it would be possible to justify acts of sadism or torture if they were carried out by the majority, no matter how perverted their pleasure. Mill's qualitative principle does go some way to addressing this weakness, however.
- Even in less extreme circumstances, we cannot assume that the majority is always right. There should be room for both the majority and the minority views to be accommodated.
- The theory relies on a single principle by which we make moral decisions. This is too simplistic. We cannot solve every dilemma by reference to one ethical theory because every ethical dilemma is multifaceted and unique in some way.
- Values such as justice can have no place, since the majority may not support that which is just.
- The responsibility for bringing about the best outcome belongs to God and not to man.
- The theory makes no allowance for personal relationships: if a man's wife were dying in a fire, reason would not tell him first to rescue an eminent politician who was also in danger, even if, arguably, greater happiness was to be gained. We have prima facie duties to those whom we love which

will always be more important to us than duties to a society of unknown individuals.

> *It remains true ... that a man must in the moment of decision do what he thinks is right. He cannot do otherwise. This does not mean that what he does will be right or even that he will not be worthy of blame or punishment. He simply has no choice, for he cannot at that moment see any discrepancy between what is right and what he thinks is right.*
>
> **William K. Frankena, *Ethics*, Prentice-Hall, 1973, p. 60**

B Kantian ethics

The material in this section is relevant to questions on:
- Kantian ethics specifically
- ethical theories in general
- solving dilemmas in practical ethics

1 *Reason and morality*

As mentioned in the last section, do not spend too much time on the history of theories: get quickly on to the evaluation.

Make sure you learn the relevant technical language and use it appropriately in your essay.

See the section 'Morality and God' (pp. 119–23) for more on this issue.

Kant was a professor of logic who aimed to establish certainty in mathematics and the sciences. He challenged the classical arguments for the existence of God and traditional ethical teaching based on revelation and natural law, divine command theory or hedonistic theories. Rather, he looked to the moral law, which any free individual would dispense in a rational and universal manner.

Kant maintained that we are obliged by duty to do what is moral. That duty cannot derive from what we desire or from the consequences of our actions. Hence Kant's theory is **deontological**, rather than **teleological**.

Kant's premise was that moral principles were not dependent on experience (**a posteriori**), but were **a priori**, i.e. independent of experience. This allowed him to argue that reason was the most reliable guide to decision making. He maintained that everyone possessed a conscience which guaranteed that they could discern moral truths without empirical proof. Kant claimed that since reason is universal, if correctly applied it will lead to the same results time and again.

Kant argued that the universe was essentially just and that the moral law would be satisfied (the good rewarded, the bad punished) in a *post-mortem* existence. In this way, he claimed, the existence of God was a necessary requirement of such a just universe.

2 The categorical imperative and a good will

Kant stated: 'It is impossible to conceive of anything at all in the world, or even out of it, which can be taken as good without qualification, except a good will.'

Kant maintained that a good will could be cultivated by the use of reason and by working to be rid of those tendencies that make rational decision making impossible. Personal preferences and inclinations, for instance, made decision making an unreliable process in terms of moral conduct. They weren't necessarily wrong, but they could not be trusted as a guide to what was morally right.

Kant used the example of a shopkeeper who made a point of not cheating his customers, but not out of a moral duty to be honest — rather to retain their business. Kant argued that the shopkeeper was acting out of prudence and a concern for the consequences of his actions, and was not therefore truly moral. He maintained that the consequences were irrelevant to moral obligation: 'Do your duty though the heavens fall!'

A moral action is the action of a morally free agent: determined actions are not morally commendable. Kant identified two types of moral command which form the basis of human moral conduct. **Hypothetical imperatives** are those commands which have a reason behind them, e.g. 'If you want to be well liked you must be generous towards your friends'. In such a case generosity is not an a priori principle and the command depends on individuals' preferences and inclinations rather than on duty. **Categorical imperatives** are commands that are not based on reason but are ends in themselves, e.g. 'Be generous'. Such imperatives can always be universalised. For Kant, actions of this kind are morally superior to all others: 'The distinction between a good man and one who is evil … must depend upon … which of the two incentives he makes the condition of the other.'

In comparison, Kant used the example of the institution of promising to illustrate his maxim. If, having promised to repay a loan, I see something I want to buy, but to do so would mean spending the money I should be repaying, I would not be acting on the universalisable principle 'Keep your promises' but would presumably be advocating another principle — 'Keep your promises unless doing so would deprive me of something I want'. This latter principle is clearly not universalisable, or the whole institution of promising would break down.

> Again, keep case studies to a minimum; the important thing is to evaluate the theory.

3 Kant's formulae

Kant outlines four further principles of right action:

(i) The **Formula of the Law of Nature** demands that human beings act in such a way that their actions become a universal law: 'Act only on that maxim through which you can at the same time will that it should become a universal law…. Act as if the maxim of your action were to become through your will a universal law of nature.' In other words, individuals are to

CHAPTER **3**   **Ethics**

consider the implications of a proposed course of action becoming a general law for mankind.

(ii) The **Formula of the End in Itself** protects minorities against ill-treatment, demanding that human actions should always be performed with the intention of treating others not as a means to an end but as an end in themselves.

(iii) The **Formula of Kingdom Ends** lays down the principle that every action should be undertaken as if the individual were 'a law-making member of a kingdom of ends'.

(iv) The **Formula of Autonomy** requires that all actions should be those of a free moral agent, working without coercion or partiality.

See the section 'New Testament ethics' (pp. 64–68) for more relevant information here.

Vardy and Grosch (in *The Puzzle of Ethics*, Fount, 1994, p. 70) observe that these principles are remarkably similar to the moral teaching of Jesus proscribing an *agape* love which puts neighbour before self. They note, however, that Jesus did teach that love for God should take precedence over love for others. Kant's principle does not eliminate the possibility of moral obligations being divine commands, but these should not be the reason for doing one's duty, otherwise they would become hypothetical imperatives.

Kant identified the performance of an individual's duty precisely because it *is* his duty as the 'greatest perfection of a human being'. The evil man, Kant maintained, does his duty only so long as it corresponds with what he feels is in his own best interests, while the good person, when faced with a conflict between self-interest and obligation, choses to do his duty. No other reason for acting morally is necessary, and in response to the question 'Why be moral?', the answer 'Because it is moral' is quite sufficient.

Contrary to some misunderstandings of Kant's moral theory, he did not suggest that divine reward was the justification for acting morally:

> *Morality must not lower herself. Her own nature must be her recommendation. All else, even divine reward, is as nothing beside her... Moral grounds of impulse ought to be presented by themselves and for themselves.*

There could, therefore, be no grounds on which morality and self-interest could coincide. Rewards and punishments may offer additional reasons for doing what we ought to do, but they cannot constitute the only reason for doing so. In this way, Kant defines virtue as being the goodwill that inclines towards the fulfilment of duty.

Duty-based morality enjoyed some revival in the twentieth century in the form of *prima facie* duties. **W. D. Ross** did not believe that the consequences of one's actions are the only way to judge their morality. Other things matter too, such as beneficence (helping others), self-improvement (developing our talents) and treating people justly. Ross calls these *prima facie* duties — duties to repay acts of generosity or to help those who are dependent upon us. However, we cannot tell in advance what the relevant *prima facie* duty will be, only the situation in

which we will reveal it, and some element of judgement is necessary before we can decide. According to Ross, the only way we can come to any moral knowledge is through experience of which moral duties matter and when they are less important.

4 Strengths of the theory

As for utilitarianism, make sure you devote enough time to evaluation, as this is where the bulk of the marks are to be gained.

Both the strengths and the weaknesses of Kant's theory revolve around its deontological nature.

- Even if the consequences of an action go drastically wrong, the motivation is worthy of credit and is valued accordingly. Conversely, it means that an action performed out of an immoral motivation which happened to bring about good consequences cannot be overlooked. Individuals must be accountable for their motivations, and should not hide behind consequences, whether they can take any credit for them or not.
- The principle is a humanitarian one. If we use reason to determine our moral actions we are less likely to be swayed by conflicting or deceiving circumstances. We shall be governed by the principles of 'universal law' and 'the end in itself' and shall treat others as human beings worthy of respect. In such a case minorities would be respected, individuals valued, and whole populations ensured of their civil rights over and above the government's political preferences.
- Unlike utilitarianism, Kant establishes justice as an absolute, irrespective of social fashions or pressures.

5 Weaknesses of the theory

- Deontological theories have been criticised for making moral obligation appear arbitrary or inexplicable except by reference to duty. There are many more factors which rightly influence our decision making.
- What happens when we are confronted with conflicting duties? We may believe that it is our moral duty not to lie, but it is also our duty to protect others. What happens when the Nazi soldier knocks at the door demanding to know where a Jewish family is concealed? Which duty does the householder obey: to tell the truth or to save life? Kant's theory insists on the absoluteness of moral rules, and in such a case two absolutes conflict. Furthermore, there are circumstances in which lying may represent a moral and benevolent course of action.
- **W. D. Ross** highlights the question of prima-facie duties. There are some people to whom we have duties that must override our duties to others, and some situations in which we must recognise our greater obligations. Any moral theory based on the principle of duty must take such *prima facie* duties into account.
- How far can a good motive, or a good will, justify an action? There must be a limit to how far this can be taken: a good will is just as likely to cause chaos if circumstances conspire, and motivation alone cannot undo the damage caused.

- Kant's theory does not allow for the range of things which man finds desirable. Reason cannot be guaranteed to draw all people to the same conclusion. Furthermore, Kant assumes that everybody is capable of using reason to make moral decisions. What about those whose reasoning faculties are impaired? Are they therefore intrinsically immoral?

Shelly Kagan supports Mill and Bentham, arguing that while under deontology individuals are bound by constraints (such as the requirement not to kill), they are also given options (such as the right not to give money to charity). Deontology can therefore lead to a decrease in moral goodness.

> *There is more to the moral point of view than being willing to universalise one's rules; Kant and his followers fail to see this fact, although they are right in thinking such a willingness is part of it.*
>
> **William K. Frankena, *Ethics*, Prentice-Hall, 1973, p. 33**

C Natural law, conscience and virtue ethics

The material in this section is relevant to questions on:
- natural law and conscience specifically
- ethical theories in general
- solving dilemmas in practical ethics

1 The principles of natural law

Cicero first touched on the principle of natural law: 'True law is right reason in agreement with nature. It is applied universally and is unchanging and everlasting ... one eternal and unchangeable law will be valid for all nations and all times, and there will be one master and rule, that is God.'

Aquinas takes up this approach to ethics in his *Summa Theologicae*, maintaining that there is a moral code towards which human beings naturally incline, and this he calls natural law. Morality consists of this natural law plus God's commands, which develop it further. The moral human being lives in accordance with this natural law; Christians are distinguished from non-Christians in that they live their lives in the knowledge that they will continue beyond the grave.

Paul claims in Romans 1–3 that the moral law of God is evident from the nature of man. However, both Jews and gentiles are guilty of violating it and are thus

In an essay, cut down on the length of time and space you devote to the history of the ethical theories. There are few marks available for biographical and historical details. Get quickly on to the evaluation.

See the section 'New Testament ethics' (pp. 64–68) for more material on the ethics of Jesus and Paul.

inclined towards unnatural behaviour: greed, envy, conflict. Jesus points out that the divorce law in the Torah is a concession to this sinful nature and not what God intended in the original order of creation (Matthew 19:3–8). Natural moral knowledge should make it clear that divorce is wrong.

Aquinas maintained that the universe was created by God, so that:
- everything has a design and a purpose
- this could be understood through an examination of the natural world and a study of the Bible
- humans were given reason and freedom — freedom to choose to follow the good, which is God's purpose for them

He called this **natural moral law** — the rational understanding and following of God's final purpose.

While laws of the land are not applicable to everyone, natural moral law is universal. For example, the owner of a plot of land cannot be prosecuted for trespassing on it, but he will face negative consequences for refusing to heed the weather when planting his field.

The principle of natural law depends on establishing the purpose of human life, which Aquinas maintains is to live, reproduce, learn, worship God and order society. All things must be in accordance with these purposes, to which man is naturally inclined. If man uses his God-given reason combined with experience, even unbelievers can make the right decisions about how to act.

When man chooses evil rather than good, he does so because he mistakenly thinks that it is good. However, it is a falling short of the good, and in so doing human beings fall short of God's best for them. Human actions should be directed towards God as the only possible end. This is the universal aim of all human beings, who desire communion with God. However, every individual also has a further purpose that is specific to their own skills and talents. Some goals are therefore applicable only to some, but the goal of a relationship with God in this life and beyond is open to all. Any action which takes human beings further along this path is good; any action which leads them further away is wrong.

Paul recognised that this was not always possible, 'since all have sinned and fallen short of the glory of God' (Romans 3:23).

Secondary precepts are rules directing people towards actions that uphold these primary purposes and away from actions that undermine them. Natural moral law identifies two subordinate principles under the primary principle:
(i) The dictates of reason flow logically from the primary principle so as to be self-evident, e.g. worship God, respect your parents and do not murder. If moral order is to be maintained, all humans must observe these dictates under all circumstances.
(ii) The dictates reached through a more complex process of reasoning are supported by human and divine law, since reason alone cannot deduce them from nature. These dictates contribute to public and private good, but may be omitted under certain conditions. For example, monogamy is good for social order, but polygamy is not incompatible with it in some societies.

Aquinas identifies four kinds of law: (i) the **eternal law**, as God's will and wisdom, revealed in (ii) **divine law**, given in scripture and through the church, made known in (iii) **natural law**, from which (iv) **human law** is derived.

The state is therefore not an artificial creation, but a natural extension of natural and divine law. Hence, as Paul writes in Romans 13:1: 'Let every person be subject to the governing authorities. For there is no authority except from God, and those that exist have been instituted by God.'

1.1 Evaluation

Natural law theory proposes a simple, universal guide for judging the moral value of human actions. The purposes that Aquinas proposes for human existence are common to all people.

However:

See the section 'Reproductive issues and sexual ethics' (pp. 167–72) for more on this area.

- Aquinas assumes that all men believe in God and have the desire to worship him.
- He assumes too that we seek to preserve humankind by reproduction. He agrees that this is not necessarily applicable to all individuals and thus allows for a celibate priesthood. But this exclusion must surely also apply to homosexuals, and yet natural law would argue that homosexuality is against divine law.
- The theory rests on being able to identify the specific function or purpose of an act. Although one purpose of sexual union is reproduction, there is no guarantee that this will always be the result. Natural law theory would therefore demand that every sexual union should at least have the **potential** for reproduction, thus eliminating not only homosexual relationships but also sterilisation and the use of contraception. It also raises the question of whether couples who know themselves to be infertile or are past the age of child-bearing should continue to enjoy a sexual relationship.
- Aquinas assumes that human beings are composed of parts that each have a distinct function and do not interrelate. **Vardy and Grosch** (in *The Puzzle of Ethics*, Fount, 1994, p. 61) suggest that this is a reflection of Aquinas's own time, in which each person had a place, be it knight, baron or serf, and accepted this as the natural order. It is reflected even in Victorian thinking: 'The rich man at his castle/The poor man at his gate/God made them high and lowly/And ordered their estate' (Mrs C. F. Alexander).
- Aquinas maintains that we have a single human reason and human nature, which should lead all humans beings to make the same moral choices. It makes no allowance for situationism, relativism or individualism.
- It is too optimistic to suppose we can extract moral rules from generalisations about human nature. At the most we might be able to say that God's creation offers certain indications of the divine purpose for man, and which we are advised to follow.
- Human nature is not unchanging, as Aquinas assumes. It could be argued that it is an evolving thing, continually in the process of change. Surely, at least, human nature is changed by the grace of God as exhibited in the life and death of Jesus, whereas Aquinas bases his theory on the nature of man at creation (Genesis 1–3).

Proportionalism works within the framework of natural law, but without insisting on preserving a static, inflexible and absolutist interpretation if a greater good

is served by laying it aside. It allows for ontic goods — qualities such as dignity, integrity and justice — which are in themselves non-moral, but are desirable to take into account when making a moral decision.

A proportionalist may argue that natural law fails to recognise the holistic nature of human beings because it makes a distinction between body and soul, rather than recognising that humans are a psycho-physical unity, combining reason and nature. The best we can aim for is a theology of compromise, which recognises that since we live in a fallen world (affected by original sin), the best that human beings can strive towards is a moral compromise, not moral perfection.

Proportionalism recognises that natural law must be allowed to change and that it is almost impossible to identify laws that are eternally valid without adaptation. However, it could be said to allow too much freedom to decide what is proportionately good and permits the rejection of authoritarian moral codes, such as those laid down by the Roman Catholic Church.

2 Conscience

> *Conscience is the inner aspect of the life of the individual where a sense of what is right and wrong is developed.*
>
> **David Atkinson and David Field (eds),** *New Dictionary of Christian Ethics and Pastoral Theology*, **IVP, 1995, p. 251**

Christians view the conscience as a guardian of their moral health; it prompts them to respond according to their moral code by stimulating feelings of guilt or well-being. Christian teaching on conscience is influenced by three biblical principles:

(i) Conscience is universal to all human beings, whether they believe or not, and is God-given (Romans 2:12ff.).

(ii) Man's conscience has been affected by the Fall (Genesis 3) and is thus corrupted and imperfect.

(iii) Jesus's death cleanses man's unhealthy conscience and enables man to retune his conscience with the divine will.

Man's conscience requires instruction, training, education and sensitising to the will of God so that it is stimulated to direct man in the way of God and away from evil. The more right choices man makes, the more his conscience will prompt him in this direction and into the likeness of God.

- Aquinas gave conscience the place of moral judge and the realm in which man exercised his reason in working out what was correct.
- **Kant** maintained it was the arena in which man turned an **is** into an **ought**: 'It is good to be kind to children: You ought to be kind to children.'
- **Freud** understood the conscience as the internalised super-ego which controlled and socialised man but was capable of doing great damage to his mental health, particularly when it was confused with religion.

See the section on atheism (pp. 109–14) for more on Freud's critique of religion.

- Sociologists would propose the view that the conscience is developed by upbringing, education and socialisation. It is therefore not inherent in human beings and does not owe its origin to God.

Different understandings of the conscience essentially distinguish between when it is God-given and discovered by man or acquired as part of the human developmental process.

Thinker	Nature of conscience and its role	Origin
Thomas Aquinas	Enables humans to act upon an innate (instinctive) knowledge of morality	Given by God, discovered by humans
Joseph Butler	Gives humans the ability to act as moral judges in ethical dilemmas; an intuitive divine voice that has absolute authority and that encourages humans to choose to act altruistically rather than selfishly	Given by God, discovered by humans
John Newman	A stern monitor of human behaviour, literally the voice of God	Given by God, discovered by humans
Sigmund Freud	A moral policeman developed from guilt learned at a pre-rational stage	Acquired and developmental
Jean Piaget	Developed as the result of cognitive development prior to the age of 10	Acquired and developmental
St Paul	Inherent in all humanity, corrupted by the Fall, redeemed by God through Jesus Christ	Given by God, discovered by humans
St Augustine	A blessing from God that enables humans to decide right from wrong and liberates them to follow the path to spiritual freedom	Given by God, discovered by humans
Erich Fromm	The means by which humans can take independent action and use reason to establish moral values rather than being constrained by authoritarian moral values	Given by God, discovered by humans, but needing to evolve
Lawrence Kohlberg	Built on Piaget's work, tracing the conscience through six stages of development	Acquired and developmental

Virtue ethics

The great Greek philosopher Aristotle was influenced in his thinking by his conviction that all things and all human beings have a purpose or function — a *telos*. A complete explanation of anything would include its final cause or purpose, which is to realise its potential and to fulfil its goal. For human beings, Aristotle maintained that the ultimate goal is human flourishing and developing those characteristics best suited to the realisation of a virtuous human being.

Aristotle's emphasis was not on what people do but on what type of person they are, although being a kind person, for example, is essentially accomplished by practising acts of kindness until the habit of being kind is firmly established in a person's character.

Natural law, conscience and virtue ethics

Aristotle maintained that the virtues are those qualities that lead to a good life — such as courage, compassion, honesty and justice. The person who aims to cultivate these qualities is maximising his or her potential for a happy life — a quality of happiness described as ***eudaimonia***, which involves being happy and living well. It is of intrinsic value, not a means to an end, and should be desired for its own sake, not only for individuals but also for the society of which they are members. For Aristotle, the right way to act is to follow the **golden mean**. This is a perfect balance between two extremes, such as cowardice and foolhardiness, which are both vices; in this example the golden mean is courage — a virtue that human beings are not born with but that they should cultivate in the way that they might cultivate good health or fitness. People should learn from good role models, train and exercise this virtue, until it becomes an automatic way of living and behaving and part of their character that they can exercise without conscious effort or will. In this way they will become courageous people.

In the twentieth century, Elizabeth Anscombe observed that ethical codes stressing moral absolutes and laws are anachronistic in a society that has effectively abandoned God, and she urged a return to a morality based on human flourishing. Similarly, Richard Taylor rejected a system of morality that is based on divine commands and that discourages people from achieving their potential.

> Taylor argued that the emphasis Christianity places on human equality does not encourage individuals to strive to be great, but rather advocates a self-negating humility.

Philippa Foot argued that although the virtues cannot guarantee happiness, they can go some way to achieving it, while Alastair MacIntyre noted that in moral dilemmas, naturalistic theories of ethics are of little value as they are time-consuming and overly complex. A virtue-based approach to ethics is more realistic and applicable to people's everyday situations.

Virtue ethics has appeal because it can be accommodated by both religious and secular morality. Jesus can be held up as a model of the virtuous person, in whom weakness becomes strength and death is transformed into life. It is a simple system based on universal well-being for the individual and the community, and in holding up models of virtuous people it does not set unrealistic goals. It is accessible by reference to the real world, and it attempts to link theoretical and practical approaches to ethics and maintains that theories of moral behaviour have objective value as part of developing a good life.

3.1 Weaknesses of virtue ethics

> The virtues valued by Aristotle are essentially masculine and frequently associated with the battlefield, such as bravery and honour. Conceivably, therefore, the approach could be seen as chauvinistic, giving little credit to more feminine virtues such as humility and empathy.

- Virtues have relative value in different cultures; while physical courage is considered highly valuable in some societies, intellectual prowess is rated more highly in others. Furthermore, not everyone values the concept of virtue as highly as Aristotle. Susan Wolf writes: 'I don't know whether there are moral saints. But if there are, I am glad that neither I nor those about whom I care most are among them' (cited in Ahluwalia, 2001).
- Aristotle's principle of the golden mean is not easy to apply to all virtues. While courage appears to be a mean between cowardice and foolhardiness,

is there a mean virtue of compassion or loyalty? Is it possible to take compassion to an extreme whereupon it becomes a vice?

- Aristotle gives no guidance in situations where virtues conflict and where we need rules to guide our actions. Because the emphasis of the approach is on being rather than doing, it can also be seen as a rather selfish theory, which places greater emphasis on personal development than the effect our actions have on others.

D Situation ethics

The material in this section is relevant to questions on:
- situation ethics specifically
- ethical theories in general
- solving dilemmas in practical ethics

See comment on p. 146 on evaluation.

1 *Background*

- **Joseph Fletcher**, an American Episcopalian moralist, coined the phrase 'situation ethics' in his 1966 book of the same title. In the spirit of the decade, he was responding to what he felt were the failures of legalism inherent in ethical systems that propose rules to govern human behaviour. At the same time, however, he rejected **antinomianism** — a total abandonment of rules and principles.
- Situation ethics are based on a single principle which enables man to enter every situation armed with the experience and precedents of past situations, but willing to lay them aside if the principle of love — *agape* — is better served by so doing.
- Fletcher's work was seized upon by **J. A. T. Robinson**, whose famous book *Honest to God* laid aside traditional values. It argued that if man operated within the spirit of love he would be prevented from performing immoral acts. No rules were therefore necessary because love would decide then and there the best course of action in the situation. Robinson wrote: 'Dr Fletcher's approach is the only ethic for "man come of age". To resist his approach in the name of religion will not stop it, it will only ensure the form it takes will be anti-Christian.'

Susan Howatch's novel *Scandalous Risks* (Harper Collins, 1990) is based on Robinson's thinking. It provides an excellent illustration of a situationist approach to an ethical dilemma.

Situationists take the example of Jesus in dialogue with the Pharisees as the model for their moral code. While the Pharisees elaborated the Torah to accommodate every possible situation, Jesus went back to first principles. When asked about divorce law, Jesus referred them back to creation (Mark 10:2–12), rather than the Law of Moses, which was designed to accommodate sinful human nature. The story of the woman caught in adultery shows Jesus adopting a classic situationist approach (John 8:2–11), demonstrating love, compassion and integrity, and revealing the weakness of using absolute laws as a means of

judging individual moral cases. Jesus touched lepers, mixed with the outcasts of society and was prepared to flout the letter of the Jewish law in ways that scandalised his opponent

2 Situationist principles

> *Whatever the pointers of the law to the demands of love, there can for the Christian be no 'packaged' moral judgements — for persons are more important even than 'standards'.*
>
> **Honest to God**, SCM, 1963, p. 66

Fletcher maintained that there was a middle way between legalism and antinomianism, and this lay in the application of *agape*, the love which Jesus commanded:

> *You shall love the Lord your God with all your heart, and with all your soul, and with all your strength and with all your mind; and your neighbour as yourself.*
>
> **Luke 10:27**
>
> *Greater love has no man than this, that a man lay down his life for his friends.*
>
> **John 15:13**
>
> *And this is his commandment, that we should believe in the name of his Son Jesus Christ and love one another, just as he has commanded us.*
>
> **1 John 3:23**

Fletcher maintained that love is the **principle of utility** — it is a principle that can be applied in every situation, and which will enable us to achieve the greatest good. He proposed four presumptions of situation ethics:

(i) **Pragmatism** demands that a proposed course of action should work, and that its success or failure should be judged according to the principle.

(ii) **Relativism** rejects absolutes such as 'never' or 'always'.

(iii) **Positivism** recognises that love is the most important criterion of all.

(iv) **Personalism** demands that people should be put first.

Fletcher carefully defined love: it was always good, and the only norm. Love and justice are the same, for love is justice distributed. It is not necessarily liking, and only the end of love justifies the means. It makes a decision there and then in each individual situation.

> Compare this with the principle of utility proposed by Jeremy Bentham: that which creates the **greatest happiness** for the greatest number is the right course of action.

William Barclay defined it as:

> ...*unconquerable good will; it is the determination to seek the other man's highest good, no matter what he does to you. Insult, injury, indifference — it does not matter; nothing but good will. It has been defined as purpose, not passion. It is an attitude to the other person.*
>
> ***Ethics in a Permissive Society*, Fontana, 1971, p. 75**

This kind of love is highly demanding or, as Barclay suggested, 'a highly intelligent thing'. It is not random, fatalistic, romantic love, which cannot be demanded. Rather, *agape* love is required of one human being to another, and demands that the whole personality be involved in a deliberate directing of the will, heart and mind.

Fletcher used real-life case studies to illustrate his theory. For example:

> A man with stomach cancer will die in 6 months without treatment that will cost $40 every 3 days. He must give up work and borrow on his life insurance to survive for 3 years if he follows this course of action. However, if he refuses treatment he will die with his life insurance valid, providing his family with $100,000 after his death. If he refuses treatment it is tantamount to suicide, but if he accepts it his family will be heavily in debt after his death. What should he do? What is the loving thing in terms of his intention and the consequences for others?

Or:

The example I see most often quoted in examination papers is the one about the German prisoner of war who becomes pregnant by one of her captors in order to be released and return to her family. This is fine, but why not offer something a bit different?

> When the Americans were attempting to decide whether to drop the atomic bomb on Hiroshima and Nagasaki the committee responsible for advising President Truman was divided. Some were totally opposed. Others felt that the Japanese should be warned about the bomb's potential by dropping it first on an uninhabited part of the country. Others still felt that the dropping of the bomb was the only way to ensure the end of the war. In the event the bomb was dropped on civilian and military targets. Was this right?

3 Strengths of situationism

- Individual cases are judged on their own merits, irrespective of what has been done in similar situations in the past.
- Individuals are not subject to rules which bind them. Nothing is intrinsically wrong or right except the principle of love.
- Love seeks the well-being of others, even if the course of action is not one of preference.
- It is modelled on the teaching of Jesus, and so could be considered a truly Christian ethic.

See the section 'New Testament ethics' (pp. 64–68) for more material on the ethics of Jesus.

4 Weaknesses of situationism

Professor Graham Dunstan wrote of Fletcher's theory: 'It is possible, though not easy, to forgive Professor Fletcher for writing this book, for he is is a generous and loveable man. It is harder to forgive the SCM Press for publishing it.'

- Despite Fletcher's attempt to be anti-legalistic, the application of one principle only makes it a legalistic approach in itself. To say no rules apply and yet also to say that the only rule is love offers something of a contradiction.
- The cases on which situation ethics are based are exceptional ones, in which general rules do not apply. Most ethical dilemmas offer an obvious course of action without our having to resort to situationism.
- The theory is **teleological**, i.e. dependent on the calculation of consequences. It is impossible to be unfailingly accurate in making such a calculation.
- The theory justifies adultery, murder and even genocide in the interests of love. Surely Fletcher is guilty of calling 'good' what is in reality evil.
- Fletcher is overly optimistic about the capacity of human beings to make morally correct choices and not to be influenced by personal preferences. Humans need the guidelines offered by rules to avoid moral chaos.
- Law and love are seen as mutually exclusive; Paul writes that love is the fulfilling of the law (Romans 13:10).

William Barclay outlined a carefully considered critique of the theory in his Baird Lectures in 1971, subsequently developed in *Ethics in a Permissive Society* (1971). Barclay's lectures were an attempt to examine the nature of Christian ethics in the last quarter of the twentieth century, aware of the drastic challenge to Christian ethics that had been posed over the previous 30 years:

> *Thirty years ago no one ever really questioned the Christian ethic... No one ever doubted that divorce was disgraceful; that illegitimate babies were a disaster; that chastity was a good thing.*

E Ethical language

1 Meta-ethics

Before we can begin to establish what constitutes good or bad moral or ethical behaviour, we need to consider whether we can define what morality *is*. The branch of moral philosophy concerned with this issue is **meta-ethics**, which examines the issue of what we mean when we say that a thing or an action is good, bad, right, wrong, moral or immoral.

The word 'good' has many meanings and most of them are not used in a moral context.

S. A. Burns identifies 36 meanings of the word 'good' but observes that only one is open to philosophical disagreement: 'Of moral excellence; upright'. Burns also identifies a further 24 meanings of the word 'right'. Some are distinct and belong to a peculiar, non-moral context. Again, only one is open to philosophical disagreement: 'Conforming with or conformable to morality. That which is just, morally good'.

I may say that a computer is 'good' because it fulfils the task that it was purchased to fulfil, but this does not ascribe moral status to it, because a computer is not a moral agent. Similarly, we use the word 'ought' in different contexts: 'Teachers ought to be kind to their students' carries quite different implications from 'You ought to take an umbrella with you'. The first statement is prescribing a particular mode of behaviour, which is based on our opinion of how teachers ought to behave and so is a moral statement, while the second recommends a course of action on the basis of certain objective facts.

If a moral opinion is independent of external facts, it essentially concerns how we feel about an ethical issue and is therefore subjective. An objective fact, however, is related to how things actually are in the real world and is the same for everyone. If moral values are objective, then they are similarly true for everyone. Whether morality deals in facts or opinions is a crucial issue for ethical debate, and the key to this is whether we can place goodness in an objective category since it is open to so many different interpretations.

If morality is objective, then it is **cognitive**. Cognitive language deals with making propositions about things that can be known and so can be held to be true or false. If it is subjective, then it is **non-cognitive** — it deals with matters that are not simply resolved by establishing if they are true or false.

2 The naturalistic fallacy

A key problem in attempting to reach a definition of morality is commonly referred to as the **'is–ought gap'**, or the naturalistic fallacy. Naturalistic theories of ethics attempt to define good in terms of something that can be identified in the world or in human nature — for example, claiming that what is natural,

David Hume observed that there is nothing in a descriptive statement that allows us to proceed from what people *actually* do (a factual statement) to making a rule about what people *ought* to do (a value judgement). For example, it would be unfair to move from a statement of fact that women are better parents (if, say, an experiment produced that result) to saying that therefore men ought not to be single parents.

John Searle argued, however, that it is possible to derive an 'ought' from an 'is' in the case of promising. If I say that 'I promise to…', I take on the obligation of fulfilling that promise; the fact of speaking the words leads me to carrying out my obligation to do so.

or what makes us happy, fit or healthy, is good. If we adopt this approach, we are effectively turning an 'is' into an 'ought'.

G. E. Moore argued that it is not acceptable to identify morality with any other concept, such as happiness, because any attempt to do so will not be able to accommodate the full measure of the concept and so will always be inadequate. Most importantly, if we say that something *is* the case, we are making a descriptive statement of how things actually are, while a normative or prescriptive statement says that something *ought* to be desired or done.

All attempts to move from an 'ought' to an 'is' face the same problem — they attempt to describe a situation that logically dictates what an individual is then obliged to do. However, there is no reason why we should not ask why we ought to do this.

In ethical terms, to say that something is good, and therefore prescribe it as a moral action that we are obliged to perform, is unconvincing to many. Why should we seek the happiness of the greatest number, do our duty, or pursue the virtues? These may be good in some circumstances, or even most, but that alone is not sufficient to make them a matter of moral obligation.

Moore's position is often called the **Open Question Argument**. A statement such as 'Anything that brings happiness is good' leads to the question 'Is it good that X leads to happiness?' This is an open question because the answer is maybe yes, maybe no, hence it does not increase our moral knowledge about X or about happiness. Put another way, we could say 'Good is that which maximises the happiness of the greatest number', but if we then ask the question 'Is it good to maximise the greatest happiness of the greatest number?' the same problem arises — sometimes it is, and sometimes it isn't.

Intuitionism

> *It may be true that all things which are good are also something else, just as it is true that all things which are yellow produce a certain kind of vibration in the light. And it is a fact, that Ethics aims at discovering what are those other properties belonging to all things which are good. But far too many philosophers have thought that when they named those other properties they were actually defining good; that these properties, in fact, were simply not 'other', but absolutely and entirely the same with goodness.*
>
> **G. E. Moore, *Principia Ethica*, CUP, 1993**

Proponents of intuitionism argue that ethical terms cannot be defined, since the properties ascribed to them, such as 'good' or 'ought', can also be defined in non-ethical terms. G. E. Moore argued, 'If I am asked "What is good?", my answer is that "good is good", and that is the end of the matter.'

In addition to categorising 'good' as indefinable, Moore also argued that it is a non-natural property, since two objects that are qualitatively identical cannot have different values. There cannot be two yellow shirts that are identical in every way (same shade of yellow, made at the same factory, the same brand name, the same style), but one is good and the other not good.

In the eighteenth century, David Hume argued that we have a motivation for acting in certain ways, although intuitionists may respond to this with the suggestion that if we feel motivated towards a particular action, it is because we have an innate desire to do it that goes beyond reason.

3.1 Strengths of intuitionism

- Intuitionism allows for objective moral values to be identified; it is not a question of dismissing the possibility of any moral facts.
- Intuitionism does not propose a subjective or emotive approach to ethics, but it does avoid the problems of identifying ethics with a natural property.
- While we might recognise the wrongness of some actions, it is difficult to specify exactly why they are wrong; instead, we interpret it through a moral sense rather than a list of moral definitions. We identify a moral sense in the same way was we might identify an aesthetic sense in art or literature.
- Intuitionism allows for moral duties and obligations, satisfying a moral absolutist, and may be associated with idea of conscience as a moral guide.
- The intuitionist points to the existence of a considerable common consensus on moral issues, such as the value of human life, as evidence of a common intuition of morality.

3.2 Problems with intuitionism

- People who intuit and those who use reason may reach different conclusions, and there is no obvious way to resolve their differences.
- How can we be sure that our intuitions are correct? Is it a gut feeling? Is it God's direction? How reliable is experience as a guide?
- Intuition may be considered to be a meaningless concept since it is non-verifiable.

4 *Emotivism*

Alastair MacIntyre defined emotivism as:

> ...*the doctrine that all evaluative judgements, and, more specifically, all moral judgements, are nothing but expressions of preference, expressions of attitude or feeling.*

The emotive theory of ethics stems from the work of the logical positivists, who sought to do away with all metaphysical language, which they deemed to be beyond empirical verification and thereby meaningless. Thus, at its extreme, emotivism argues that if we make a claim such as 'Abortion is wrong', we are not making a value judgement based on an objective point of reference, but rather we are simply saying 'I don't like abortion'. A. J. Ayer (1936) reduced all moral talk to an expression of the speaker's feelings and maintained that to say, for example, 'Abortion (or murder) is wrong' is making a kind of primitive noise. Ethical claims are not designed to make factual statements but to invoke certain emotional responses in the hearer, and so what they mean is less important than what they accomplish.

In his famous book *Language, Truth and Logic* (Penguin, 1936), A. J. Ayer declared:

> *Exhortations to moral virtue are not propositions at all, but ejaculations or commands which are designed to provoke the reader to action of a certain sort. Accordingly, they do not belong to any branch of philosophy or science… A strictly philosophical treatise on ethics should therefore make no ethical pronouncements. But it should, by giving an analysis of ethical terms, show what is the category to which all such pronouncements belong.*

C. L. Stevenson argues that ethical judgements express the speaker's attitude and seek to evoke a similar attitude in the audience, but he allows that our attitudes are based on beliefs that provide reasonable grounds for holding them. We may know that a certain course of action will bring about particular results and thus argue in its favour. Nevertheless, even our most fundamental attitudes may not be rooted in any particular beliefs, in which case we cannot reason about them.

Alastair MacIntyre observes:

> *Emotivism rests upon a claim that every attempt, whether past or present, to provide a rational justification for an objective morality has in fact failed.*
>
> **Alistair MacIntyre, *After Virtue*, Duckworth, 1997**

Emotivism rejects absolutism because absolutism is an impossible position to hold — there are no facts, empirical or metaphysical, that an ethical statement can assert. The fallacy that emotivism attempts to expose, however, is that ethical statements are treated as if they assert facts. 'Tell the truth' is overtly a command to be truthful based on a preference for truth telling, and covertly a claim that 'It is a fact that truthfulness is morally right'. For the emotivist, all we can do is recognise the power to persuade that lies behind moral statements, but we should not be deceived into thinking they have factual value.

Alastair MacIntyre argues that emotivism has become:

> *…embodied in our culture. Of course, in saying this I am … contending that … what was once morality has to some large degree disappeared — and that this marks a degeneration, a grave cultural loss.*

4.1 Problems with emotivism

- Ethical statements are not usually judged according to the response of the listener but on the claims themselves. 'Abortion is wrong' makes a claim that can be discussed and evaluated. Its power does not simply lie in how others respond to it.

As part of the linguistic philosophy of the logical positivists, Ayer's approach to ethical language may be largely discredited, since it proposed a method of analysing the meaningfulness of language which it was itself unable to satisfy.

- If ethical claims were contingent on emotions, they would change as emotions changed. Neither could they be universal claims, since the emotions of different speakers would vary.
- Even when moral statements are carried by a weight of public emotion, that does not make them the reason that they are adopted and it does not make them right.
- Emotivism effectively prescribes complete freedom of action on the basis that everyone's opinion is equally valid, and hence everyone is free to do what they choose, irrespective of the opinion of others.
- How can we judge between two people's moral opinions? What criteria are there — if any — for judging the relative merits of a moral viewpoint?
- Emotions can unite people in a common moral bond, but they can also isolate individuals and groups.
- The emotional force with which a moral view is expressed is no recommendation of its value.

F Abortion

The material in this section is relevant to questions on:
- abortion specifically
- the sanctity of life
- biblical ethics
- applying ethical theory to practical ethical dilemmas
- rights and freedoms in medical ethics and reproduction

1 Definitions and legalities

Therapeutic or **procured abortion** involves evacuating the uterus of the foetus before the baby has been carried to full term. It is distinguished from a **miscarriage** or a **spontaneous abortion**, when the foetus is expelled naturally. Some pregnancies end in miscarriage without the woman even knowing that she is pregnant. If the womb is too weak to carry the child to full term, or if the foetus itself is not viable, the body will protect itself against further harm. Therapeutic abortion may involve the use of drugs or surgery, and some contraceptive devices such as the IUD and the drug RU486 act as aborto-facients. Although Roman Catholic teaching considers all unnatural contraceptives and aborto-facients as wrong, in many countries abortion has been legalised under certain circumstances.

- **Time-scale:** usually up to 28 weeks in the UK, but India allows abortion up to 40 weeks. Applications are regularly made to reduce the legal time limit for abortion.
- **Circumstances:** if the woman, or her existing children, will suffer physically, psychologically or economically from the birth of the child, or if the baby itself is likely to be born handicapped, deformed or congenitally ill. In this way the suffering of the family, carers and the baby itself is prevented by the abortion.

Limit factual
information and
make sure that the
bulk of your essay is
concerned with an
evaluation of the
religious and ethical
dilemmas raised by
abortion.

- **Recommendation** for abortion in the UK must be provided by two doctors. Hence abortion is not illegal, but those carrying out abortions must comply with these regulations under the current Abortion Law. Those opposed to abortion claim that these provisions effectively allow for abortion on demand, and few doctors refuse to carry out an abortion.

2 Ethical and religious dilemmas

2.1 When does life begin?

The decision as to when life begins will have serious implications for the ethics of abortion and whether it can be considered the termination of human life, or even murder. Life may be considered to have begun at one of five points in the development of the foetus:

(i)   **Fertilisation:** the extreme conservative view. Sperm and egg unite and the full genetic potential of the foetus is established. At this point over 40% of fertilised eggs are lost naturally.

(ii) **Implantation:** the fertilised egg is implanted onto the wall of the womb.

(iii) **Quickening:** when the child moves in the womb. Traditionally this was associated with **ensoulment** — when the soul entered the body of the foetus. Aquinas claimed that this was at 40 days for a male foetus and 90 days for a female!

(iv) **Viability:** the point at which the foetus can be considered independent of the mother for the purposes of medical care.

(v)   **Birth:** the extreme liberal view. When genuine independent existence can be established.

2.2 The sanctity of life

Accurate biblical
references are essential
to support this point.
Simply to say 'Life
is sacred because
it is created by God'
is inadequate.

The principle of the sanctity of life is based on the teaching of Genesis 2:7: 'Then the Lord God formed man of dust from the ground, and breathed into his nostrils the breath of life, and man became a living being.' Psalm 139:13ff. also supports the view that God is responsible for the existence of all human life: 'For thou didst form my inward parts, thou didst knit me together in my mother's womb. I praise thee, for I am fearfully and wonderfully made.' The prophet Jeremiah was told by God: 'Before I formed you in the womb I knew you, and before you were born I consecrated you' (Jeremiah 1:5). The New Testament continues to support the principle, e.g. in Acts 17:25 Paul declares: 'He himself gives to all men life and breath and everything.'

If life is **sacred** (set apart for God's purposes) and created by him, then by definition he must be the one who has control over its end as well as its beginning. Once a life has been set in motion by God it can only be ended by him. Thus a miscarriage represents a complete life brought to an end by God within his own timing and purpose, but a procured abortion represents a challenge to God's divine will. The principle maintains that outside certain circumstances (in themselves arguable) innocent human beings have the right not to be deliberately killed. Life is precious to God, and while it is not necessary to preserve it **at all costs** (e.g. prohibitively expensive

and ultimately futile medical care), it must not be disposable for utilitarian reasons.

2.3 Whose rights anyway?

This is the primary area of debate, which is as applicable to non-believers as it is to believers. In your essay you should spend some time on this issue and not get bogged down in biblical debates.

There are arguably many parties who we might claim have rights in the abortion issue: the foetus, the mother, the father, the law, the church and the medical profession.

2.3a The mother's rights

During pregnancy the mother performs a unique function — the provision of the appropriate conditions in which the child can form, develop and from which it is born. She is a host to the foetus, whose survival depends on her continued willingness to be a host.

> Judith Jarvis Thompson argues the case of the famous violinist (in 'A Defence of Abortion', *Philosophy and Public Affairs*, Vol. 1, No. 1, 1971). If a woman were to wake to find that a famous violinist whose kidneys had failed had been plugged into her blood supply and would continue to be so for 9 months, she would be under no moral obligation to agree. If she did agree, it would not be out of moral compulsion but out of compassion. Thompson argues that pregnancy is an analogous situation, and the woman should be able to choose whether or not to carry the child to full term without the moral obligation to do so.

If the mother's life is considered to be of greater value than that of the foetus, then she clearly must have considerable rights. She may exercise her right to continue that life without danger to physical or mental health. The **doctrine of double effect** may come into play here, allowing even opponents of abortion to grant that the woman's life has value: an abortion in this case is to save the life of the mother, and the loss of the foetus is a secondary, not primary, effect and is thus morally permissible.

The woman may feel equally justified in asserting other rights: the right to make the choice whether to bear a child or not; the right to pursue educational or career goals without the possible hindrances of having a child to care for. However, this may not be considered as justifiable since even though the woman's right to life may be greater than that of the foetus, it is not to say that her right to live her life as she chooses is just as great.

2.3b The rights of the foetus

Defenders of the rights of the foetus may claim that even if the mother does not feel able to carry the child to full term and to provide its care thereafter, it is not justifiable to deprive it of life. Once conception has taken place, the foetus has a right to life which must be honoured, even if the care of the child is handed over to others after birth. This is just as important if the child is handicapped or ill. It may be that the child will live a life of pain and suffering, but it is impossible to make an accurate a priori judgement: a child born with every

conceivable advantage may still suffer greatly in later life. The decision to abort a deformed or sick foetus implies a particular view of human worth: life is not worthwhile in the case of disability. This sets dangerous precedents about the right to life of those who do not conform to society's standard of so-called normality.

G Euthanasia

This is a topic that can be spoiled by overly emotional or subjective answers. Make sure you follow a clear structure and provide plenty of evidence for your argument.

The material in this section is relevant to questions on:
- euthanasia specifically
- the sanctity of life
- biblical ethics
- applying ethical theory to practical ethical dilemmas
- rights and freedoms in medical ethics

1 Definitions and legalities

> *Euthanasia is the intentional killing by act or omission, of one whose life is deemed not worth living.*
>
> **David Atkinson and David Field (eds),** *New Dictionary of Christian Ethics and Pastoral Theology***, IVP, 1995, p. 357**

The word 'euthanasia', based on the Greek terms *eu* and *thanatos*, is defined in the Oxford English Dictionary as referring to a good or happy death, and in its current sense it is used to refer to the deliberate bringing about of such a death, often described as 'mercy killing'. It is seen to be a key issue in modern medical ethics, although the practice of euthanasia was endemic in the ancient world. In recent years sympathy towards euthanasia has risen, especially in the Netherlands, described in the *New Dictionary of Christian Ethics and Pastoral Theology* as 'one of the most striking evidences of the development of the post-Christian society in contemporary Europe'. The modern preoccupation with pain-free existence had led to an increasing lobby for the legalisation of euthanasia. On the other hand, those who claim that pain is part of life, and should not be avoided at all costs, will find the euthanasia lobby objectionable.

There are various types of euthanasia:
- **Active euthanasia:** the result of positive action (e.g. lethal injection) on the part of a carer.
- **Passive euthanasia:** the omission or termination of treatment which is prolonging the patient's life.
- **Voluntary euthanasia:** carried out at the express wish of the patient.

- **Involuntary euthanasia:** carried out without the permission of the patient, which may or may not be because they are not capable of expressing a view.
- **Assisted suicide:** the provision of means and/or opportunity whereby a patient may terminate his or her life.

2 *Ethical and religious dilemmas*

2.1 In support of euthanasia

2.1a Freedom from pain

The assumption that death is preceded by serious pain which can only be controlled to a limited extent by drugs gives rise to considerable support for euthanasia.

2.1b Death with dignity

Many fear a prolonged death, drawn out by the application of medical technology with the express purpose of delaying death as long as possible. During this time the patient may become increasingly dependent on others, and unable to control bodily and mental functions. An earlier death is frequently considered more desirable.

> *In a certain state it is indecent to live longer. To go on vegetating in cowardly dependence on physicians and machinations, after the meaning of life, the right to life, has been lost, that ought to prompt a profound contempt in society.... I want to die proudly when it is no longer possible to live proudly.*
>
> **Friedrich Nietzsche, in John Wyatt, *Matters of Life and Death*, IVP, 1998, p. 177**

2.1c Social fears and pressures

The breakdown of traditional family structures, which provided care for ill and elderly people, has led to an increasing fear of the old and sick being abandoned to a faceless and ill-equipped health service, or left alone to die. Medical advances too may encourage a philosophy in favour of euthanasia, as expensive, glamorous life-extending — but ultimately futile — treatments are promoted way above palliative care. Where there is a desperate need for organs for transplantation, death may be encouraged while the organs are still healthy enough to be of use to others. Finally, a fear of dementia and the effects of Alzheimer's disease may encourage thoughts of euthanasia in the elderly.

2.2 Against euthanasia

2.2a The sanctity of life

The principle of the sanctity of life is based on the teaching of Genesis 2:7: 'Then the Lord God formed man of dust from the ground, and breathed into his nostrils the breath of life, and man became a living being.' Psalm 139:13ff. also supports the view that God is responsible for the existence of all human life: 'For thou didst form my inward parts, thou didst knit me together in my

Limit factual information and make sure that the bulk of your essay is concerned with an evaluation of the religious and ethical dilemmas raised by euthanasia.

mother's womb. I praise thee, for I am fearfully and wonderfully made.' The prophet Jeremiah was told by God: 'Before I formed you in the womb I knew you, and before you were born I consecrated you' (Jeremiah 1:5). The New Testament continues to support the principle, for example in Acts 17:25 Paul declares: 'He himself gives to all men life and breath and everything.'

If life is sacred (set apart for God's purposes) and created by him, then by definition he must be the one who has control over its end as well as its beginning. Once a life has been set in motion by God it can only be ended by him. Thus an illness which ends in natural death represents a complete life, brought to an end by God within his own timing and purpose, whereas euthanasia represents a challenge to God's divine will. The principle maintains that outside certain circumstances (in themselves arguable) innocent human beings have the right not to be deliberately killed (i.e. involuntary euthanasia), nor should they seek to end their life (i.e. voluntary euthanasia). Life is precious to God, and while it is not necessary to preserve it **at all costs** (e.g. prohibitively expensive and ultimately futile medical care), it must not be disposable for utilitarian reasons — to save money, or to avoid inconvenience to others.

Ultimately, Christians believe that this life is lived from the perspective of the next, and decisions made about it should be made in the context of man's relationship with God. The influential evangelical Joni Eareckson Tada, herself a quadriplegic, writes:

> *God knows you're heading for a hereafter. For those who, apart from Him, prematurely end their lives hoping to find relief there will only be a hereafter of vast and utter disappointment. For those who believe in Jesus, the dying process becomes the most significant passage of their lives.*
>
> **Joni Eareckson Tada, When is it Right to Die?,**
> **Marshall Pickering, 1992, p. 120**

> In an exam essay it doesn't really matter which side you come down in favour of when dealing with issues such as euthanasia or abortion. You should, however, consider both sides of the debate in a thoughtful and academic way and shouldn't use the essay as an opportunity to preach, lecture or condemn.

2.2b Errors and misunderstandings

- Even patients in a persistent vegetative state have been known to recover. Recovery from brain injury takes place at different rates, and it is only after a period of 12 months that it is diagnosed as persistent, i.e. permanent. There are, however, well-documented cases of recovery after this time, although as every month goes by the likelihood of recovery is diminished.
- All illnesses diagnosed as terminal will not necessarily end in death. Cases of patients given a terminal prognosis, only to live significantly longer than anticipated or to recover entirely, are by no means rare. For believers there is always the possibility of God's divine intervention, either through the channels of medicine or through a miraculous healing. Believers will be confident to leave their healing, or otherwise, in God's hands.
- The development of effective palliative care means that it is certainly not the case that all terminal patients will face a painful, undignified death. The work of the hospice movement exists to care for terminal patients and to educate

the public and the medical profession in alternatives to the extremes of a painful death or euthanasia. At present, however, access to hospice care is limited and expensive, and palliative care does not attract significant numbers of healthcare professionals.

- Death is not necessarily an evil. We live in an age in which we are so protected from the reality of frequent, apparently premature death that we come to see it as an outrage. In response we tend to have a paradoxical relationship with death: we pursue treatments as far as medical care can allow, and yet we seek to avoid a long-drawn-out dying process:

> *Human life span is limited, not just as a curse, but out of God's grace.... Even though human death is an evil to be fought against, and a reality which can never be sought intentionally, it may also at times be accepted, even welcomed, as a sign of God's mercy.*
>
> John Wyatt, *Matters of Life and Death*, p. 195

- If human beings were able to feel more comfortable about death and dying, seeing each life as complete and perfect in God's sight, then the conflict between those who support euthanasia and those who oppose it may be resolved.

- **Living wills** — instructions left by individuals regarding future healthcare — may be intended to guard against the resuscitation of a patient who will be seriously brain damaged or otherwise incapacitated. However, such documents rarely have legal status and are made in times of health. At the time when they are applied, the patient may hold different views but be unable to express them.

- Why not legalise euthanasia? In 1993 the House of Lords unanimously rejected any change in the law to permit euthanasia, arguing: 'It would be next to impossible to ensure that all acts of euthanasia were truly voluntary and that any liberalisation of the law was not abused.'

> *I once cornered Dr J. L. Packer, a prominent evangelical theologian, and asked him this question: 'What would you suggest to a severely handicapped man with cerebral palsy who was totally bedridden, non-verbal, and relegated to a back bedroom in a nursing home? No one visits him and no nurse takes time to benefit from his good attitude. What can that handi-capped man do?' ...Dr Packer replied, 'A man like that can worship and glorify God'.*
>
> Joni Eareckson Tada, *When Is It Right To Die?*,
> Marshall Pickering, 1992, p. 147

H Reproductive issues and sexual ethics

These are all topics that could be spoiled by overly emotional or subjective answers. Make sure you follow a clear structure and provide plenty of evidence for your arguments.

The material in this section is relevant to questions on:

- conception and contraception
- embryo experimentation and eugenics
- homosexuality
- pornography
- premarital and extramarital sexual relationships

1 *Conception and contraception*

The process of conception has gone beyond human control since the emergence of technologies which permit fertility treatment, IVF, egg and sperm donation, surrogacy, and the freezing of embryos. There are several ethical and religious matters to be considered.

1.1 The sanctity of life

The principle of the sanctity of life is based on the teaching of Genesis 2:7: 'Then the Lord God formed man of dust from the ground, and breathed into his nostrils the breath of life, and man became a living being.' Psalm 139:13ff. also supports the view that God is responsible for the existence of all human life: 'For thou didst form my inward parts, thou didst knit me together in my mother's womb. I praise thee, for I am fearfully and wonderfully made.' The prophet Jeremiah was told by God: 'Before I formed you in the womb I knew you, and before you were born I consecrated you' (Jeremiah 1:5). The New Testament continues to support the principle, for example in Acts 17:25 Paul declares: 'He himself gives to all men life and breath and everything.'

All attempts by human beings to involve themselves in the 'creation' of life must be carefully scrutinised. Humans are open to the corruption of techniques which may be good in themselves, but which in their hands can be employed for evil ends. Ultimately, the power to give or to withhold life belongs to God. Furthermore, the practice of freezing eggs and embryos which are later destroyed is seen by some as tantamount to the destruction of human life.

1.2 The pain of infertility

While some religious believers may object to the use of medical technology and funds to increase fertility, it is important to remember that those who are infertile often suffer great psychological and emotional pain. It is in the spirit of Christian compassion to minister to them — not necessarily only to help them come to terms with infertility but, where appropriate, to find ways of overcoming it.

1.3 'Designer babies'

For most would-be parents there is no question of taking the opportunity to create a 'perfect' baby, but reproductive technologies have created the potential to pursue the quest for the so-called 'designer baby'. However, such technologies may mean embryos can be screened for congenital disorders, so eradicating inherited conditions from the family tree. Is this meddling in God's will for the child?

1.4 Relationships

If the primary purpose of the sexual relationship within marriage is reproduction, then there may be much to say for reproductive technology. However, if the couple are unable to have a child by natural means, it may equally be the case that they are not intended by natural and divine intention to have a child. Persistent, unsuccessful attempts at conception put immense strain on relationships. The option of surrogacy presents difficult questions about the role of the surrogate — even without sexual intercourse with the father, has she become a second wife? Is there an implied unfaithfulness? What about the rights of the surrogate before and after birth?

1.5 Contraception

Whereas many people pursue their 'right' to conceive, just as many pursue their 'right' not to conceive. The church has traditionally been more concerned with contraception, which for the Catholic Church is still traditionally forbidden (except by natural means). According to natural law thinking, every act of sexual intercourse must be open to the possibility of procreation. Augustine maintained that contraception introduced moral corruption into the marital relationship. However, many Christian couples practise contraception in order to plan the timing of their family responsibly. Some methods of contraception may be considered less viable than others: the IUD acts as an aborto-facient, and the 'morning-after pill' prevents implantation but not fertilisation. Remaining childless can be seen by some as a calling, freeing the couple for religious or social service in other ways. Some Christian thinkers, however, may claim that while contraception in itself is not an evil, a Christian couple should not entirely eliminate the possibility of bearing children at some point in their marriage.

> Make sure that the bulk of your essay is concerned with an evaluation of the religious and ethical dilemmas raised by eugenics and related issues.

2 Eugenics and embryo experimentation

Experimentation with embryos has the potential to allow many future developments in fertility treatments, the control of congenital disease, and the genetic screening for predisposition to illnesses such as cancer and heart disease. In themselves these developments may be seen as good. However, there are several points that must be taken into consideration.

2.1 Selection of characteristics

Conceivably, an embryo can be manipulated before implantation in order to encourage, if not determine, the development of certain characteristics such as intelligence, physical features, sexuality and gender. In principle this stands in opposition to the Christian viewpoint (see the note about Psalm 139:13ff. earlier in this section). Such selection could also encourage the notion that certain characteristics are more desirable than others, and in societies where males are considered more economically viable than females, a dramatic decrease in the number of female babies could lead to serious problems for future generations. A distinction can be made between positive and negative selection, however. Is it more acceptable to screen out negative characteristics than to screen in positive ones? In either case it may be argued that human beings are meddling in matters which are not their responsibility.

2.2 Discarding of unused embryos

Eggs and sperm can be fused in the laboratory to enable infertile couples to achieve pregnancies by returning *in vitro* conceptions to the womb. Many more embryos may be created than are needed, however, and some religious believers maintain that the discarding of unused embryos is unacceptable. Aborted embryos are often used in experimentation, raising other important ethical issues: since the embryo has already been aborted, is it at least being used to do some good, or does it merely condone the practice of abortion?

2.3 The image of God

Genesis 1:27 claims that man was made in the image of God. It is mankind's relationship with God that sets it apart from the rest of creation, and it could be argued that the embryo is therefore special. Should we seek to know as much about the process of life and death that embryo experimentation permits us? Perhaps some element of mystery should be allowed to remain.

3 Homosexuality

This is an area of huge debate for religious believers, and one over which they are deeply divided.

See comment on p. 165.

There are many examples of websites that reveal extreme conservative Christian opposition to homosexuality, e.g. the Westboro Baptist Church runs www.godhatesfags.com.

3.1 Opposition to homosexuality

- Genesis 2:24 advocates that the only divinely ordained sexual relationship is between two consenting partners of the opposite sex. Woman is described as being created specifically and specially as a partner for man — 'a helper fit for him' (Genesis 2:18). The relationship is clearly open to the possibility of procreation: they are instructed to 'be fruitful and multiply' (Genesis 1:28).
- Leviticus 20:13 warns against homosexual practices, which carry the death penalty, and the story of Lot and the angelic visitors suggests that it is an even more serious sin than heterosexual rape (Genesis 19). Any Israelites who 'lie

with a man as with a woman' (Leviticus 18:22) will be 'vomited out of the land' (18:28). In Judges 19:22–30 a concubine is murdered in order to avoid the worse sin — 'this vile thing' — of homosexual rape.

- In the New Testament Paul continues this condemnation: 'Do not be deceived; neither the immoral ... nor sexual perverts ... will inherit the Kingdom of God' (1 Corinthians 6:9–10). He suggests that homosexuality was a result of the Fall, after which 'men ... gave up natural relations with women' (Romans 1:27).
- Contemporary Christian counselling, especially that which adopts an evangelical perspective, often views homosexuality not as an illness or a natural condition, but as a sin which can only be dealt with through repentance, forgiveness, prayer and spiritual healing. Rejection of the homosexual would not be considered useful in this process, however.

3.2 Responses

- It is not clear whether the sin of Sodom was homosexuality or inhospitality. The Hebrew verb *yada* — 'to know' — may allude to sexual knowledge, but could simply mean 'to become acquainted'.
- Condemnation of homosexual practices in the Bible may be effectively a condemnation of pagan practices in the Canaanite world in which Israel dwelt.
- Paul admits that some of his teaching is 'no command of the Lord, but I give my opinion as one who by the Lord's mercy is trustworthy' (1 Corinthians 7:25). Paul does not derive his teaching on homosexuality directly from Jesus, and so it may be culturally relative.
- Homosexuality may be an inherited or genetic trait over which we have no control. It would be as pointless to condemn someone for homosexuality as to condemn them for having blue eyes.
- Canon Anthony Harvey argued that 'Christian teaching should be revised in this area as it has been in other areas such as the acceptance of slavery and the subordination of woman to men' ('Church Must Defend Gay Rights', *The Times*, 21 June 1994).
- The Church of England acknowledges the need to respect the decision of those 'who are conscientiously convinced that they have more hope of growing in love for God and neighbour with the help of a loving and faithful homophile partnership, in intention lifelong, where mutual self-giving includes the expression of their attachment' (*What the Churches Say*, 2nd edn, CEM, 1995).

Homosexuality is a human rights issue, and for many years it was felt that gay and lesbian marriage should be permitted in the same way as heterosexual marriage. To this end, the government passed the Civil Partnership Act 2004, which became law in December 2005, allowing same-sex couples to register their partnership legally in a civil ceremony. Civil partnerships give to the partners the same legal rights as married couples over such matters as property, inheritance tax and pension benefits. In the same way that a married couple must seek a divorce if the marriage breaks down, so the partners in a civil partnership must go through a formal court action to dissolve their union. However, despite such public moves to win acceptance for homosexual couples,

there are still problems and many people hold very strongly to the view that homosexuality is immoral. Others are openly hostile, as attacks on homosexual individuals and organisations demonstrate.

4 Pornography

This is not an issue that is specifically discussed in many exam answers. Consider it a useful addition to your bank of material about sexual attitudes and relationships.
It can also be used as a coursework topic.

- Religious believers are universally opposed to pornography.
- Pornography is associated with violence. Ted Bundy, the American serial killer, admitted in an interview with James Dobson of the organisation 'Focus on the Family' that pornography had had a decisive effect on his life and the crimes he committed.
- Pornography violates the status of human beings as being in the image of God. It degrades those who use it and who are used by it, discouraging dignity, equality and holiness.
- Pornography involves addiction, from which millions of pounds are made every year.
- The subordination and demeaning of women is encouraged by the practice of pornography, and the view of the sexual relationship as being a beautiful and creative thing between husband and wife is undermined.
- The Christian call to holiness is threatened by pornography. Paul writes in Romans 12:2: 'Do not be conformed to this world but be transformed by the renewal of your mind, that you may prove what is the will of God, what is good and acceptable and perfect.'
- Christians are called to recognise that the freedom which is theirs in Christ should be tempered by a sensitivity to what is upbuilding: 'All things are lawful to me, but not all things are helpful.... So glorify God with your body' (1 Corinthians 6:20).

5 Premarital and extramarital relationships

This is a huge area, which could conceivably include a discussion of divorce. These are a few suggestions to set you on your way on what should be a straight-forward, but always carefully thought-out, debate.

- The biblical concept of marriage suggests that it is divinely ordained and the only legitimate sexual relationship. It is between two heterosexual partners who voluntarily give up all other potential sexual partners to 'cleave' to a spouse (Genesis 2:24).
- The 'one flesh' principle suggests that the sexual relationship between marriage partners is its primary, although not its only, characteristic.
- The biblical writers used the analogy of marriage to describe the relationship between Yahweh and Israel (Hosea 2:16) and between Jesus and the church (Revelation 21:2), affirming its unique and exclusive nature. The exclusive commitment which is characteristic of marriage makes it different from all other relationships.
- As a result, all sexual relationships outside marriage are usually seen to be wrong. Premarital sexual relationships anticipate the marriage relationship but without the structure which provides trust, security and the protective acceptance of the couple within society. Extramarital sexual relationships undermine that trust and violate a partner's right to an exclusive sexual relationship with their spouse.

- Matthew 5:27–28 declares that adultery begins in the heart, and the consummation of a sexual relationship is not necessary to determine that adultery has taken place.

> *Marriage is a total troth communion which can be broken by any kind of prolonged infidelity, whether through the squandering of monies, unwillingness to share of self, breaking of confidences, or other betrayals of trust.*
>
> **David Atkinson and David Field (eds),** *New Dictionary of Christian Ethics and Pastoral Theology*, **IVP, 1995, p. 146**

- Similarly, impurity before marriage need not involve the act of sexual intercourse, but impure thoughts and feelings towards others. Christians are encouraged to adopt holiness in thoughts as well as actions, in order to guard against sexual immorality.

War, peace and punishment

The material in this section is relevant to questions on:
- war specifically
- punishment specifically
- justice
- religious responses to wrongdoing
- relating ethical theory to issues in practical ethics

1 Can a religious believer ever participate in war?

> *Thus says the Lord of hosts, 'I will punish what Amalek did to Israel in opposing them on the way, when they came up out of Egypt. Now go and smite Amalek and utterly destroy all that they have; do not spare them, but kill both man and woman, infant and suckling, ox and sheep, camel and ass.'*
>
> **1 Samuel 15:2–3**
>
> *Beloved, never avenge yourselves, leave it to the wrath of God; for it is written, 'Vengeance is mine, I will repay, says the Lord'. No, if your enemy is hungry, feed him; if he is thirsty, give him drink; for by so doing you will heap burning coals upon his head.*
>
> **Romans 12:19–20**

At face value it seems that the Old Testament advocates aggressive attack on enemies whereas the New Testament teaches unconditional love. Which should the believer adopt in their attitude to war? Should conflict and violence against legitimate enemies be initiated by man or left to God? Perhaps, since the biblical

writers understood that the vehicles which God uses to execute his will on earth are usually human beings, man will inevitably become embroiled in conflict.

1.1 How does this apply to modern warfare?

Early Christians adopted the principle of non-retaliation: 'Do not resist one who is evil. But if anyone strikes you on the right cheek, turn to him the other also' (Matthew 5:39). However, 100 years after Christianity had become the official religion of Rome, the empire believed that the reluctance of Christians to fight was weakening their defences. Augustine responded with the **'just war' theory**, which consists of nine principles:

1.1a Resort to war: *jus ad bellum*

(i) War must be in a just cause. To save life or protect human rights would normally be considered a just cause.

(ii) War must be declared by a competent authority. In most cases the government would be the legitimate authority to declare war.

(iii) There must be comparison of justice on both sides.

(iv) There must be right intention, i.e. not with the deliberate intention of assassinating a country's leader.

(v) It must be a last resort — after all negotiation has failed.

(vi) There should be a reasonable likelihood of success.

1.1b Conduct in war: *jus in bello*

(vii) The injustice being fought and the suffering inflicted by war should be in reasonable proportion.

(viii) Proportionality must be exercised in the use of armaments, i.e. their use must be proportional to the threat.

(ix) Warfare must be discriminate. That is, civilians must be protected as far as possible, and should not be direct targets.

However:

- The theory is just that — a theory — and it does not guarantee that it will be appropriately applied or that it will necessarily be applicable to all circumstances.
- Some religious believers hold an absolute pacifist stance which does not allow them to fight in any war, even if it is allegedly 'just'. However, pacifism is not the official stance of many denominations. The Quakers, Mennonites and Amish are notable exceptions.
- The theory can be applied to any war to make it appear to be just. Both sides will apply it in such a way that their claim is apparently just, and yet both claims cannot surely be equally valid.
- The existence and the use of nuclear arms goes way beyond the conditions in warfare envisaged by Augustine. Modern weapons are capable of destroying the whole of human civilisation, and attempts to refine attacks to hit only military targets are open to human error. In a nuclear age, therefore, the only possibility for a Christian may be to revert to pacifism rather than risk the escalation of a war which originally appeared to be containable.
- The principle of the sanctity of life demands that all deliberate acts of killing — including those in war — are forbidden.

It would be useful to have some examples of relatively modern warfare to use to illustrate these points.

See the section on euthanasia (pp. 163–66) for a discussion of the principle of the sanctity of life. You should use accurate biblical references to support this point.

2 Pacifism

Pacifists are opposed to war and violence and believe that it is wrong to harm or kill other people. There are several types of pacifism:

- **Absolute pacifism** — the belief that it is never right to take part in war because nothing can justify the killing of human beings.
- **Relative pacifism** — war is wrong but there may be circumstances when it is the lesser of two evils.
- **Selective/nuclear pacifism** — opposition to wars involving weapons of mass destruction because of the devastating consequences and the fact that such wars cannot be won.
- **Active pacifism** — active engagement in political activity and campaigns to promote peace.

In time of war, therefore, pacifists may become 'conscientious objectors'. However, they may still play an active part, for example as emergency workers in hospitals or the fire service. Many pacifists served in both world wars by caring for the wounded and dying on the battlefield — a job that required considerable courage. In peacetime, pacifists may campaign and demonstrate against warfare and work to change society by removing the causes of war, such as injustice, oppression and exploitation.

For pacifists, war is cruel, immoral, unjust and a waste of life and resources. They claim that disputes should be solved in peaceful ways, for example the non-violent campaigns led by Ghandi and Martin Luther King. The aim of non-violent conflict is to convert opponents and to help them to change their mind away from aggression.

For Christians, pacifism comes from the Sermon on the Mount (Matthew 5:38–48), where Jesus taught his followers not to resist evil people, but to turn the other cheek, love their enemies, pray for their persecutors, and give up their right to *lex talionis* — justifiable and limited retribution for injustice.

He refused to rebel against the occupying Roman power, and did not advocate tax avoidance or civil disobedience. In Romans 13, Paul teaches that the state should be respected as the legitimate bearer of God's authority to rule, and that rebellion against the state is disobedience to God. He proposes that in dealings in general with the world, Christians should meet their enemies not with violence but with kindness, and so 'heap burning coals upon their heads', while respecting the legitimacy of the ruling authority to punish evil-doers.

Those who take the view that violent struggle for justice is sometimes legitimate may adopt relative, selective, or nuclear pacifism. They would argue that the Bible emphasises the importance of avoiding the 'shedding of innocent blood' (Genesis 9:4, Leviticus 17:11). The view is that the authority God has given to the legitimate rulers of the state must only be used to protect civilians and to bring about a just end by just means. However, a problem with pacifism is that if all warfare is rejected, this also means rejecting the possibility of fighting against a cruel aggressor in order to protect innocent civilians. For example, if Britain had not taken up arms against Hitler, the country may have been

Absolute or total pacifism allows no engagement in military activity, even if it is allegedly just.

conquered by the Nazis. Furthermore, pacifism cannot be a national policy; if a nation declares that it will never fight, it lays itself open to attack and invasion. Many argue that nations have a moral obligation to protect their citizens, and pacifism does not work in the face of extreme evil.

3 Punishment: its purpose and nature

Punishment is the intentional inflicting of pain by an authority on those who have breached its standards of behaviour. It can be inflicted by parents, employers and private organisations, but ethical concerns most often involve the meting out of punishment by the legal representatives of society for criminal activity.

3.1 Why punish?

Retribution stems from the notion of deserving. Those who do wrong should bear the consequences of so doing. Retribution defines community values, asserts individual responsibility in the performance of free acts, satisfies the desire for redress and vindicates the victims of crime. It is **opposed** by those who claim that education and rehabilitation are more effective ways to reinforce values. If a lawbreaker is incapable of making a free choice to obey the law or to disobey it, then retributive punishment has no valuable purpose.

Rehabilitation aims to change the offender's personality or circumstances so that they will not reoffend. The theory of **deterrence** proposes that sufficiently severe punishment will discourage future crimes. **Incapacitation** prevents the offender from committing further crimes. Such theories of punishment are **opposed** by those who argue that there is no evidence that such methods work any better than others which are more economically viable and which impose less on the offender.

3.2 Forms of punishment

- **Harm to the body:** corporal punishment and execution.
- **Harm to property:** seizing of goods or restriction of ownership, fines, or restitution to the victim.
- **Restriction of movement:** house arrest, imprisonment, electronic tagging.
- **Harm to reputation:** public shaming in some way.

Imprisonment has traditionally been the favoured method, on the basis that prisoners can effectively be rehabilitated.

3.3 Biblical view of punishment

Justice was to be administered in the interest of restoring broken relationships between man and God, and between human beings. **Restitution** was key, restoring the social norms within society (Exodus 22:6, 11–12; Luke 19:8). Most Western forms of punishment consider a prisoner's 'debt to society' to be paid more in terms of a custodial sentence than in restitution of property.

See comment on p. 165.

3.4 Capital punishment

This extreme form of punishment is only used by a few Western countries outside some states of the USA. While the Old Testament appears to sanction and use capital punishment, the teachings of Jesus do not support it (albeit indirectly). Opponents of capital punishment stress the failure it represents in rehabilitating or deterring the offender. Although both the Old Testament and the New Testament cite examples of capital punishment (including the death of Jesus), the blood of Jesus is spilt to make any further bloodshed unnecessary. In the confrontation with the Jewish leaders over the adulterous woman (John 8), Jesus does not appear to condone the practice. On the other hand, the Law of Moses orders the death penalty for 18 different offences, including rape and rebellion against parents. Those who argue that the Bible represents unchanging moral standards would, technically, see no contradiction in continuing to impose the death penalty for these offences.

3.5 Freedom

It is implicit in the execution of punishment that an offender should have committed a crime as an autonomous moral agent. Limits are placed on the extent to which an individual can be punished if there is doubt as to their moral freedom through mental illness, coercion or other restrictions on their liberty.

3.6 Human rights

It is incumbent on society to ensure that forms of punishment do not impinge on the human rights of the offender. Punishment should be proportional, humane (an argument against capital punishment) and respectful of the equal dignity of all human beings.

Specification summary

The following table relates the contents of these Exam Revision Notes to the specifications published by the major examining boards. It is not meant as a substitute for a specification, however, and it is important that you are aware of the details that are appropriate a far as your own specification is concerned. Not all topics are relevant to every specification, and some appear in different guises; for example, medical ethics topics are relevant for the investigations paper for AS on the Edexcel specification but not for the foundation paper (these topics are indicated by a *). On the other hand, some examined topics appear on Edexcel examination papers but are not covered at all by AQA or OCR. Be very clear what relates to you, and check with your teacher if in doubt. Some topics are quite broad — those to do with political and cultural background, or biblical ethics, for example, and should be used to throw light on the more specific topics which you will be asked about in the examination. Note that many topics in Chapters 2 and 3 are relevant for the AQA AS Philosophy specification.

BOARD	OCR	AQA	EDEXCEL
Specification code for AS	AS H172	AS 2060	AS 8RS01
Specification code for A2	A2 H572	A2 2060	A2 9RS01

CHAPTER 1 New Testament

	OCR	AQA	EDEXCEL
A Biblical criticism			
1 Source criticism and the synoptic problem	AS	AS	AS
2 Form criticism	AS	AS	AS
3 Redaction criticism	AS	AS	AS
B Issues of authorship and dating			
1 Authorship		AS	
2 Dating		AS	
C Birth and resurrection narratives			
1 Birth narratives		AS	
2 Resurrection narratives		AS/**A2**	AS*/**A2**
D New Testament miracles			
1 The place of miracles in the gospel tradition		AS	AS
2 Background to New Testament miracles		AS	AS
3 The purpose of miracles in the gospel tradition		AS	AS
4 Johannine signs		**A2**	AS
E Parables and the teaching of Jesus			
1 Jesus the teacher	**A2**	AS	AS
2 Setting	**A2**	AS	AS
3 Types of teaching	**A2**	AS	AS
4 Parables	**A2**	AS	AS
F Special features of the Fourth Gospel			
1 The Prologue		AS	**A2**
2 Purpose		AS	**A2**
G The ministry of Jesus in the Fourth Gospel		AS/**A2**	AS/**A2**
H Social themes in Luke's gospel			
1 Outcasts		AS	AS
2 Women		AS	AS
3 Rich and poor		AS	AS

CHAPTER 2   Philosophy of religion

		OCR	AQA	EDEXCEL
B	**Kantian ethics**			
1	Reason and morality	AS/**A2**	AS	**A2**
2	The categorical imperative and a good will	AS/**A2**	AS	**A2**
3	Kant's formulae	AS/**A2**	AS	**A2**
4	Strengths of the theory	AS/**A2**	AS	**A2**
5	Weaknesses of the theory	AS/**A2**	AS	**A2**
C	**Natural law, conscience and virtue ethics**			
1	The principles of natural law	AS	AS	**A2**
2	Conscience	**A2**		AS
3	Virtue ethics	AS/**A2**	AS/**A2**	**A2**
D	**Situation ethics**			
1	Background	AS/**A2**	AS/**A2**	AS
2	Situationist principles	AS/**A2**	AS/**A2**	AS
3	Strengths of situationism	AS/**A2**	AS/**A2**	AS
4	Weaknesses of situationism	AS/**A2**	AS/**A2**	AS
E	**Ethical language**			
1	Meta-ethics	AS		**A2**
2	The naturalistic fallacy	AS		**A2**
3	Intuitionism	AS		**A2**
4	Emotivism	AS		**A2**
F	**Abortion**			
1	Definitions and legalities	AS/**A2**	AS	AS*
2	Ethical and religious dilemmas	AS/**A2**	AS	AS*
G	**Euthanasia**			
1	Definitions and legalities	AS/**A2**	AS	AS*
2	Ethical and religious dilemmas	AS/**A2**	AS	AS*
H	**Reproductive issues and sexual ethics**			
1	Conception and contraception	AS/**A2**	AS	AS*
2	Eugenics and embryo experimentation	AS/**A2**	AS	AS*
3	Homosexuality	AS/**A2**	AS	AS
4	Pornography	**A2**		AS
5	Premarital and extramarital relationships	**A2**		AS
I	**War, peace and punishment**			
1	Can a religious believer ever participate in war?	**A2**		AS
2	Pacifism	AS/**A2**	AS/**A2**	AS
3	Punishment: its purpose and nature	**A2**		**A2**